·中英对照全译本·

丛林之书

The Jungle Books

[英] 约瑟夫·鲁德亚德·吉卜林 著

Joseph Rudyard Kipling

盛世教育西方名著翻译委员会 译

主　任：杜　毅　尚慧诗

本册委员：毛金凤　肖俊英

世界图书出版公司

上海·西安·北京·广州

图书在版编目（CIP）数据

丛林之书：中英对照全译本：汉英对照/（英）约瑟夫·鲁德亚德·吉卜林著；盛世教育西方名著翻译委员会译. —上海：上海世界图书出版公司，2018.11
ISBN 978-7-5192-4870-3

Ⅰ. ① 丛… Ⅱ. ① 约… ② 盛… Ⅲ. ① 英语—汉语—对照读物 ② 儿童故事—作品集—英国—近代 Ⅳ. ①H319.4：I

中国版本图书馆CIP数据核字（2018）第177093号

书　　名	丛林之书 The Jungle Book
著　　者	［英］约瑟夫·鲁德亚德·吉卜林
译　　者	盛世教育西方名著翻译委员会
责任编辑	孙妍捷
封面设计	张　力
出版发行	上海世界图书出版公司
地　　址	上海市广中路88号9-10楼
邮　　编	200083
网　　址	http://www.wpcsh.com
经　　销	新华书店
印　　刷	杭州恒力通印务有限公司
开　　本	880mm×1230mm　1/32
印　　张	8.5
字　　数	285千字
版　　次	2018年11月第1版　2018年11月第1次印刷
书　　号	ISBN　978-7-5192-4870-3/H·1417
定　　价	31.80元

前 言

通过阅读文学名著学语言，是掌握英语的绝佳方法。既可接触原汁原味的英语，又能享受文学之美，一举两得，何乐不为？

对于喜欢阅读名著的读者，这是一个最好的时代，因为有成千上万的书可以选择；这又是一个不好的时代，因为在浩繁的卷帙中，很难找到适合自己的好书。

然而，你手中的这套丛书，值得你来信赖。

这套精选的中英对照名著全译丛书，未改编改写、未删节削减，且配有权威注释，部分书中还添加了精美插图。

要学语言、读好书，当读名著原文。如习武者切磋交流，同高手过招方能渐明其间奥妙，若一味在低端徘徊，终难登堂入室。积年流传的名著，就是书中"高手"。然而这个"高手"，却有真假之分。初读书时，常遇到一些挂了名著名家之名改写改编的版本，虽有助于了解基本情节，然而所得只是皮毛，你何曾真的就读过了那名著呢？一边是窖藏了50年的女儿红，一边是贴了女儿红标签的薄酒，那滋味，怎能一样？"朝闻道，夕死可矣。"人生短如朝露，当努力追求真正的美。

本套丛书的英文版本，是根据外文原版书精心挑选而来；对应的中文译文以直译为主，以方便中英文对照学习，译文经反复推敲，对忠实理解原著极有助益；在涉及重要文化习俗之处，添加了精当的注释，以解疑惑。

读过本套丛书的原文全译，相信你会得书之真意、语言之精髓。

送君"开卷有益"之书，愿成文采斐然之人。

CONTENTS
目 录

CHAPTER 1　MOWGLI'S BROTHERS

第一章　莫格里的兄弟们

NOW Chil the Kite brings home the night

That Mangthe Bat sets free –

The herds are shut in byre and hut,

For loosed till dawn are we.

This is the hour of pride and power,

Talon and tush and claw.

Oh, hear the call! – Good hunting all

That keep the Jungle Law!

Night-Song in the Jungle

IT was seven o'clock of a very warm evening in the Seeonee hills when Father Wolf woke up from his day's rest, scratched himself, yawned, and spread out his paws one after the other to get rid of the sleepy feeling in their tips. Mother Wolf lay with her big gray nose dropped across her four tumbling, squealing cubs, and the moon shone into the mouth of the cave where they all lived. "Augrh!" said Father Wolf, "it

此时老鹰奇尔将黑夜带回家

是蝙蝠芒恩释放了它

牛群被关进了牛棚

黎明前我们可以尽情欢乐

这是彰显力量、耀武扬威的时刻

舞爪长牙

哦，听号角声！——祝捕猎好运

遵守丛林法则的兽民们！

《丛林夜歌》

此时是晚间七点钟，西奥尼山中很是温暖，狼爸爸从白天的休息中清醒过来。他舒展一下筋骨，打个哈欠，一个接一个把爪子伸开，摆脱残存的睡意。狼妈妈还趴着，用她的大灰鼻子拱着四个正在翻滚尖叫着的幼崽。月光洒进他们所住的洞穴口。"嗷！"狼爸爸说，"到了去打猎的时候了。"他要下山的时候，一个小小的身影来到洞中，它的尾巴毛茸茸的。小家伙说："愿

is time to hunt again." And he was going to spring downhill when a little shadow with a bushy tail crossed the threshold and whined: "Good luck go with you, O Chief of the Wolves; and good luck and strong white teeth go with the noble children, that they may never forget the hungry in this world."

It was the jackal – Tabaqui, the Dish-licker – and the wolves of India despise Tabaqui because he runs about making mischief, and telling tales, and eating rags and pieces of leather from the village rubbish-heaps. But they are afraid of him too, because Tabaqui, more than any one else in the jungle, is apt to go mad, and then he forgets that he was ever afraid of any one, and runs through the forest biting everything in his way. Even the tiger hides when little Tabaqui goes mad, for madness is the most disgraceful thing that can overtake a wild creature. We call it hydrophobia, but they call it dewanee – the madness – and run.

"Enter, then, and look," said Father Wolf, stiffly; "but there is no food here."

"For a wolf, no," said Tabaqui; "but for so mean a person as myself a dry bone is a good feast. Who are we, the

好运相伴，狼首领。希望您的这些贵族子女都走好运，有健康洁白的牙齿，永远不会忘记这个世界上还有动物在忍饥挨饿。"

进来说话的是豺——名字是塔巴克，他专门捡残羹冷炙。印度的狼鄙视塔巴克，因为他总是惹是生非，胡说八道，还吃村子垃圾堆里的破布和皮革。不过与此同时，塔巴克也让大家感到恐惧，因为他比丛林中的其他动物更容易发疯。他只要一发疯，就不记得自己怕什么其他的动物，开始在丛林里乱跑，逮谁咬谁。就算是老虎看到他发疯话的话，也会躲得远远的，野生动物们最受不了的事物中，疯病是让他们感到最丢脸的。我们把这种疯病叫作"狂犬病"，他们称之为"地瓦泥"，看见发疯的就赶紧跑开。

"你进里面来看看，"狼爸爸语气生硬地说，"但是家里没有食物。"

"在狼的眼里是没有，"塔巴克说，"不过对我这样的一只卑微的豺，一块干巴的骨头就是美食一

Gidur-log, to pick and choose?" He scuttled to the back of the cave, where he found the bone of a buck with some meat on it, and sat cracking the end merrily.

"All thanks for this good meal," he said, licking his lips. "How beautiful are the noble children! How large are their eyes! And so young too! Indeed, indeed, I might have remembered that the children of kings are men from the beginning."

Now, Tabaqui knew as well as any one else that there is nothing so unlucky as to compliment children to their faces; and it pleased him to see Mother and Father Wolf look uncomfortable.

Tabaqui sat still, rejoicing in the mischief that he had made, and then he said spitefully.

"Shere Khan, the Big One, has shifted his hunting-grounds. He will hunt among these hills during the next moon, so he has told me."

Shere Khan was the tiger who lived near the Waianganga River, twenty miles away.

"He has no right!" Father Wolf

顿。我们是谁呀，饥度尔－洛格[1]，怎么还能挑挑拣拣呢？"说罢它奔着洞穴的深处跑去，在那里发现了一些带着肉星的骨头，然后坐下开始大快朵颐。

"谢谢这顿美餐，"塔巴克舔了舔嘴唇说，"高贵的孩子们长得就是美啊！看他们的眼睛长得多大！多么青春年少！确实，确实，我应该记得，国王的孩子们出生的一刻就是男人了。"

塔巴克和其他任何一种动物一样，都知道在父母面前称赞他们的孩子是很不吉利的。但是眼看着狼爸爸和狼妈妈不舒畅的样子，塔巴克感到很高兴。

塔巴克一动不动地坐着，陶醉于自己制造的不快之中，然后没好气地说道：

"谢尔可汗，大头领，已经转移了他的狩猎场。他下个月会在这些山丘之间捕猎，他告诉我的。"

谢尔可汗是住在韦恩根格河附近、离此处二十英里[2]远的那只老虎。

"他没有权利那样做！"狼爸

---

[1] 豺民，"饥度尔"是印度语中"豺"的谐音，"洛格"是"民"的谐音。
[2] 英制长度单位，1 英里等于 1609.344 米。

began angrily. "By the Law of the Jungle he has no right to change his quarters without fair warning. He will frighten every head of game within ten miles; and I – I have to kill for two, these days."

"His mother did not call him Lungri for nothing," said Mother Wolf, quietly. "He has been lame in one foot from his birth. That is why he has only killed cattle. Now the villagers of the Wainganga are angry with him, and he has come here to make our villagers angry. They will scour the jungle for him when he is far away, and we and our children must run when the grass is set alight. Indeed, we are very grateful to Shere Khan!"

"Shall I tell him of your gratitude?" said Tabaqui.

"Out!" snapped Father Wolf. "Out and hunt with thy master. Thou hast done harm enough for one night."

"I go," said Tabaqui, quietly. "Ye can hear Shere Khan below in the thickets. I might have saved myself the message."

Father Wolf listened, and below in the valley that ran down to a little river, he heard the dry, angry, snarly,

爸开始生气了，"按照丛林法则的规定，他没有权利在不预先警告的情况下改变狩猎地。他这样会吓到每一个十英里之内的动物。而且我——这些天我不得不狩猎到两份，才够一家子吃的。"

"他妈妈可不是随便叫他郎格离[1]的，"狼妈妈静静说道，"他出生的时候就瘸了一条腿，这就是为什么他只猎杀牛。现在，韦恩根格村的村民对他很恼火，他就要转到这里来。这里的村民会生气并放火烧丛林来搜寻他，那时候他肯定自己跑得老远。可是一旦草地起火，我们和我们的孩子必须得逃离这里。真的，对此我们得感谢谢尔可汗啊！"

"我要告诉他你们的感激吗？"塔巴克说。

"你出去！"狼爸爸厉声喝道，"滚到你主子那里一起狩猎吧。一晚上你已经干尽坏事了。"

"我这就走，"塔巴克平静地说，"你可以听到下面茂密的树林中谢尔可汗的声响。我本可以为了自己不告诉你这个消息的。"

狼爸爸仔细听了听，河边的山谷下面，有老虎单调的、干涩的怒吼声。这是老虎什么也没抓到发出

---

[1] 印度语中"瘸腿"的意思。

singsong whine of a tiger who has caught nothing and does not care if all the jungle knows it.

"The fool!" said Father Wolf. "To begin a night's work with that noise! Does he think that our buck are like his fat Wainganga bullocks?"

"Hsh! It is neither bullock nor buck that he hunts to-night," said Mother Wolf; "it is Man." The whine had changed to a sort of humming purr that seemed to roll from every quarter of the compass. It was the noise that bewilders wood-cutters, and gipsies sleeping in the open, and makes them run sometimes into the very mouth of the tiger.

"Man!" said Father Wolf, showing all his white teeth. "Faugh! Are there not enough beetles and frogs in the tanks that he must eat Man – and on our ground too!"

The Law of the Jungle, which never orders anything without a reason, forbids every beast to eat Man except when he is killing to show his children how to kill, and then he must hunt outside the hunting-grounds of his pack or tribe. The real reason for this is that man-killing means, sooner or later, the arrival of white men on elephants, with

的声音，他也不介意整个丛林都听到。

"蠢货！"狼爸爸说，"要开始干夜活的时候，竟然这么大动静！他是以为我们的雄鹿与韦恩根格河的公牛一样吗？"

"嘘！他晚上要猎的不是公牛，也不是鹿，"狼妈妈说，"他要狩猎的是人。"呜呜声变成了一种嗡嗡的叫声，就像是从各个角度发出似的。这样的声音就是要伐木工人和睡在野外的吉普赛人被迷惑，分不清要往哪里跑，常常恰巧就跑到老虎的嘴边。

"人类！"狼爸爸露出雪白的牙齿说道，"呸！难道水里的甲虫和青蛙还不够多吗，他必须要去吃人？还在我们的地盘干这种事。"

丛林法则从来不会无缘无故规定任何东西，法则禁止野兽吃人。除非他在杀人的时候是想要跟他的孩子展示如何杀人。而且，猎杀人类的野兽必须在他的部落之外做这件事。这么规定的真正原因是，猎杀了人类意味着有朝一日白人会骑着大象，手里拿着枪，还有数百个棕色人类带着锣鼓、火箭和

guns, and hundreds of brown men with gongs and rockets and torches. Then everybody in the jungle suffers. The reason the beasts give among themselves is that Man is the weakest and most defenseless of all living things, and it is unsportsmanlike to touch him. They say too – and it is true – that man-eaters become mangy, and lose their teeth.

The purr grew louder, and ended in the full-throated "Aaarh!" of the tiger's charge.

Then there was a howl – an untigerish howl – from Shere Khan. "He has missed," said Mother Wolf. "What is it?"

Father Wolf ran out a few paces and heard Shere Khan muttering and mumbling savagely, as he tumbled about in the scrub.

"The fool has had no more sense than to jump at a wood-cutters' camp-fire, so he has burned his feet," said Father Wolf, with a grunt. "Tabaqui is with him."

"Something is coming uphill," said Mother Wolf, twitching one ear. "Get ready."

The bushes rustled a little in the thicket, and Father Wolf dropped with

火把来找兽类算账。然后丛林里的每个民众都会因此受难。兽族定下这样的法则给自己的理由是：人类是一切生物中最柔弱、最没有防护能力的，攻击人类是不体面的。而且他们还说，食用了人以后的兽身体会长疥癣，还会掉牙，这可是真的。

咆哮声越来越大，最后以老虎一声响亮的"啊哈！"告终。

紧接着是一声号叫——听起来不像是老虎发出的叫声——这是谢尔可汗发出的声音。"他失败了，"狼妈妈说，"这是什么？"

狼爸爸跑到了洞外不远处，听到了谢尔可汗在凶狠地嘟囔着什么，因为他跌进了灌木丛中。

"那个蠢货笨得自己跳到了伐木工堆起的篝火上面了，所以烧到了脚，"狼爸爸嘟囔着说，"塔巴克跟他在一起呢。"

"有什么东西上来了，"狼妈妈说的时候一只耳朵抽动着，"准备好。"

灌木丛中有灌木沙沙作响的声音，狼爸爸蹲下来，准备起跳。

his haunches under him, ready for his leap. Then, if you had been watching, you would have seen the most wonderful thing in the world – the wolf checked in mid-spring. He made his bound before he saw what it was he was jumping at, and then he tried to stop himself. The result was that he shot up straight into the air for four or five feet, landing almost where he left ground.

"Man!" he snapped. "A man's cub. Look!"

Directly in front of him, holding on by a low branch, stood a naked brown baby who could just walk – as soft and as dimpled a little thing as ever came to a wolf's cave at night. He looked up into Father Wolf's face, and laughed.

"Is that a man's cub?" said Mother Wolf. "I have never seen one. Bring it here."

A wolf accustomed to moving his own cubs can, if necessary, mouth an egg without breaking it, and though Father Wolf's jaws closed right on the child's back, not a tooth even scratched the skin, as he laid it down among the cubs.

"How little! How naked, and – how

接下来，如果你一直注视着一切，你会看到世界上最美妙的场景，狼爸爸起跳之后戛然静止。因为在起跳时，狼爸爸没有看清攻击目标，看清之后又想停止出击，所以他是直线向上跳起四五英尺[1]，最后几乎着陆在他起跳的原地点。

"是人类！"他厉声说道，"人类的幼崽，看！"

站在他正前面的是一个手握低矮的树枝、全身光溜溜的棕色皮肤的小孩儿，他刚刚能走路。这么柔软还长着小酒窝的小东西还是第一次出现在狼的洞穴中。他抬头看看狼爸爸的脸，笑了起来。

"那是一个人类的幼崽吗？"狼妈妈说，"我从未见过。把它带过来。"

狼习惯于用嘴叼着移动自己的幼崽，有必要的时候，就是用嘴叼一枚蛋也不会将其咬碎。尽管狼爸爸的嘴紧紧咬住孩子的背，但皮肤上一点牙印都没有留下，他把小孩儿放在了他那些幼崽中间。

"好小啊！好光溜，也好勇

---

[1] 英制长度单位，1 英尺等于 0.3048 米。

bold!" said Mother Wolf, softly. The baby was pushing his way between the cubs to get close to the warm hide. "Ahai! He is taking his meal with the others. And so this is a man's cub. Now, was there ever a wolf that could boast of a man's cub among her children?"

"I have heard now and again of such a thing, but never in our pack or in my time," said Father Wolf. "He is altogether without hair, and I could kill him with a touch of my foot. But see, he looks up and is not afraid."

The moonlight was blocked out of the mouth of the cave, for Shere Khan's great square head and shoulders were thrust into the entrance. Tabaqui, behind him, was squeaking: "My Lord, my Lord, it went in here!"

"Shere Khan does us great honor," said Father Wolf, but his eyes were very angry. "What does Shere Khan need?"

"My quarry. A man's cub went this way," said Shere Khan. "Its parents have run off. Give it to me."

Shere Khan had jumped at a wood-cutter's camp-fire, as Father Wolf had said, and was furious from the pain of his burned feet. But Father

敢！"狼妈妈轻声说道。小孩挤近狼幼崽中间，就为了靠近暖和的狼皮。"啊嗨！他正在和其他的孩子一起用餐呢。原来这就是人类的幼崽。现在，有没有一只狼可以吹嘘在她的孩子中间竟然会有人类幼崽的存在？"

"我听到过几次这样的事儿，不过从来没有在我们这群狼当中发生过，年代也不是我们这时候，"狼爸爸说，"他周身一点毛都没有，我能用我的一只脚杀死他。但是您看看，他抬起头来并不害怕我们。"

月光在洞口被挡住了，因为谢尔可汗的大方头和肩膀钻了进来。在他的身后是塔巴克的尖叫声："主人，主人，它进到这个洞里了！"

"谢尔可汗光临寒舍，令我们蓬荜生辉，"狼爸爸这样说着的时候，眼神里却充满愤怒，"谢尔可汗需要什么？"

"我要我的猎物。一个人类的孩子走到这儿来了，"谢尔可汗说，"他父母已经跑掉了，把它给我。"

就像狼爸爸说的那样，谢尔可汗跳到了一个伐木工人的篝火堆上，他因为烧伤的脚感到愤怒。不过狼爸爸清楚，洞口太窄，一只老

Wolf knew that the mouth of the cave was too narrow for a tiger to come in by. Even where he was, Shere Khan's shoulders and fore paws were cramped for want of room, as a man's would be if he tried to fight in a barrel.

"The Wolves are a free people," said Father Wolf. "They take orders from the Head of the Pack, and not from any striped cattle-killer. The man's cub is ours – to kill if we choose."

"Ye choose and ye do not choose! What talk is this of choosing? By the Bull that I killed, am I to stand nosing into your dog's den for my fair dues? It is I, Shere Khan, who speak!"

The tiger's roar filled the cave with thunder. Mother Wolf shook herself clear of the cubs and sprang forward, her eyes, like two green moons in the darkness, facing the blazing eyes of Shere Khan.

"And it is I, Raksha, who answer. The man's cub is mine, Lungri – mine to me! He shall not be killed. He shall live to run with the Pack and to hunt with the Pack; and in the end, look you, hunter of little naked cubs – frog-eater – fish-killer, he shall hunt thee! Now get hence, or by the Sambhur that I killed (I eat no starved cattle), back thou

虎是进不来的。尽管是眼下这个情况,谢尔可汗的肩膀和前爪也因为空间太小动不了了,好比是人类窝在酒桶里面要打架一样。

"狼是自由的族群,"狼爸爸说,"狼只听命于狼群的首领,而不是任何长着斑纹的猎杀老牛的家伙。那个人类幼崽是属于我们的——杀或不杀我们说了算。"

"你们选择杀或者不杀?你们在说选择什么?以我杀死的牛起誓,我要这样一直在你们的狗窝门口闻着属于我的猎物吗?跟你讲话的是我,谢尔可汗。"

老虎的吼声如雷声一般充斥在洞中。狼妈妈离开幼崽,向前跳了起来。她的眼睛就像黑暗中绿色的月亮一般,直面谢尔可汗愤怒的双眼。

"是我,拉克夏,在回答你的问题。人类幼崽是属于我的,郎格离——是我的!他不会遭到猎杀。他会和活着与狼群一起奔跑一起捕猎。而最终,你,只会捕猎小的没毛的幼崽,吃青蛙、吃鱼的家伙,他以后会猎杀你的!现在立马滚开,以我猎杀的黑鹿发誓(我不知道忍饥挨饿的牛),回到你妈妈身

goest to thy mother, burned beast of the jungle, lamer than ever thou camest into the world! Go!"

Father Wolf looked on amazed. He had almost forgotten the days when he won Mother Wolf in fair fight from five other wolves, when she ran in the Pack and was not called the Demon for compliment's sake. Shere Khan might have faced Father Wolf, but he could not stand up against Mother Wolf, for he knew that where he was she had all the advantage of the ground, and would fight to the death. So he backed out of the cave-mouth growling, and when he was clear he shouted:

"Each dog barks in his own yard! We will see what the Pack will say to this fostering of man-cubs. The cub is mine, and to my teeth he will come in the end, O bush-tailed thieves!"

Mother Wolf threw herself down panting among the cubs, and Father Wolf said to her gravely:

"Shere Khan speaks this much truth. The cub must be shown to the Pack. Wilt thou still keep him, Mother?"

"Keep him!" she gasped. "He came naked, by night, alone and very hungry; yet he was not afraid! Look, he has pushed one of my babes to one side

边去，活该被烧的丛林野兽，比出生的时候更瘸的家伙！滚蛋！"

狼爸爸惊奇地看着她。他差点忘记了当初自己是在与其他五只狼的公平竞争中，赢得了狼妈妈。狼妈妈在狼群中被冠以"恶魔"的称号，也不是恭维的意思。谢尔可汗可能能对付一下狼爸爸，但是却不能站起来还击狼妈妈。因为他知道，跟他相比，狼妈妈占据位置上的绝对优，一旦开战就是生死之战。于是他从洞口咆哮着退了出来，当他确认自己没有危险的时候，他喊道：

"每只狗都会在自己的院子里狂吠！我们就看看狼群对抚育人类幼崽这件事给个什么说法。这幼崽是属于我的。我最终会用牙齿咬碎他，毛尾巴贼！"

狼妈妈瘫倒在幼崽中间，喘着粗气。狼爸爸严肃地对她说：

"谢尔可汗说得很有道理。幼崽是必须展示给狼群看的。你还要留下他吗，妈妈？"

"留下他！"她喘着气说，"他在夜里光溜溜地来到这里，独自一人，非常饥饿，可是他并不害怕！看看，他已经把我的一个宝贝推到

already. And that lame butcher would have killed him, and would have run off to the Wainganga while the villagers here hunted through all our lairs in revenge! Keep him? Assuredly I will keep him. Lie still, little frog. O thou Mowgli, – for Mowgli, the Frog, I will call thee, – the time will come when thou wilt hunt Shere Khan as he has hunted thee!"

"But what will our Pack say?" said Father Wolf.

The Law of the Jungle lays down very clearly that any wolf may, when he marries, withdraw from the Pack he belongs to; but as soon as his cubs are old enough to stand on their feet he must bring them to the Pack Council, which is generally held once a month at full moon, in order that the other wolves may identify them. After that inspection the cubs are free to run where they please, and until they have killed their first buck no excuse is accepted if a grown wolf of the Pack kills one of them. The punishment is death where the murderer can be found; and if you think for a minute you will see that this must be so.

Father Wolf waited till his cubs could run a little, and then on the night

一边了。那跛脚的屠夫原本要将他捕杀，之后就跑到韦恩根格河的。真要是那样，这里的村里会找遍所有的巢穴进行报复，留下他，我要留下他。安静地躺着吧，小青蛙。哦，你这个莫格里——青蛙莫格里，我以后就这么叫你。有朝一日你就会猎杀谢尔可汗，因为他捕杀过你。"

"但我们族群会说些什么呢？"狼爸爸说。

丛林法则很清楚地规定，任何狼在结婚后都能退出所属的群体。不过他的幼崽长到可以站起来的时候，他们必须把幼崽带到每月一次的狼群大会，好让别的狼能够认识这些幼狼。狼群大会通常是满月的时候召开一次。经过检查后，幼崽可以自由地奔跑到任何他们想去的地方。直到他们杀死了他们的第一只公鹿之前，狼族里成年的狼不能以任何理由杀死一只幼狼。若是有谋杀行为被发现，成年狼面临的惩罚就是死，如果你思考一分钟，你就明白必须要定这样的规矩。

狼爸爸等到他的小狼们能跑一段路了，就在狼群大会的晚上带

of the Pack Meeting took them and Mowgli and Mother Wolf to the Council Rock – a hilltop covered with stones and boulders where a hundred wolves could hide. Akela, the great gray Lone Wolf, who led all the Pack by strength and cunning, lay out at full length on his rock, and below him sat forty or more wolves of every size and color, from badger-colored veterans who could handle a buck alone, to young black three-year-olds who thought they could. The Lone Wolf had led them for a year now. He had fallen twice into a wolf-trap in his youth, and once he had been beaten and left for dead; so he knew the manners and customs of men.

There was very little talking at the Rock. The cubs tumbled over one another in the center of the circle where their mothers and fathers sat, and now and again a senior wolf would go quietly up to a cub, look at him carefully, and return to his place on noiseless feet. Sometimes a mother would push her cub far out into the moonlight, to be sure that he had not been overlooked. Akela from his rock would cry: "Ye know the Law – ye know the Law! Look well, O Wolves!"

着他们和莫格里，与狼妈妈一起到会议岩石去。岩顶上被石头和巨石覆盖着，这个地方可以藏下一百只狼。那只伟大的灰色的独行狼阿克拉凭借力量和灵活的头脑成为这个狼群的首领。大会召开的时候，阿克拉伸展着他的四肢，躺在他的岩石上面，在他下面坐着四十多只大小不一、毛色不同的狼。这里有毛色跟獾子一般的单独就能捕杀一头公鹿的老狼，也有毛色暗黑、觉得自己也可以一样了不起的三岁大的狼。孤狼已经领导大家一年了。他在年少的时候曾两次陷入捕狼的圈套，有一次还被狠狠打了一顿后扔掉等死，所有他很清楚人类的行事方式和习惯。

岩石上很少听到狼在交流。小狼崽们在母亲和父亲围坐的圆圈中间来回翻滚。偶尔有年长的狼悄悄地来到一只幼崽身边，仔细看着他，接着再默默地回到自己的地方。有时候，一个母亲会把她的幼崽推到远处的月光下，以确保他没有被大家忽略掉。阿克拉就在岩石上大喊："你们是知道法则的，你们是知道法则的。大家伙儿，都看仔细些！"焦虑的母亲们会接着说道："看哪——看仔细些，狼伙计们！"

And the anxious mothers would take up the call: "Look – look well, O Wolves!"

At last – and Mother Wolf's neck-bristles lifted as the time came – Father Wolf pushed "Mowgli, the Frog," as they called him, into the center, where he sat laughing and playing with some pebbles that glistened in the moonlight.

Akela never raised his head from his paws, but went on with the monotonous cry, "Look well!" A muffled roar came up from behind the rocks – the voice of Shere Khan crying, "The cub is mine; give him to me. What have the Free People to do with a man's cub?"

Akela never even twitched his ears. All he said was, "Look well, O Wolves! What have the Free People to do with the orders of any save the Free People? Look well!"

There was a chorus of deep growls, and a young wolf in his fourth year flung back Shere Khan's question to Akela: "What have the Free People to do with a man's cub?"

Now the Law of the Jungle lays down that if there is any dispute as to the right of a cub to be accepted by the Pack, he must be spoken for by at least

终于，这一时刻到了，狼妈妈的颈毛都竖起来了，狼爸爸将"青蛙莫格里"推到中间，他坐在那里笑着玩一些在月光下闪闪发光的鹅卵石。

阿克拉从未将头从爪子上抬起，不过继续单调地喊着："好好看看吧！"一个沉闷的喊叫声此刻从岩石后面发出，那是谢尔可汗的声音。"幼崽是属于我的，将他给我。自由的民众和人类的幼崽有什么关系？"

阿克拉耳朵甚至动都没动，他只说："我的狼伙计，好好看看吧！自由的民众怎么会管其他族类的命令呢？看仔细一些吧！"

会场上出现了一阵深深的咆哮声，有只四岁的小狼将谢尔可汗的问题扔给了阿克拉："自由民众与人类的幼崽有什么关系？"

此刻不得不说一说丛林法则的规定了。假如一只幼崽是否被狼群接受出现了异议，至少应该由两个不是他父母的族群的成员肯为

two members of the Pack who are not his father and mother.

"Who speaks for this cub?" said Akela. "Among the Free People, who speaks?" There was no answer, and Mother Wolf got ready for what she knew would be her last fight, if things came to fighting.

Then the only other creature who is allowed at the Pack Council – Baloo, the sleepy brown bear who teaches the wolf cubs the Law of the Jungle; old Baloo, who can come and go where he pleases because he eats only nuts and roots and honey – rose up on his hind quarters and grunted.

"The man's cub – the man's cub?" he said. "I speak for the man's cub. There is no harm in a man's cub. I have no gift of words, but I speak the truth. Let him run with the Pack, and be entered with the others. I myself will teach him."

"We need yet another," said Akela. "Baloo has spoken, and he is our teacher for the young cubs. Who speaks besides Baloo?"

A black shadow dropped down into the circle. It was Bagheera, the Black Panther, inky black all over, but with the panther markings showing up in

他说话。

"谁为这只幼崽讲话吗?"阿克拉说,"在自由民众中,有谁要说吗?"没有回应。狼妈妈准备好了,如果情况演变成战斗,她知道这会是她最后一场战斗。

然后,唯一一个被允许参加狼族大会的他族动物站直了后半身,哼了一声。他是棕熊巴洛,总是一副睡眼惺忪的模样,教狼崽们丛林法则的伙计。老巴洛可以按照自己的喜好想去哪儿就去哪儿,因为他只食用坚果、根和蜂蜜。

"人类的幼崽——人类的幼崽?"他说,"我为这个人类的幼崽发言。人类的幼崽不会带来害处。我没有语言天赋,不过我说的是实话。就让他和其他的幼崽们一起奔跑,融入这个群体当中。我会亲自教导他的。"

"我们需要再有一个人发声,"阿克拉说,"巴洛已经为他开口了,而且他是我们幼崽的老师。除了巴洛之外,谁为他说话?"

有个黑影落在了圆圈当中。这是巴赫拉,一只黑豹,周身漆黑,可是在一定的光线条件下,看起来就是波纹丝绸样的豹纹。每一个动

certain lights like the pattern of watered silk. Everybody knew Bagheera, and nobody cared to cross his path; for he was as cunning as Tabaqui, as bold as the wild buffalo, and as reckless as the wounded elephant. But he had a voice as soft as wild honey dripping from a tree, and a skin softer than down.

"O Akela, and ye, the Free People," he purred, "I have no right in your assembly; but the Law of the Jungle says that if there is a doubt which is not a killing matter in regard to a new cub, the life of that cub may be bought at a price. And the Law does not say who may or may not pay that price. Am I right?"

"Good! Good!" said the young wolves, who are always hungry. "Listen to Bagheera. The cub can be bought for a price. It is the Law."

"Knowing that I have no right to speak here, I ask your leave."

"Speak then," cried twenty voices.

"To kill a naked cub is shame. Besides, he may make better sport for you when he is grown. Baloo has spoken in his behalf. Now to Baloo's word I will add one bull, and a fat one, newly killed, not half a mile from here, if ye will accept the man's cub

物都知道巴赫拉，没有谁有胆量挡他的路。他就像塔巴克一样聪慧，像野生水牛一样大胆，像受伤的大象一样横冲直撞。可他的嗓音又那么轻柔，像从树上滴落的蜂蜜，还有他的皮肤比鸟的羽毛还要柔软。

"哦，阿克拉，还有自由的民众，"他咕哝着，"我没有权利出现在你们的族会，但是丛林法则规定，倘若涉及一个新的幼崽让大家有了异议，而且事情并没有严重到要杀死他那么严重，那这只幼崽的性命可以出价买下。法则没有规定谁可以或者谁不可以支付这个价钱。我讲得对吗？"

"好啊！好啊！"年轻的狼们一起说道，他们总是吃不饱的状态，"听巴赫啦说的。幼崽可以被出价买下。这是法则。"

"我清楚我没有权利在这里讲话，我渴求你们允许。"

"那就说吧，"二十个声音喊道，"杀一个没毛的幼崽是件蒙羞的事情。此外，他长大后可能会捕杀到更多的猎物给你们。巴洛代表他自己为他讲话了。现在以巴洛的话来讲，假设你们愿意就接受这个幼崽，我再加一头公牛，很肥的一头，刚被杀死的，距离此处不到半

according to the Law. Is it difficult?"

There was a clamor of scores of voices, saying: "What matter? He will die in the winter rains. He will scorch in the sun. What harm can a naked frog do us? Let him run with the Pack. Where is the bull, Bagheera? Let him be accepted." And then came Akela's deep bay, crying: "Look well – look well, O Wolves!"

Mowgli was still playing with the pebbles, and he did not notice when the wolves came and looked at him one by one. At last they all went down the hill for the dead bull, and only Akela, Bagheera, Baloo, and Mowgli's own wolves were left. Shere Khan roared still in the night, for he was very angry that Mowgli had not been handed over to him.

"Aye, roar well," said Bagheera, under his whiskers; "for the time comes when this naked thing will make thee roar to another tune, or I know nothing of Man."

"It was well done," said Akela. "Men and their cubs are very wise. He may be a help in time."

"Truly, a help in time of need; for none can hope to lead the Pack forever," said Bagheera.

英里那里。根据法则接受人类的幼崽，你们觉得难吗？"

狼群响起一阵喧哗的声音，说道："能有什么关系？一场冬雨他就会死去。他会被太阳烤焦的。一只光溜的青蛙会伤害我们什么？就让他和狼群们一起奔跑。公牛在哪里，巴赫拉？他被大家接受了。"接着是阿克拉低沉的叫喊声，他喊道："看好喽——看好喽，狼群伙计们。"

莫格里还在玩石子，他没有注意到一只又一只狼过来看他。最后这些狼都下山去找死公牛了，只有阿克拉、巴赫拉、巴洛还有莫格里所在的狼的一家留下了。谢尔可汗还在黑夜中咆哮，因为他真的生气了，对于莫格里没有交到他手上这件事。

"哎，好好吼着吧，"巴赫拉在他的胡须下面的嘴巴说道，"因为有一天，这个光溜的小家伙会让你的咆哮变成另外一种声音，除非我对人类一无所知。"

"做得很好，"阿克拉说，"人类和他们的孩子是非常聪慧的。他可能会在某一天帮到我们。"

"真的是这样，在需要的时候帮到我们，因为没有谁可以期望一直领导狼群。"

Akela said nothing. He was thinking of the time that comes to every leader of every pack when his strength goes from him and he gets feebler and feebler, till at last he is killed by the wolves and a new leader comes up – to be killed in his turn.

"Take him away," he said to Father Wolf, "and train him as befits one of the Free People."

And that is how Mowgli was entered into the Seeonee wolf-pack for the price of a bull and on Baloo's good word.

Now you must be content to skip ten or eleven whole years, and only guess at all the wonderful life that Mowgli led among the wolves, because if it were written out it would fill ever so many books. He grew up with the cubs, though they of course were grown wolves almost before he was a child, and Father Wolf taught him his business, and the meaning of things in the jungle, till every rustle in the grass, every breath of the warm night air, every note of the owls above his head, every scratch of a bat's claws as it roosted for a while in a tree, and every splash of every little fish jumping in a

阿克拉什么也没说。他想着以后的日子里，每一个族群的首领都会变得越来越没有力量，越来越弱，直到最后被其他的狼杀死，一个新的首领产生。然后，新的首领又会被杀死。

"把他带走，"他对狼爸爸说，"将他训练成为一名自由的民众。"

莫格里就是这样凭借一头公牛作为代价，加上巴洛为他说好话，而进入了西奥尼狼群。

现在你必须要在内容上跳过十或者十一年之久，莫格里是如何在狼群中度过这段美妙人生的，只能由你自己去猜测了。因为这些都写出来的话，那得要写好多本书。莫格里和其他的狼崽们共同长大，不过在他几乎还是个孩子的时候，其他的狼崽们就已经成年了。狼爸爸把自己的本领教给莫格里，让他知道丛林里那些事物的意义。直到每一片草的沙沙声，夜晚温暖的空气中的每一次呼吸，猫头鹰在他头顶上发出的每一个音符，蝙蝠栖息在树上停留片刻爪子的抓挠声，每一条小鱼在池塘中跳跃的水滴溅落的声音，对他来说都像是一个商

pool, meant just as much to him as the work of his office means to a business man. When he was not learning he sat out in the sun and slept, and ate, and went to sleep again; when he felt dirty or hot he swam in the forest pools; and when he wanted honey (Baloo told him that honey and nuts were just as pleasant to eat as raw meat) he climbed up for it, and that Bagheera showed him how to do.

Bagheera would lie out on a branch and call, "Come along, Little Brother," and at first Mowgli would cling like the sloth, but afterward he would fling himself through the branches almost as boldly as the gray ape. He took his place at the Council Rock, too, when the Pack met, and there he discovered that if he stared hard at any wolf, the wolf would be forced to drop his eyes, and so he used to stare for fun.

At other times he would pick the long thorns out of the pads of his friends, for wolves suffer terribly from thorns and burs in their coats. He would go down the hillside into the cultivated lands by night, and look very curiously at the villagers in their huts, but he had a mistrust of men because Bagheera showed him a square box

务人员对自己办公室的工作那么熟悉。当他不学习的时候，就坐在太阳下面睡觉、吃饭，接着再睡。当他觉得自己身上脏了或者热了，他就到森林里的池塘游泳；当他想吃蜂蜜（巴洛告诉他，蜂蜜和坚果就跟生肉一样美味）的时候，他就爬到树上去找，巴赫拉教他怎么做。

巴赫拉会趴在树枝上，喊道："来吧，小兄弟。"最初，莫格里就像个树懒一样紧紧抱着树不撒手，不过后来他就像灰猿一样大胆地在树枝间跳来跳去了。在狼群大会的岩石上，莫格里也有了他自己的位置。在大会上狼群相见的时候，他发现如果他紧紧地盯着任何一只狼，那只狼就会被迫将眼睛垂下。所以他常常盯着一只狼看，纯粹是为了好玩。

其他时候，他会从他朋友掌心拔出那些长刺，因为狼脚心或者皮毛扎到刺，会非常遭罪的。夜晚来临的时候，莫格里会沿着山坡进入耕地，十分好奇地看着小屋里的村民。不过他却不信任人类，因为巴赫拉给他看过一个有闸门的方形的盒子，它被巧妙地隐藏在丛林中，他差点落入圈套，巴赫拉说那

with a drop-gate so cunningly hidden in the jungle that he nearly walked into it, and told him it was a trap.

He loved better than anything else to go with Bagheera into the dark warm heart of the forest, to sleep all through the drowsy day, and at night see how Bagheera did his killing. Bagheera killed right and left as he felt hungry, and so did Mowgli – with one exception. As soon as he was old enough to understand things, Bagheera told him that he must never touch cattle because he had been bought into the Pack at the price of a bull's life. "All the jungle is thine," said Bagheera, "and thou canst kill everything that thou art strong enough to kill; but for the sake of the bull that bought thee thou must never kill or eat any cattle young or old. That is the Law of the Jungle." Mowgli obeyed faithfully.

And he grew and grew strong as a boy must grow who does not know that he is learning any lessons, and who has nothing in the world to think of except things to eat.

Mother Wolf told him once or twice that Shere Khan was not a creature to be trusted, and that some day he must kill Shere Khan; but though a young

是陷阱。

跟其他任何事情比起来，莫格里最喜欢的就是和巴赫拉一起去黑暗温暖的森林中心，昏天暗地地睡上一天，晚上的时候看看巴赫拉如何猎杀食物。巴赫拉要是感到饿了，他不分谁是谁地一顿猛杀，莫格里也是如此——只有一个例外。莫格里长大能理解道理以后，巴赫拉告诉他，他绝对不能碰牛，因为他已经以牛的生命为代价进入狼群。"丛林里的一切都是你的，"巴赫拉说，"只要你足够强壮，你可以杀死一切要杀死的动物。不过为了祭奠买你的那头公牛，你绝不能杀也不能吃年轻或者年老的牛。这就是丛林法则的规定。"莫格里忠实地服从着。

随着男孩的不断成长，他变得越来越强壮了。男孩是注定要长大的，可他不知道他正在学习着。除了吃的东西以外，这个世界上没有什么能让他去思考。

曾经有一两次，狼妈妈告诉他，不要相信谢尔可汗，日后他必须杀了谢尔可汗。但是，这样的建议一只狼会无时无刻不记在心上，

wolf would have remembered that advice every hour, Mowgli forgot it because he was only a boy – though he would have called himself a wolf if he had been able to speak in any human tongue.

Shere Khan was always crossing his path in the jungle, for as Akela grew older and feebler the lame tiger had come to be great friends with the younger wolves of the Pack, who followed him for scraps, a thing Akela would never have allowed if he had dared to push his authority to the proper bounds. Then Shere Khan would flatter them and wonder that such fine young hunters were content to be led by a dying wolf and a man's cub. "They tell me," Shere Khan would say, "that at Council ye dare not look him between the eyes"; and the young wolves would growl and bristle.

Bagheera, who had eyes and ears everywhere, knew something of this, and once or twice he told Mowgli in so many words that Shere Khan would kill him some day; and Mowgli would laugh and answer: "I have the Pack and I have thee; and Baloo, though he is so lazy, might strike a blow or two for my sake. Why should I be afraid?"

莫格里却不记得。如果他能说任何人类的发音，他会把自己称为狼，可他毕竟只是一个男孩。

谢尔可汗总是在他身边的丛林中穿行，阿克拉变得越来越老，身体也越来越弱了。瘸腿的老虎就和狼群中相对年轻的狼们成了很好的朋友，年轻的狼们跟在谢尔可汗身后捡一些碎肉吃，这件事情若是阿克拉还敢于行使他的首领权威的话，是一定不会允许的。然后谢尔可汗就趁机奉承这些跟随的狼，说他想知道如此年轻的猎手为什么要甘于接受一只将死的狼和一个人类幼崽的领导。"他们告诉我，"谢尔可汗说，"在狼群大会上，你们不敢与他对视。"年轻的狼们听到这话会咆哮起来。

哪里都有巴赫拉的耳目，他也听到了一些风声。有一两次，他和莫格里讲了好多话，告诉他谢尔可汗有一天会杀了他。莫格里笑着回答："我有狼群和你，我有巴洛，尽管他那么懒惰，为了我也还是会打他两拳的。我为什么要害怕？"

It was one very warm day that a new notion came to Bagheera – born of something that he had heard. Perhaps Ikki, the Porcupine, had told him; but he said to Mowgli when they were deep in the jungle, as the boy lay with his head on Bagheera's beautiful black skin: "Little Brother, how often have I told thee that Shere Khan is thy enemy?"

"As many times as there are nuts on that palm," said Mowgli, who, naturally, could not count. "What of it? I am sleepy, Bagheera, and Shere Khan is all long tail and loud talk– like Mor, the Peacock."

"But this is no time for sleeping. Baloo knows it, I know it, the pack know it, and even the foolish, foolish deer know. Tabaqui has told thee too."

"Ho! Ho!" said Mowgli. "Tabaqui came to me not long ago with some rude talk that I was a naked man's cub, and not fit to dig pig-nuts; but I caught Tabaqui by the tail and swung him twice against a palm-tree to teach him better manners."

"That was foolishness; for though Tabaqui is a mischief-maker, he would have told thee of something that concerned thee closely. Open those

这是温暖的一天。一个新的想法突然从巴赫拉脑子冒出来——来源于他听到的某件事，可能是那个豪猪伊基跟他讲的，当他和莫格里已经到了丛林深处的时候。男孩投靠在巴赫拉美丽的黑色皮毛上躺下来，巴赫拉对他说："小兄弟，我跟你说过多少次，谢尔可汗是你的敌人？"

"次数多得就像那颗棕榈树上的果子，"莫格里说，他当然是数不过来，"怎么了？我困了，巴赫拉。谢尔可汗就是一个长着长尾巴、说话大嗓门、像孔雀莫尔一样的家伙。"

"但现在不是该睡觉的时候。巴洛知道，我知道，狼群知道，甚至是愚蠢的、愚蠢的鹿都知道这个。塔巴克也告诉了你。"

"嗬！嗬！"莫格里说，"塔巴克不久之前来找我，说了一些很粗鲁的话，他说我是一个没长毛的人类幼崽，不应该挖坚果。不过我抓住塔巴克的尾巴，将他两次磕在棕榈树上，教他以后礼貌一些。"

"那样是很愚蠢的。虽然塔巴克是个捣蛋鬼，可他却会告诉你与你密切相关的一些事情。睁开眼睛吧，小兄弟。谢尔可汗是不敢在丛

eyes, Little Brother! Shere Khan dares not kill thee in the jungle for fear of those that love thee; but remember, Akela is very old, and soon the day comes when he cannot kill his buck, and then he will be leader no more. Many of the wolves that looked thee over when thou wast brought to the Council first are old too, and the young wolves believe, as Shere Khan has taught them, that a man-cub has no place with the Pack. In a little time thou wilt be a man."

"And what is a man that he should not run with his brothers?" said Mowgli. "I was born in the jungle; I have obeyed the Law of the Jungle; and there is no wolf of ours from whose paws I have not pulled a thorn. Surely they are my brothers!"

Bagheera stretched himself at full length and half shut his eyes. "Little Brother," said he, "feel under my jaw."

Mowgli put up his strong brown hand, and just under Bagheera's silky chin, where the giant rolling muscles were all hid by the glossy hair, he came upon a little bald spot.

"There is no one in the jungle that knows that I, Bagheera, carry that mark – the mark of the collar; and yet, Little

林中杀死你，因为他害怕那些爱你的伙计。但请记住，阿克拉很老了，很快就会到了他不能猎杀公鹿的那一天，那时他就不会是首领了。很多你第一次被带到狼族大会上见过你的狼也都老了。年轻的狼们相信，正如谢尔可汗告诉他们的那样，一个人类的幼崽是不应该出现在狼群的地盘的。过不了多长时间，你就会成为一个真正的人。"

"一个人怎么就不能和他的弟兄们一起奔跑呢？"莫格里说，"我出生在丛林，我遵守了丛林法则。我给每一只我们的狼都拔过刺。他们当然是我的兄弟！"

巴赫拉伸展了一下身躯，半闭上眼睛。"小弟弟，"他说，"摸摸我的下巴。"

莫格里举起他壮实的棕色手掌，摸着巴赫拉柔滑的下巴。硕大的圆滚滚的地方都被有光泽的毛发遮住了，不过他还是摸到了一块光秃秃的地方。

"丛林之中没有谁知道这件事，我巴赫拉带着这个标记——带过项圈的标记。然而，小兄弟，我

Brother, I was born among men, and it was among men that my mother died – in the cages of the King's Palace at Oodeypore. It was because of this that I paid the price for thee at the Council when thou wast a little naked cub. Yes, I too was born among men. I had never seen the jungle. They fed me behind bars from an iron pan till one night I felt that I was Bagheera, the Panther, and no man's plaything, and I broke the silly lock with one blow of my paw, and came away; and because I had learned the ways of men, I became more terrible in the jungle than Shere Khan. Is it not so?"

"Yes," said Mowgli; "all the jungle fears Bagheera – all except Mowgli."

"Oh, thou art a man's cub," said the Black Panther, very tenderly; "and even as I returned to my jungle, so thou must go back to men at last, – to the men who are thy brothers, – if thou art not killed in the council."

"But why – but why should any wish to kill me?" said Mowgli.

"Look at me," said Bagheera; and Mowgli looked at him steadily between the eyes. The big panther turned his head away in half a minute.

"That is why," he said, shifting his

在人类中间出生,我的母亲是在乌代浦国王宫殿的笼子里去世的。这就是为什么当初你是一个全身光溜溜的幼崽时,我在狼族大会上出价将你留下。是的,我就是出生在人类中间的,我从未见过丛林什么样。他们拿铁盘里的食物隔着栅栏喂我。直到有一天晚上,我感觉到我是巴赫拉,我是黑豹,我不是人类的玩物。我用爪子一下子打破了愚蠢的锁头,然后逃走了。因为我已经了解了人类的行事方式,我比丛林中的谢尔可汗更加可怕,不是吗?"

"是这样的,"莫格里说,"丛林里所有动物都惧怕巴赫拉——所有的,除了莫格里。"

"哦,因为你是人类的幼崽,"黑豹很温柔地说着,"正如我回到我的丛林之中一样,你最后必须要回到人类中间——如果你没有在狼族大会上被杀的话,你就要回到你人类的兄弟当中去。"

"但是为什么——为什么有动物希望将我杀死?"

"看看我。"巴赫拉说。莫格里眼神坚定地望着他。大黑豹半分钟不到就把头转向一边。

"这就是原因,"他说着,爪

paw on the leaves. "Not even I can look thee between the eyes, and I was born among men, and I love thee, Little Brother. The others they hate thee because their eyes cannot meet thine; because thou art wise; because thou hast pulled out thorns from their feet – because thou art a man."

"I did not know these things," said Mowgli, sullenly; and he frowned under his heavy black eyebrows.

"What is the Law of the Jungle? Strike first and then give tongue. By thy very carelessness they know that thou art a man. But be wise. It is in my heart that when Akela misses his next kill, – and at each hunt it costs him more to pin the buck, – the Pack will turn against him and against thee. They will hold a jungle Council at the Rock, and then – and then ... I have it!" said Bagheera, leaping up. "Go thou down quickly to the men's huts in the valley, and take some of the Red Flower which they grow there, so that when the time comes thou mayest have even a stronger friend than I or Baloo or those of the Pack that love thee. Get the Red Flower."

By Red Flower Bagheera meant fire, only no creature in the jungle will call

子移到树叶上面，"即使我都不能与你对视，我可是出生在人类中间的，并且我是爱你的，小兄弟。他们恨你，因为他们不能直视你的眼睛，因为你聪明，因为你从他们脚上拔出了刺，因为你是一个人。"

"我不明白这怎么回事。"莫格里郁闷地说，他浓密的黑色眉毛皱了起来。

"丛林法则是什么？先打然后再开口。你毫不在乎的样子，让他们明白你是一个人。你得学着聪明些。我心想的是，当阿克拉下一次猎杀失败的时候——现在他每一次捕杀都要花费更大的力气才能捕到公鹿——那时候狼群就会反对他的领导，同时也反对你。他们将在岩石上举行丛林大会，然后，然后……我有办法了!"巴赫拉跳起来说，"你迅速下山，到山谷中人类居住的小屋，取一些红色的花，它们生长在那里。以便到时候你拥有更强大的朋友，这个朋友比我、巴洛或者其他狼群中爱你的那些朋友更厉害。取红色的花过来。"

巴赫拉口中的红花就是指火，只不过丛林中没有动物会用火这

fire by its proper name. Every beast lives in deadly fear of it, and invents a hundred ways of describing it.

"The Red Flower?" said Mowgli. "That grows outside their huts in the twilight. I will get some."

"There speaks the man's cub," said Bagheera, proudly. "Remember that it grows in little pots. Get one swiftly, and keep it by thee for time of need."

"Good!" said Mowgli. "I go. But art thou sure, O my Bagheera" – he slipped his arm round the splendid neck, and looked deep into the big eyes – "art thou sure that all this is Shere Khan's doing?"

"By the Broken Lock that freed me, I am sure, Little Brother."

"Then, by the Bull that bought me, I will pay Shere Khan full tale for this, and it may be a little over," said Mowgli; and he bounded away.

"That is a man. That is all a man," said Bagheera to himself, lying down again. "Oh, Shere Khan never was a blacker hunting than that frog-hunt of thine ten years ago!"

Mowgli was far and far through the forest, running hard, and his heart was hot in him. He came to the cave as the evening mist rose, and drew breath, and

个名字来称呼它。每种动物都对它有着致命的恐惧，并创造了一百种描述它的方式。

"红色的花？"莫格里说，"黄昏时分在他们小屋外面生长。我会取一些的。"

"这是人类幼崽应该说的话，"巴赫拉说这话时，显得很骄傲，"记着，它生长在小盆里。要迅速把它弄来，在需要的时候把它留在你身边。"

"好！"莫格里说，"我走了。但是你确定吗，我的巴赫拉"——他用胳膊搂住巴赫拉闪亮的脖子，并深深地看着他的大眼睛——"你确定这一切都是谢尔可汗在搞鬼？"

"以我获得自由损坏的那把锁发誓，我确定，小兄弟。"

"那么，以买下我的那头公牛发誓，我会让谢尔可汗为这一切付出代价，也许要付出更多。"莫格里说，随后就走开了。

"这是一个人的样子，这完全就是一个人，"巴赫拉自言自语说着，再次躺了下来，"哦，再也没有比谢尔可汗十年前捕杀青蛙莫格里更不幸的捕猎了。"

莫格里在树林中跑得越来越远，他拼命地跑着，心里火热。黄昏时分，他回到山洞。他吸了口气，

looked down the valley. The cubs were out, but Mother Wolf, at the back of the cave, knew by his breathing that something was troubling her frog.

"What is it, Son?" she said.

"Some bat's chatter of Shere Khan," he called back. "I hunt among the plowed fields to-night"; and he plunged downward through the bushes, to the stream at the bottom of the valley. There he checked, for he heard the yell of the Pack hunting, heard the bellow of a hunted Sambhur, and the snort as the buck turned at bay. Then there were wicked, bitter howls from the young wolves: "Akela! Akela! Let the Lone Wolf show his strength. Room for the leader of our Pack! Spring, Akela!"

The Lone Wolf must have sprung and missed his hold, for Mowgli heard the snap of his teeth and then a yelp as the Sambhur knocked him over with his fore foot.

He did not wait for anything more, but dashed on; and the yells grew fainter behind him as he ran into the crop-lands where the villagers lived.

"Bagheera spoke truth," he panted, as he nestled down in some cattle-fodder by the window of a hut. "To-morrow is one day for Akela and

俯视着山谷。小狼们都出去了，不过狼妈妈在山洞深处，从他的呼吸声，狼妈妈知道了她的青蛙此刻很困扰。

"怎么了，儿子？"她说。

"谢尔可汗喋喋不休搞的鬼，"他喊着回应，"晚上我在犁过的田地中捕猎。"他从灌木丛中向下飞奔到山谷底部的小溪里。在那里他侦查了一下，因为他听到了狼群狩猎的呐喊，听到被猎公鹿的惨叫，听到了公鹿被逼绝路时发出的鼻息声。然后是一群年轻的狼邪恶的、愤愤的号叫声："阿克拉！阿克拉！让孤狼展示一下他的力量。给我们狼群的首领让地方！跳啊，阿克拉！"

孤狼肯定是失手了，因为莫格里听到他咬牙切齿的声音，接下来那只公鹿用他的前蹄把他踹翻了，他发出了痛苦的叫声。

他没有继续等待发生更多的事情，向前冲着。在他后面，叫喊声越来越弱，他跑进了庄稼地，就是村民生活的那个地方。

"巴赫拉说的是真的，"莫格里喘着气说，他坐在一间小屋的窗户旁边的牛饲料堆里，"对于阿克拉，也对于我，明天是个大日子。"

for me."

Then he pressed his face close to the window and watched the fire on the hearth. He saw the husbandman's wife get up and feed it in the night with black lumps; and when the morning came and the mists were all white and cold, he saw the man's child pick up a wicker pot plastered inside with earth, fill it with lumps of red-hot charcoal, put it under his blanket, and go out to tend the cows in the byre.

"Is that all?" said Mowgli. "If a cub can do it, there is nothing to fear"; so he strode around the corner and met the boy, took the pot from his hand, and disappeared into the mist while the boy howled with fear.

"They are very like me," said Mowgli, blowing into the pot, as he had seen the woman do "This thing will die if I do not give it things to eat"; and he dropped twigs and dried bark on the red stuff. Half-way up the hill he met Bagheera with the morning dew shining like moonstones on his coat.

"Akela has missed," said the panther. "They would have killed him last night, but they needed thee also. They were looking for thee on the hill."

"I was among the plowed lands. I am

然后他把脸紧贴在窗户上,看着壁炉上的炉火。他瞧见农夫的妻子黑夜当中站起来,往里面喂一些黑色的东西。清晨时分,薄雾又白又冷,他看到那个人类的小孩拿起一个柳条的泥罐子,装满了红彤彤的炭块,放在毯子下面,然后走出来,照管牛棚里的牛。

"就这样?"莫格里说,"如果一个小孩子能做到的,那没什么可怕的。"于是他大步走到拐角处,走向那个男孩,从他的手中抢了盆子,就消失在雾中了,那个男孩被吓得哭了起来。

"他们和我真的很像。"莫格里说着,往盆子里吹着气,他看见那个女人就这么做的。"如果我给他吃东西,这东西就会死。"他把树枝和树皮放在红色的东西上。上山途中他遇到巴赫拉,晨露在他的皮毛上就像月光石一样闪闪发亮。

"阿克拉不见了,"黑豹说,"他们打算昨天晚上就把他杀了,但他们需要把你一起杀了。他们正在山上寻找你。"

"我昨晚在耕地。我准备好

ready. Look!" Mowgli held up the fire-pot.

"Good! Now, I have seen men thrust a dry branch into that stuff, and presently the Red Flower blossomed at the end of it. Art thou not afraid?"

"No. Why should I fear? I remember now – if it is not a dream – how, before I was a wolf, I lay beside the Red Flower, and it was warm and pleasant."

All that day Mowgli sat in the cave tending his fire-pot and dipping dry branches into it to see how they looked. He found a branch that satisfied him, and in the evening when Tabaqui came to the cave and told him, rudely enough, that he was wanted at the Council Rock, he laughed till Tabaqui ran away. Then Mowgli went to the Council, still laughing.

Akela the Lone Wolf lay by the side of his rock as a sign that the leadership of the Pack was open, and Shere Khan with his following of scrap-fed wolves walked to and fro openly, being flattered. Bagheera lay close to Mowgli, and the fire-pot was between Mowgli's knees. When they were all gathered together, Shere Khan began to speak – a thing he would never have dared to do when Akela was in his

了。瞧!"莫格里举起火盆。

"好样的!现在是这样,我看过人们把一根干树枝插进这个东西里,不久红色的花朵就在它的顶端开花。你不感到害怕吗?"

"不害怕,我为什么要害怕?我现在还记得——如果那不是梦的话——在我变成狼之前,我就躺在红色的花朵旁边,它是温暖宜人的。"

那一整天,莫格里一直坐在山洞中照料他的火盆。他将干燥的树枝放进去,看着它们一点点燃尽的样子。他找到了一枝让他满意的树枝。傍晚的时候,塔巴克来到山洞,态度粗鲁地告诉他,他们想要他到会议岩石那里。莫格里大笑,直到塔巴克跑了。接着莫格里来到大会当中,还保持着大笑。

孤狼阿克拉躺在了岩石旁边,这说明狼群的首领现在是空缺。谢尔可汗和那些追随他捡食残羹冷炙的狼们来回地走着,享受着大家的巴结。巴赫拉靠近莫格里,火盆就放在莫格里的膝盖中间。当全部聚齐的时候,谢尔可汗开始说话。这是在阿克拉巅峰期间,他从未敢做的事情。

prime.

"He has no right," whispered Bagheera. "Say so. He is a dog's son. He will be frightened."

Mowgli sprang to his feet. "Free People," he cried, "does Shere Khan lead the Pack? What has a tiger to do with our leadership?"

"Seeing that the leadership is yet open, and being asked to speak –" Shere Khan began.

"By whom?" said Mowgli. "Are we all jackals, to fawn on this cattle-butcher? The leadership of the Pack is with the Pack alone."

There were yells of "Silence, thou man's cub!" "Let him speak; he has kept our law!" And at last the seniors of the Pack thundered: "Let the Dead Wolf speak!"

When a leader of the Pack has missed his kill, he is called the Dead Wolf as long as he lives, which is not long, as a rule.

Akela raised his old head wearily:

"Free People, and ye too, jackals of Shere Khan, for twelve seasons I have led ye to and from the kill, and in all that time not one has been trapped or maimed. Now I have missed my kill. Ye know how that plot was made. Ye

"他无权这样做，"巴赫拉低声说，"就这么说，他是一个狗的儿子，他会感到害怕的。"

莫格里跳起来。"自由民众，"他大喊，"谢尔可汗现在领导着狼群吗？他一只老虎和我们的首领有什么关系？"

"看看现在首领是空缺的，我是受大家请求发言的。"谢尔可汗开始说。

"谁请求你发言了？"莫格里说，"我们竟然是豺狗吗？要对你这个牛屠夫卑躬屈膝？狼群的首领问题是狼群自己的事。"

群体中出现了喊声："闭嘴，你这个人类的幼崽！""让他说话，他一直都遵从我们的法则。"最后是群体中年纪大一些的狼大声疾呼道："让死狼讲话。"

按照规定，当一个狼群的首领猎杀失败的时候，他还没死就会被称作死狼，不过通常他也不会活得太久了。

阿克拉疲惫地抬起他的头：

"自由的民众啊，还有你们这些谢尔可汗的豺狼，我已经带领你们十二载春秋，带领你们从搏杀中生存，在这期间没有一只狼掉进陷阱或者受伤致残。如今我捕杀失败了。你们清楚这阴谋是怎么回事。

know how ye brought me up to an untried buck to make my weakness known. It was cleverly done. Your right is to kill me here on the Council Rock now. Therefore I ask, 'Who comes to make an end of the Lone Wolf?' For it is my right, by the Law of the Jungle, that ye come one by one."

There was a long hush, for no single wolf cared to fight Akela to the death. Then Shere Khan roared: "Bah! What have we to do with this toothless fool? He is doomed to die! It is the man-cub who has lived too long. Free People, he was my meat from the first. Give him to me. I am weary of this man-wolf folly. He has troubled the jungle for ten seasons. Give me the man-cub, or I will hunt here always, and not give you one bone! He is a man – a man's child, and from the marrow of my bones I hate him!"

Then more than half the Pack yelled: "A man – a man! What has a man to do with us? Let him go to his own place."

"And turn all the people of the villages against us?" snarled Shere Khan. "No; give him to me. He is a man, and none of us can look him between the eyes."

Akela lifted his head again, and said:

你们知道你们是如何把我带入到一个未经试探的公鹿面前,使我的虚弱人尽皆知。这事儿错得很巧妙。现在你们有权在这个会议岩石上把我结果掉。因此我请问,谁来终结我这条孤狼的性命?这是我的权利,根据丛林法则,你们只能一个一个来。"

很长一段时间没有任何动静,没有一只狼想要独自与阿克拉决一死战。接下来谢尔可汗喊道:"呸!我们跟这个没牙的蠢货有什么关系?他注定是要死的!活得太久的是那个小男孩。自由的兽民,最开始他就是我的嘴边肉。把他交给我吧。我讨厌这个人狼的蠢笨,他在丛林中制造麻烦已经十个春秋。将人类的幼崽给我,要不然我就在这儿捕猎,不给你们留一根骨头。他是人——人类的孩子,我对他恨之入骨。"

超过一半的狼大声喊道:"一个人,一个人!人和我们有什么关系呢?让他回到他自己的地盘去。"

"然后村庄里所有的人反过来对付我们?"谢尔可汗咆哮着说,"不要,将他给我。他是个人,我们中任何一个人都不能与他对视。"

"He has eaten our food; he has slept with us; he has driven game for us; he has broken no word of the Law of the Jungle."

"Also, I paid for him with a bull when he was accepted. The worth of a bull is little, but Bagheera's honor is something that he will perhaps fight for," said Bagheera in his gentlest voice.

"A bull paid ten years ago!" the Pack snarled. "What do we care for bones ten years old?"

"Or for a pledge?" said Bagheera, his white teeth bared under his lip. "Well are ye called the Free People!"

"No man's cub can run with the people of the jungle!" roared Shere Khan. "Give him to me."

"He is our brother in all but blood," Akela went on; "and ye would kill him here. In truth, I have lived too long. Some of ye are eaters of cattle, and of others I have heard that, under Shere Khan's teaching, ye go by dark night and snatch children from the villager's doorstep. Therefore I know ye to be cowards, and it is to cowards I speak. It is certain that I must die, and my life is of no worth, or I would offer that in the man-cub's place. But for the sake of the

阿克拉再次抬起头，说："他吃着我们的食物，同我们一同入眠，他为我们追捕食物，他一点也不曾破坏丛林法则。"

"并且，他被大家接受的时候，我是用公牛赎买的。一头牛没什么价值，但是巴赫拉的荣誉并非一文不值，他也许会为此而战斗的。"巴赫拉用他温柔的声音说。

"十年前的一头公牛！"狼群厉声地说，"十年的几根骨头，我们在乎它干什么？"

"为了承诺呢？"巴赫拉说着，露出他白色的牙齿，"你们这就叫自由民众啊！"

"没有什么人类的幼崽能和丛林里的兽众一起奔跑，"谢尔可汗吼叫着，"把他交给我。"

"他在所有方面都是我们的兄弟，除了血脉，"阿克拉接着说，"你们要在这里把他杀死。事实上，我活得太久了。你们当中现在有些成了食牛狼，我已经听说了，在谢尔可汗的教唆下，你们深夜的时候从村民的家门口抢夺孩子。所以我很清楚你们就是懦夫，我此刻就在对懦夫讲话。我一定会死，这毋庸置疑。我的性命毫无价值，要不然我会代人类的幼崽一死。但是，为了狼群的荣誉——这件小

Honor of the Pack, – a little matter that, by being without a leader, ye have forgotten, – I promise that if ye let the man-cub go to his own place, I will not, when my time comes to die, bare one tooth against ye. I will die without fighting. That will at least save the Pack three lives. More I cannot do; but, if ye will, I can save ye the shame that comes of killing a brother against whom there is no fault – a brother spoken for and bought into the Pack according to the Law of the Jungle."

"He is a man – a man – a man!" snarled the Pack; and most of the wolves began to gather round Shere Khan, whose tail was beginning to switch.

"Now the business is in thy hands," said Bagheera to Mowgli. "We can do no more except fight."

Mowgli stood upright – the fire-pot in his hands. Then he stretched out his arms, and yawned in the face of the Council; but he was furious with rage and sorrow, for, wolf-like, the wolves had never told him how they hated him.

"Listen, you!" he cried. "There is no need for this dog's jabber. Ye have told me so often to-night that I am a man

事，没有首领，你们已经忘了什么是荣誉——我承诺倘若你们让人类的幼崽去他自己的地盘，当我要死的时候，我不会对你们露出一颗牙。我不与你们决斗就死。那至少能够拯救三条狼的性命。再多的我就做不了了。但是，如果你们愿意，我可以拯救你们免于蒙羞，去杀死一个没有过错的兄弟——他是根据丛林法则，有兄弟为他讲话才被带进狼群的。"

"他是个人——一个人——一个人！"狼群咆哮着。大多数狼开始围着谢尔可汗，他的尾巴开始摇摆起来。

"此时一切在你手中了，"巴赫拉对莫格里说，"除了战斗，我们别无选择。"

莫格里站起来——火盆在他的手里。然后他伸展了下胳膊，打了个哈欠。但是他心中充满了愤怒和悲痛，因为，狼真是狼心，这些狼从未告诉他他们如何讨厌他。

"听着，你们这帮家伙！"他喊道，"没有必要像条狗一样。这个晚上你们说了那么多次我是一

(though indeed I would have been a wolf with you to my life's end) that I feel your words are true. So I do not call ye my brothers any more, butsag, as a man should. What ye will do, and what ye will not do, is not yours to say. That matter is with me; and that we may see the matter more plainly, I, the man, have brought here a little of the Red Flower which ye, dogs, fear."

He flung the fire-pot on the ground, and some of the red coals lit a tuft of dried moss that flared up as all the Council drew back in terror before the leaping flames.

Mowgli thrust his dead branch into the fire till the twigs lit and crackled, and whirled it above his head among the cowering wolves.

"Thou art the master," said Bagheera, in an undertone. "Save Akela from death. He was ever thy friend."

Akela, the grim old wolf who had never asked for mercy in his life, gave one piteous look at Mowgli as the boy stood all naked, his long black hair tossing over his shoulders in the light of the blazing branch that made the shadows jump and quiver.

"Good!" said Mowgli, staring

个人（虽然我确实想要一辈子都和你们在一起做一只狼）。我觉得你们说的话是真心的，因此我再也不会将你们叫作兄弟。我要像一个人原本的样子，叫你们傻狗。你们将做什么，不做什么，不是由你们说的，那是我说了算。我们可以更清楚地看清事态，我，人类，带来了让你们这群狗惧怕的红色花朵。"

他将火盆粗暴地扔在地上，一些红色的炭块点燃了一簇干苔藓，火苗烧了起来。在跳跃的火苗面前，所有狼都吓得往后退缩。

莫格里把枯枝放在火上点燃，等到枝杈噼啪作响的时候，他把树枝举到头顶摇晃。整个狼群都吓得畏畏缩缩。

"现在你是老大，"巴赫拉低声说，"救救阿克拉，他永远都是你的朋友。"

阿克拉，一生中从未请求怜悯的冷酷老狼，现在却可怜兮兮地看着莫格里。莫格里赤裸裸地站在那里，黑色的长发披在肩膀上，燃烧的树枝的光亮使一个个影子不断跳跃和颤抖着。

"好吧！"莫格里说着，慢慢

around slowly. "I see that ye are dogs. I go from you to my own people – if they be my own people. The jungle is shut to me, and I must forget your talk and your companionship; but I will be more merciful than ye are. Because I was all but your brother in blood, I promise that when I am a man among men I will not betray ye to men as ye have betrayed me." He kicked the fire with his foot, and the sparks flew up. "There shall be no war between any of us and the Pack. But here is a debt to pay before I go." He strode forward to where Shere Khan sat blinking stupidly at the flames, and caught him by the tuft on his chin. Bagheera followed close, in case of accidents. "Up, dog!" Mowgli cried. "Up, when a man speaks, or I will set that coat ablaze!"

Shere Khan's ears lay flat back on his head, and he shut his eyes, for the blazing branch was very near.

"This cattle-killer said he would kill me in the Council because he had not killed me when I was a cub. Thus and thus, then, do we beat dogs when we are men! Stir a whisker, Lungri, and I ram the Red Flower down thy gullet!" He beat Shere Khan over the head with the branch, and the tiger whimpered

地凝视了四周，"我了解了你们是狗。我从你们身边走开，我回到我的同族里去——如果他们是我的同族的话。丛林对我来说关闭了，我必须忘记你们对我说过什么，也忘记与你们的伙伴情，不过我会比你们更慈悲。因为只有血脉不是，其他方面我都是你们的兄弟，我保证，我在人类中间的时候，我不会像你们出卖我那样背叛你们。"莫格里用脚蹬了一下火，火花飞了起来，"我们之间，还有狼群内部不应该有战争。不过我离开之前，这里有笔账要算一下。"他大步走到谢尔可汗面前，谢尔可汗正傻傻地对着火光眨巴着眼睛，莫格里抓住了他下颚上的一簇毛。巴赫拉紧随身后，以防不测。"站起来，你这只狗！"莫格里喊道，"当一个人讲话的时候，你要站起来，要不然我把你的皮毛烧了。"

谢尔可汗的耳朵平贴在脑后，而且把眼睛闭上了，因为炽热的树枝近在眼前。

"这个牛屠夫说要在大会上杀死我，因为我是一个幼崽的时候，他没将我干掉。既然这样，那我们称之为人的时候，我必然打狗。郎格离，若是敢动一根胡须，我把红色的花插进你的喉咙！"莫格里用树枝击打谢尔可汗的脑壳，

and whined in an agony of fear.

"Pah! Singed jungle-cat – go now! But remember when next I come to the Council Rock, as a man should come, it will be with Shere Khan's hide on my head. For the rest, Akela goes free to live as he pleases. Ye will not kill him, because that is not my will. Nor do I think that ye will sit here any longer, lolling out your tongues as though ye were somebodies, instead of dogs whom I drive out – thus! Go!"

The fire was burning furiously at the end of the branch, and Mowgli struck right and left round the circle, and the wolves ran howling with the sparks burning their fur. At last there were only Akela, Bagheera, and perhaps ten wolves that had taken Mowgli's part. Then something began to hurt Mowgli inside him, as he had never been hurt in his life before, and he caught his breath and sobbed, and the tears ran down his face.

"What is it? What is it?" he said. "I do not wish to leave the jungle, and I do not know what this is. Am I dying, Bagheera?"

"No, Little Brother. That is only tears such as men use," said Bagheera. "Now I know thou art a man and a

这只老虎非常害怕，哀号着、呜咽着。

"呸！你这只被烧焦的丛林猫——现在就滚！不过记得下次我来到会议岩石的时候，是作为一个人来的，我会把谢尔可汗的皮顶在脑袋上。另外，阿克拉可以自由地按照自己的意愿生活。你们不准杀他，因为我不允许你们那样做。我想你们也不要坐在这里了，舌头都伸出来好像自己是个大人物，不是我要赶走的狗似的——所以，滚吧！"

树枝末端的火愈加猛烈。莫格里左右轮了一圈，那些狼都逃走了，因为火花烧到了他们的皮毛，吓得他们直叫。最后，只有阿克拉、巴赫拉和大约十来只和莫格里站在一边的狼留下了。莫格里的内心感到了伤痛。因为他以前从来没有受过伤害，他吸了一口气，抽泣着，泪水顺着脸颊流了下来。

"这是什么东西？这是什么东西？"他说，"我不愿意离开丛林，我不知道这是什么东西。我快死了吧，巴赫拉？"

"不是的，小兄弟。这只是像人类会流的眼泪，"巴赫拉说，"此时我知道了，你不再是一个人类的

man's cub no longer. The jungle is shut indeed to thee henceforward. Let them fall, Mowgli; they are only tears." So Mowgli sat and cried as though his heart would break; and he had never cried in all his life before.

"Now," he said, "I will go to men. But first I must say farewell to my mother"; and he went to the cave where she lived with Father Wolf, and he cried on her coat, while the four cubs howled miserably.

"Ye will not forget me?" said Mowgli.

"Never while we can follow a trail," said the cubs. "Come to the foot of the hill when thou art a man, and we will talk to thee; and we will come into the crop-lands to play with thee by night."

"Come soon!" said Father Wolf. "Oh, wise little Frog, come again soon; for we be old, thy mother and I."

"Come soon," said Mother Wolf, "little naked son of mine; for, listen, child of man, I loved thee more than ever I loved my cubs."

"I will surely come," said Mowgli; "and when I come it will be to lay out Shere Khan's hide upon the Council Rock. Do not forget me! Tell them in the jungle never to forget me!"

幼崽了，你已经长大成人。丛林从此就对你关闭了。让眼泪流吧，莫格里，他们只是眼泪而已。"于是莫格里坐下来大哭，就好像他的心要碎了。而他以前从来没有哭过。

"如今，"莫格里说，"我会回到人类中间，不过首先我要跟我的母亲告别。"他去了狼妈妈狼爸爸一起居住的山洞，在她的皮毛上趴着痛哭，而四只小狼也悲惨地号叫着。

"你们不会把我忘掉吧？"莫格里说。

"我们只要能追踪猎物，就绝不会忘了你，"小狼们说，"当你成为人之后，来山脚下，我们和你聊天。晚上的时候我们去庄稼地和你一起玩。"

"快点来！"狼爸爸说，"聪慧的小青蛙，快点再来，因为我们，你妈妈和我老了。"

"快点来，"狼妈妈说，"我光溜的小儿子，因为，听着，人类的孩子，我对你的爱超越我爱自己的孩子。"

"我一定会来的，"莫格里说，"当我来的时候，我会把谢尔可汗的皮放在会议岩石上。一定不要忘了我！要告诉丛林里的兽众们绝对不要忘了我！"

The dawn was beginning to break when Mowgli went down the hillside alone to the crops to meet those mysterious things that are called men.

黎明破晓时分,莫格里独自走下山坡,他去见那些被称作人类的神秘生物。

HUNTING-SONG OF THE SEEONEE PACK

西奥尼狼群狩猎之歌

AS the dawn was breaking the Sambhur belled

Once, twice, and again!

And a doe leaped up – and a doe leaped up

From the pond in the wood where the wild deer sup.

This I, scouting alone, beheld,

Once, twice, and again!

黎明破晓，黑鹿鸣叫，

一声，两声，又一声！

一只母鹿跳起来，一只母鹿跳起来，

就在野鹿啜饮的树林池塘边。

我独自一人观察，

一声，两声，又一声！

As the dawn was breaking the Sambhur belled

Once, twice, and again!

And a wolf stole back – and a wolf stole back

To carry the word to the waiting Pack;

And we sought and we found and we bayed on his track

Once, twice, and again!

黎明破晓，黑鹿鸣叫，

一声，两声，又一声！

一只狼偷偷折返——一只狼偷偷折返，

把话带给等待的狼群。

我们寻找，我们发现，我们正循着他的踪迹，

一声，两声，又一声！

As the dawn was breaking the Wolf-pack yelled

Once, twice, and again!

黎明破晓，狼群齐声号叫，

一声，两声，又一声！

Feet in the jungle that leave no mark!

Eyes that can see in the dark – the dark!

Tongue – give tongue to it! Hark! O Hark!

Once, twice, and again!

丛林之中没有留下痕迹的脚！

能在黑暗之中看清的眼，黑暗之中看得清！

舌头——吐出舌头！听着！哦，听着！

一声，两声，又一声！

CHAPTER 2   KAA'S HUNTING

第二章   卡阿的狩猎

*HIS spots are the joy of the Leopard:
his horns are the Buffalo's pride –*

*Be clean, for the strength of the
hunter is known by the gloss of his
hide.*

*If ye find that the Bullock can toss
you, or the heavy-browed Sambhur can
gore;*

*Ye need not stop work to inform us:
we knew it ten seasons before.*

*Oppress not the cubs of the stranger,
but hail them as Sister and Brother,*

*For though they are little and fubsy,
it may be the Bear is their mother.*

*"There is none like to me!" says the
Cub in the pride of his earliest kill;*

*But the Jungle is large and the Cub
he is small. Let him think and be still.*

Maxims of Baloo

ALL that is told here happened some
time before Mowgli was turned out of
the Seeonee Wolf Pack, or revenged
himself on Shere Kham the Tiger. It

　　身上的斑点是猎豹的喜乐，头上的犄角是水牛的自尊。

　　一定要洁净，因为猎手的力量凭他身上的光泽就可窥见一斑。

　　如果发觉公牛能把你踢翻，黑鹿也用角顶你，

　　不必停下捕杀知会我们，十年之前我们就已经知晓。

　　不要欺负陌生的幼崽，要把他们当作兄弟姐妹，

　　尽管他们很小，胖乎乎的，可他们没准儿是大熊的宝宝。

　　"没有谁像我一样！"幼崽最初捕猎时自豪地说，

　　丛林很大，幼崽很小。让他静静地思考。

　　——巴洛格言

　　这里所说的一切都发生在莫格里被赶出西奥尼狼群之前，或者说是他自己还没有向谢尔可汗那只老虎复仇之前。那段日子，巴洛

was in the days when Baloo was teaching him the Law of the Jungle. The big, serious, old brown bear was delighted to have so quick a pupil, for the young wolves will only learn as much of the Law of the Jungle as applies to their own pack and tribe, and run away as soon as they can repeat the Hunting Verse: "Feet that make no noise; eyes that can see in the dark; ears that can hear the winds in their lairs, and sharp white teeth – all these things are the marks of our brothers except Tabaqui and the Hyena, whom we hate." But Mowgli, as a man-cub, had to learn a great deal more than this. Sometimes Bagheera, the Black Panther, would come lounging through the jungle to see how his pet was getting on, and would purr with his head against a tree while Mowgli recited the day's lesson to Baloo. The boy could climb almost as well as he could swim, and swim almost as well as he could run; so Baloo, the Teacher of the Law, taught him the Wood and Water laws: how to tell a rotten branch from a sound one; how to speak politely to the wild bees when he came upon a hive of them fifty feet aboveground; what to say to Mang, the

教会他什么是丛林法则。高大严肃的老棕熊非常开心能有学得这么快的学生。因为年轻的狼刚刚知道了适用于他们自己族群或者部落的法则，能够重复狩猎的诗句就急忙跑走了："脚掌莫要出声响，双眼深夜擦清亮；耳朵辨出巢穴风，尖白牙齿不能少；除了我们讨厌的塔巴克和豺狗，大家都是兄弟。"不过莫格里，这个人类的幼崽，不得不学习更多的东西。有些时候，大黑豹巴赫拉会穿过丛林闲逛一番，来看看他喜爱的小兄弟学得怎么样。当莫格里给巴洛背诵一天的功课时，巴赫拉就将头靠在树上发出满意的咕噜声。这个男孩爬树厉害，游泳出色，奔跑也是一级棒。因此，法则老师巴洛不仅教他森林中的法则，还教他水中的法则；教他如何辨别腐烂的树枝与新鲜的树枝；当他遇见距地面有五十英尺的蜂巢时，如何礼貌地与野蜂讲话；该对午间时分被惊扰了的树上休息的蝙蝠芒恩说什么；以及在跳进去溅起水花之前，如何警告池中的水蛇。没有任何一个丛林居民喜欢被打扰，所有居民都准备好向侵犯者飞扑过来。接下来，莫格里也学会了陌生者的狩猎招呼。当一个丛林居民在自己地盘之外进行狩猎时，必须大声地重复，直到得到

Bat, when he disturbed him in the branches at midday; and how to warn the water-snakes in the pools before he splashed down among them. None of the Jungle People like being disturbed, and all are very ready to fly at an intruder. Then, too, Mowgli was taught the Strangers' Hunting Call, which must be repeated aloud till it is answered, whenever one of the Jungle People hunts outside his own grounds. It means, translated: "Give me leave to hunt here because I am hungry"; and the answer is: "Hunt, then, for food, but not for pleasure."

All this will show you how much Mowgli had to learn by heart, and he grew very tired of repeating the same thing a hundred times; but, as Baloo said to Bagheera one day when Mowgli had been cuffed and had run off in a temper: "A man's cub is a man's cub, and he must learn all the Law of the Jungle."

"But think how small he is," said the Black Panther, who would have spoiled Mowgli if he had had his own way. "How can his little head carry all thy long talk?"

"Is there anything in the jungle too little to be killed? No. That is why I

答复才可以进行捕杀。这意思翻译过来是说："让我在这里狩猎吧，因为我饿了。"回复是："狩猎吧。不过只是为了食物，不是享乐的。"

所有这些都会告诉你，莫格里必须用心学会很多东西。他厌倦了重复同样的事情一百多遍。不过，正如那天莫格里被打了一巴掌，生气跑掉了时巴洛对巴赫拉说的："人类的幼崽终归是人类的幼崽，他必须学会丛林的所有法则。"

"但是想想他才多小，"黑豹说，如果让他用自己的方式教授莫格里，会把他娇惯坏的，"他那个小脑袋如何能装下你所有的冗词赘句？"

"丛林里有任何生物因为太小就免于被杀吗？没有。这就是为

teach him these things, and that is why I hit him, very softly, when he forgets."

"Softly! What dost thou know of softness, old Iron-feet?" Bagheera grunted. "His face is all bruised to-day by thy – softness. Ugh!"

"Better he should be bruised from head to foot by me who love him than that he should come to harm through ignorance," Baloo answered, very earnestly. "I am now teaching him the Master Words of the Jungle that shall protect him with the Birds and the Snake People, and all that hunt on four feet, except his own pack. He can now claim protection, if he will only remember the Words, from all in the jungle. Is not that worth a little beating?"

"Well, look it then that thou dost not kill the man-cub. He is no tree-trunk to sharpen thy blunt claws upon. But what are those Master Words? I am more likely to give help than to ask it" – Bagheera stretched out one paw and admired the steel-blue ripping-chisel talons at the end of it – "Still I should like to know."

"I will call Mowgli and he shall say them – if he will. Come, Little Brother!"

什么我教他这些东西，这就是为什么他忘掉的时候我打了他，而且打得很轻。"

"轻轻地！你知道什么是很轻吗，老铁掌？"巴赫拉哼了一声，"他的脸一天都因你轻轻一掌瘀紫呢。哼！"

"我是爱他的，我把他打得从头到脚都肿了，也好过他因愚昧无知受到伤害，"巴洛非常认真地回答，"我现在正在教他丛林主人要说的话。让他免于鸟类、蛇类和所有他自己狼群之外的四条腿的生物的伤害。他可以用丛林之语寻求保护，只要他记得这些话，就能应对所有的丛林兽众。小小地挨一顿打不值得吗？"

"好吧，那你留神一些。不要把人类幼崽给打死。他不是树干，能磨尖你的牙齿。不过那些主人的话语是什么？我是想提供些帮助，不是非得要问，"巴赫拉伸展他的爪子，欣赏着钢铁般的蓝色凿子爪，"但是我还是想知道怎么回事。"

"我叫莫格里，如果他愿意，他会说那是什么。来吧，小兄弟！"

"My head is ringing like a bee-tree," said a sullen voice over their heads, and Mowgli slid down a tree-trunk, very angry and indignant, adding, as he reached the ground: "I come for Bagheera and not for thee, fat old Baloo!"

"That is all one to me," said Baloo, though he was hurt and grieved. "Tell Bagheera, then, the Master Words of the Jungle that I have taught thee this day."

"Master Words for which people?" said Mowgli, delighted to show off. "The jungle has many tongues. I know them all."

"A little thou knowest, but not much. See, O Bagheera, they never thank their teacher! Not one small wolfling has come back to thank old Baloo for his teachings. Say the Word for the Hunting People, then– great scholar!"

"We are of one blood, ye and I," said Mowgli, giving the words the Bear accent which all the Hunting People of the Jungle use.

"Good! Now for the Birds."

Mowgli repeated, with the Kite's whistle at the end of the sentence.

"Now for the Snake People," said Bagheera.

"我的头一直在响,好像树上满是蜜蜂。"在他们的头上,一个愠怒的声音说道。莫格里滑下树来,非常生气,到了地上又愤愤地补充一句:"我是为了巴赫拉过来的,不是为你,老胖巴洛!"

"对我而言是一回事,"巴洛说,尽管他受到了伤害有些伤心,"那么告诉巴赫拉,我今天教你的丛林主人的话语。"

"哪一族群的主人话语?"莫格里高兴地炫耀道,"丛林中有很多种语言,我全部都知晓。"

"你是知道一些,但不太多。瞧瞧,巴赫拉,他们从来不会感谢他们的老师,没有一只小狼回来感谢老巴洛的教导。那么说说狩猎居民的话语吧——了不起的学者。"

"我们血脉相通,你和我。"莫格里说。他用棕熊的语气说着丛林狩猎居民使用的主人话语。

"很好!现在说说鸟类的。"
莫格里以每句末尾带着老鹰的声音背诵着。
"再来蛇类居民的。"巴赫拉说。

The answer was a perfectly indescribable hiss, and Mowgli kicked up his feet behind, clapped his hands together to applaud himself, and jumped on Bagheera's back, where he sat sideways, drumming with his heels on the glossy skin and making the worst faces that he could think of at Baloo.

"There – there! That was worth a little bruise," said the Brown Bear, tenderly. "Some day thou wilt remember me." Then he turned aside to tell Bagheera how he had begged the Master Words from Hathi, the Wild Elephant, who knows all about these things, and how Hathi had taken Mowgli down to a pool to get the Snake Word from a water-snake, because Baloo could not pronounce it, and how Mowgli was now reasonably safe against all accidents in the jungle, because neither snake, bird, nor beast would hurt him.

"No one then is to be feared," Baloo wound up, patting his big furry stomach with pride.

"Except his own tribe," said Bagheera, under his breath; and then aloud to Mowgli: "Have a care for my ribs, Little Brother! What is all this

答案是一种莫名其妙的嘘声。莫格里朝后踢了踢脚，拍了拍手为自己欢呼，接着跳上了巴赫拉的后背，侧坐着，在他的皮毛上击鼓，对巴洛做出他认为最丑陋的鬼脸。

"得了，得了！受点伤还是值得的，"棕熊温柔地说，"有朝一日你会记得我的。"然后他把脸转了过去，跟巴赫拉说，他如何恳求野象哈提教他学习主人话语，哈提知晓所有的一切。还有哈提是如何把莫格里带到池塘中跟水蛇学习蛇的话，因为巴洛不会说蛇语。他说莫格里现在在丛林中基本安全了，没有什么意外。因为蛇、鸟或者野兽都不会伤害他。

"就是说没有谁需要惧怕了。"巴洛拍拍他毛茸茸的大肚子，自豪地说。

"他自己的部落除外，"巴赫拉压低声音说，然后又大声对莫格里说，"照顾下我的肋骨，小兄弟！你上下乱窜是干什么？"

dancing up and down?"

Mowgli had been trying to make himself heard by pulling at Bagheera's shoulder-fur and kicking hard. When the two listened to him he was shouting at the top of his voice: "And so I shall have a tribe of my own, and lead them through the branches all day long."

"What is this new folly, little dreamer of dreams?" said Bagheera.

"Yes, and throw branches and dirt at old Baloo," Mowgli went on. "They have promised me this, ah!"

"Whoof!" Baloo's big paw scooped Mowgli off Bagheera's back, and as the boy lay between the big fore paws he could see the bear was angry.

"Mowgli," said Baloo, "thou hast been talking with the Bandar-log – the Monkey People."

Mowgli looked at Bagheera to see if the panther was angry too, and Bagheera's eyes were as hard as jade-stones.

"Thou hast been with the Monkey People – the gray apes – the people without a Law – the eaters of everything. That is great shame."

"When Baloo hurt my head," said Mowgli (he was still down on his

莫格里一直努力让他们听自己讲话，所以拽着巴赫拉的肩毛，并且用力踢他。当他们两个听他说话的时候，他高声喊道："因此我应该有自己的部落，并带领他们整天穿梭在树枝之间。"

"这个新的蠢念头是什么意思？爱做梦的小梦想家？"巴赫拉说。

"是的，朝老巴洛扔树枝和脏东西，"莫格里继续说，"他们跟我承诺过这个，啊！"

"呜！"巴洛的大爪子把莫格里从巴赫拉的背上抱下来。男孩躺在大熊的两个大前爪之间，能够看见他很不高兴。

"莫格里，"巴洛说，"你和那些班达尔-洛格[1]——猴民讲话了？"

莫格里看着巴赫拉，想瞧瞧是不是另一个伙计也生气了，巴赫拉的眼神坚硬得就如绿宝石一样。

"你和猴子们——那些灰色的猿猴——那些不遵从法则的——什么东西都吃的民众混在一起，真是让人感到羞耻。"

"当我被巴洛打伤了头以后，"莫格里（依然靠在大熊的掌

---

[1] "班达尔"是印度语中"猴子"的谐音，"洛格"是"民"的谐音。

back), "I went away, and the gray apes came down from the trees and had pity on me. No one else cared." He snuffled a little.

"The pity of the Monkey People!" Baloo snorted.

"The stillness of the mountain stream! The cool of the summer sun! And then, man-cub?"

"And then – and then they gave me nuts and pleasant things to eat, and they – they carried me in their arms up to the top of the trees and said I was their blood-brother, except that I had no tail, and should be their leader some day."

"They have no leader," said Bagheera. "They lie. They have always lied."

"They were very kind, and bade me come again. Why have I never been taken among the Monkey People? They stand on their feet as I do. They do not hit me with hard paws. They play all day. Let me get up! Bad Baloo, let me up! I will go play with them again."

"Listen, man-cub," said the bear, and his voice rumbled like thunder on a hot night. "I have taught thee all the Law of the Jungle for all the Peoples of the Jungle – except the Monkey Folk who live in the trees. They have no Law. They are outcaste. They have no speech

间）说，"我就走了，那些灰猿们就从树上跳下来，表现出对我的怜悯。其他的动物都没有在乎我。"他抽动着鼻子，感觉要哭了。

"猴子的怜悯！"巴洛哼了一声说道。

"除非是山涧溪流静止，夏日阳光变凉。接下来呢，人类的幼崽？"

"后来，后来他们给了我坚果和美食，然后他们把我抱在树顶上，说我是他们的亲兄弟，除了我没有尾巴，终有一日我会成为他们的首领。"

"他们才没有首领呢，"巴赫拉说，"他们撒谎了，他们总是在说谎。"

"他们很善良，还叫我再去。为什么你从未把我带到猴子中间？就像我一样，他们也是两只脚站着。他们没有用坚硬的爪子打我，他们一整天都在玩耍。让我起来吧！臭巴洛，快让我起来呀！我要再和他们一起去玩。"

"挺好，崽子，"棕熊说，他的声音在炎热的夜晚就像雷声一样响亮，"我已经把丛林中针对所有居民的法则教给了你，除了住在树上的猴子们。他们是没有法则的，他们是抛弃的贱民。他们没有

of their own, but use the stolen words which they overhear when they listen and peep and wait up above in the branches. Their way is not our way. They are without leaders. They have no remembrance. They boast and chatter and pretend that they are a great people about to do great affairs in the jungle, but the falling of a nut turns their minds to laughter, and all is forgotten. We of the jungle have no dealings with them. We do not drink where the monkeys drink; we do not go where the monkeys go; we do not hunt where they hunt; we do not die where they die. Hast thou ever heard me speak of the Bandar-log till to-day?"

"No," said Mowgli in a whisper, for the forest was very still now that Baloo had finished.

"The Jungle People put them out of their mouths and out of their minds. They are very many, evil, dirty, shameless, and they desire, if they have any fixed desire, to be noticed by the Jungle People. But we do not notice them even when they throw nuts and filth on our heads."

He had hardly spoken when a shower of nuts and twigs spattered down through the branches; and they

自己的语言，却使用偷来的话语。他们在树枝上窥视，静待时机。他们和我们的做事方式不同。没有首领带领他们，他们不长记性。他们爱吹嘘，假装他们是一个了不起的家伙，在丛林里做伟大的事。可是只要看到一颗坚果落下，他们心意马上转移，笑着忘记一切。丛林中的我们不和他们打交道。我们不喝猴子喝的东西，我们不去猴子去的地方。我们不去猴子狩猎的地方狩猎，我们不会死在他们死的地方。到目前为止，你可曾听过我说过班达尔-洛格？"

"没说过。"莫格里低声说。就在巴洛说完这些话的时候，森林里非常安静。

"丛林中的民众嘴上不谈论他们，脑子中也想不起他们。他们数量很多，既邪恶又肮脏，很无耻，欲壑难填。假如说他们有什么欲望是不变的，想必就是被丛林中的居民注意到吧。可是我们不会去注意他们的，就算他们往我们的头上扔坚果和污秽的东西。"

话还没说完，一大堆坚果和小树枝就飞落下来。他们能听见上方树枝间传来的此起彼伏的咳嗽声

could hear coughings and howlings and angry jumpings high up in the air among the thin branches.

"The Monkey People are forbidden," said Baloo, "forbidden to the Jungle People. Remember."

"Forbidden," said Bagheera; "but I still think Baloo should have warned thee against them."

"I – I? How was I to guess he would play with such dirt? The Monkey People! Faugh!"

A fresh shower came down on their heads, and the two trotted away, taking Mowgli with them. What Baloo had said about the monkeys was perfectly true. They belonged to the tree-tops, and as beasts very seldom look up, there was no occasion for the monkeys and the Jungle People to cross one another's path. But whenever they found a sick wolf, or a wounded tiger or bear, the monkeys would torment him, and would throw sticks and nuts at any beast for fun and in the hope of being noticed. Then they would howl and shriek senseless songs, and invite the Jungle People to climb up their trees and fight them, or would start furious battles over nothing among themselves, and leave the dead

和愤怒的跳脚声。

"猴民是禁区，"巴洛说，"记着，对丛林居民而言是禁区。"

"禁区，"巴赫拉说，"不过我还以为巴洛一定早警告你了，离他们远些。"

"我——你是说我吗？我怎么能猜到他会和那些脏货玩到一块去？那些猴子！呸！"

一轮新的坚果树枝雨来临，他们俩带上莫格里小跑着离开了。巴洛所说的关于猴子的那些话完全正确。猴子们是属于树顶的，野兽们很少抬头看，因此猴子与丛林居民没有机会碰面。不过每当发现一只生病的狼，或者一只受伤的老虎或者熊，猴子就会折磨他。他们把树枝和坚果扔向野兽来取乐，就是希望居民们可以注意到他们。然后他们会号叫，唱些无聊的歌，邀请丛林里的民众爬上树和他们战斗，或者他们内部就会发生无缘由的争斗，战死的猴子就留在丛林中，以便让居民们看到。

monkeys where the Jungle People could see them.

They were always just going to have a leader and laws and customs of their own, but they never did, because their memories would not hold over from day to day, and so they settled things by making up a saying: "What the Bandar-log think now the Jungle will think later"; and that comforted them a great deal. None of the beasts could reach them, but on the other hand none of the beasts would notice them, and that was why they were so pleased when Mowgli came to play with them, and when they heard how angry Baloo was.

They never meant to do any more, – the Bandar-log never mean anything at all, – but one of them invented what seemed to him a brilliant idea, and he told all the others that Mowgli would be a useful person to keep in the tribe, because he could weave sticks together for protection from the wind; so, if they caught him, they could make him teach them. Of course Mowgli, as a wood-cutter's child, inherited all sorts of instincts, and used to make little play-huts of fallen branches without thinking how he came to do it. The

他们一直吹嘘马上就有自己的首领，自己的法则和准则，但是他们从来没有实现过，因为他们的记忆不会一天天地延续下去。所以他们就通过编造一句话来敷衍此事："班达尔-洛格此刻想到的，就是日后丛林居民要想的。"这让他们非常安心。没有什么野兽能把他们怎么样，不过另一方面，也没有什么野兽会注意他们。这就是为什么莫格里和他们一起玩的时候，巴洛知道这件事情以后非常愤怒的时候，他们非常高兴。

他们从来没有想过要做什么，班达尔-洛格从未打算做些什么。不过他们当中的一员想到他自认为是绝妙的主意，他告诉其他的猴子，莫格里留在部落中会是一个有用的家伙。因为他可以将树枝编织在一起挡风，只要抓住了他，就让他教他们。这是自然，莫格里作为一个伐木工人的孩子，继承了各种的本能，用掉落的树枝搭建小屋子，想都不用想他就可以做。猴子们在树上看着，认为这些小屋非常棒。这一次，猴子们说他们真的要有一个首领了，他们会成为丛林中

Monkey People, watching in the trees, considered these huts most wonderful. This time, they said, they were really going to have a leader and become the wisest people in the jungle – so wise that every one else would notice and envy them. Therefore they followed Baloo and Bagheera and Mowgli through the jungle very quietly till it was time for the midday nap, and Mowgli, who was very much ashamed of himself, slept between the panther and the bear, resolving to have no more to do with the Monkey People.

The next thing he remembered was feeling hands on his legs and arms, – hard, strong little hands, – and then a swash of branches in his face; and then he was staring down through the swaying boughs as Baloo woke the jungle with his deep cries and Bagheera bounded up the trunk with every tooth bared. The Bandar-log howled with triumph, and scuffled away to the upper branches where Bagheera dared not follow, shouting: "He has noticed us! Bagheera has noticed us! All the Jungle People admire us for our skill and our cunning!" Then they began their flight; and the flight of the Monkey People through tree-land is one of the things

最有智慧的族类——他们是那么聪明，以至于每个丛林居民都会注意到并且羡慕他们。因此，他们悄无声息地跟着巴洛、巴赫拉还有莫格里，穿过丛林，直到午睡的时候。莫格里为自己的做法感到非常羞愧，他睡在黑豹和棕熊的中间，决心不再与猴子们扯上关系。

他记得接下来的事就是他的胳膊腿上面，有很多结实强壮的小手，他的脸划过很多树枝；接着是他正通过摇曳的树枝向下凝望，巴洛用他深沉的呐喊唤醒了丛林；而巴赫拉龇着牙，跳上树干。班达尔-洛格心满意足地吼叫着，你推我搡地跳到更高的树枝，巴赫拉不敢继续跟上了，猴子们喊着："他已经注意到我们了！巴赫拉已经注意到我们了！丛林里的民众都钦佩我们的技巧和智慧。"然后，他们就飞行一般跳远了。猴子们通过树林飞荡而行，是人们无法描述的事情之一。他们的路线是规律的，有十字路口，有上下坡，全部在地面之上五十到七十或者是一百英尺。若是

nobody can describe. They have their regular roads and cross-roads, uphills and downhills, all laid out from fifty to seventy or a hundred feet aboveground, and by these they can travel even at night if necessary.

Two of the strongest monkeys caught Mowgli under the arms and swung off with him through the tree-tops, twenty feet at a bound. Had they been alone they could have gone twice as fast, but the boy's weight held them back. Sick and giddy as Mowgli was he could not help enjoying the wild rush, though the glimpses of earth far down below frightened him, and the terrible check and jerk at the end of the swing over nothing but empty air brought his heart between his teeth.

His escort would rush him up a tree till he felt the weak topmost branches crackle and bend under them, and, then, with a cough and a whoop, would fling themselves into the air outward and downward, and bring up hanging by their hands or their feet to the lower limbs of the next tree. Sometimes he could see for miles and miles over the still green jungle, as a man on the top of a mast can see for miles across the sea, and then the branches and leaves

有必要，他们甚至可以在晚上穿行。

其中两个最强壮的猴子抓住莫格里的手臂，在树顶间穿行，跳一下就有二十英尺的距离。假如是他们独自穿行的话，他们的速度是现在的两倍，但是男孩的体重滞缓了他们。莫格里感到头晕目眩，不过他也不由自主地享受着狂野的匆忙，尽管向下看一眼都让他震撼。每一次突然停下、骤然跃起，穿过除了空气空无一物的空间时，莫格里都吓得心提到了嗓子眼。

他的护送者把他带到树顶，直到他感觉到最细的树枝在他们身下啪啪作响。紧接着，一阵咳嗽和呐喊，他们往前向下方飞跃空中，用手或者脚钩住一棵树比较低的树枝上飞荡起来。有时候，他们还能在绿色的丛林中看到数英里之外的情况，就像桅杆顶端的人，在海面上可以看到数英里之远。树枝和树叶甩在他的脸上，他和他的两个护卫几乎再次回到了地面。

would lash him across the face, and he and his two guards would be almost down to earth again.

So bounding and crashing and whooping and yelling, the whole tribe of Bandar-log swept along the tree-roads with Mowgli their prisoner.

For a time he was afraid of being dropped; then he grew angry, but he knew better than to struggle; and then he began to think. The first thing was to send back word to Baloo and Bagheera, for, at the pace the monkeys were going, he knew his friends would be left far behind. It was useless to look down, for he could see only the top sides of the branches, so he stared upward and saw, far away in the blue, Rann, the Kite, balancing and wheeling as he kept watch over the jungle waiting for things to die. Rann noticed that the monkeys were carrying something, and dropped a few hundred yards to find out whether their load was good to eat. He whistled with surprise when he saw Mowgli being dragged up to a tree-top, and heard him give the Kite call for "We be of one blood, thou and I." The waves of the branches closed over the boy, but Rann balanced

班达尔-洛格一族围在一起，弹跳着、喊叫着，带着他们的俘虏莫格里沿着他们的树林间的路线扬长而去。

有一段时间，他害怕自己掉下去，然后他很生气，可他清楚不应该反抗，然后他开始思考。首要的事情是要给巴洛和巴赫拉捎信儿，因为依照猴子的速度，他知道他的朋友将会远远落在后面。向下瞧是没用的，因为他目前只能看到树枝的顶端。因此他就盯着上面，他瞧见了远处的蓝色天空中，老鹰兰恩缓慢地飞翔，盘旋在上空，视线却是丛林方向，他在守候着什么东西死去。兰恩注意到，猴子们携带了什么东西，他向下降了几百码[1]，想知道这东西是否是美食，他惊讶地吹了声口哨，当他看见被拽到树顶上的是莫格里的时候，他还听到莫格里给他发出信号："我们血脉相连，你和我。" 树枝的巨浪淹没了男孩，但是兰恩飞到了下一棵树上空，恰巧又看到了那张棕色的小脸露出来。"把我的踪迹标记下来！"莫格里喊道，"将这告诉西奥尼狼群的巴洛，还有会议岩石的巴

---

[1] 英制长度单位，1 码等于 91.44 厘米。

away to the next tree in time to see the little brown face come up again. "Mark my trail!" Mowgli shouted. "Tell Baloo of the Seeonee Pack, and Bagheera of the Council Rock."

"In whose name, Brother?" Rann had never seen Mowgli before, though of course he had heard of him.

"Mowgli, the Frog. Man-cub they call me! Mark my trail!"

The last words were shrieked as he was being swung through the air, but Rann nodded, and rose up till he looked no bigger than a speck of dust, and there he hung, watching with his telescope eyes the swaying of the tree-tops as Mowgli's escort whirled along.

"They never go far," he said, with a chuckle. "They never do what they set out to do. Always pecking at new things are the Bandar-log. This time, if I have any eyesight, they have pecked down trouble for themselves, for Baloo is no fledgling and Bagheera can, as I know, kill more than goats."

So he rocked on his wings, his feet gathered up under him, and waited.

Meanwhile, Baloo and Bagheera were furious with rage and grief. Bagheera climbed as he had never

赫拉。"

"以谁之名？兄弟？"兰恩从未见过莫格里，不过当然听说过他。

"青蛙莫格里，他们叫我人类的幼崽，记好我的踪迹！"

最后这句话是莫格里尖叫着喊出来的，因为他被甩到空中。兰恩点头答应，直飞上空，看起来他就像一粒尘埃那般大小时，才停驻在那里，用如同望远镜的眼睛看着莫格里护送者呼啸而去过后摇曳的树梢。

"他们绝不会走远的，"他笑着说，"他们做事一向虎头蛇尾，一直在寻找新花样儿，班达尔-洛格就这样。这一次，如果我没看错的话，他们是给自己惹下麻烦了，因为巴洛可不是一只雏鸟，就我所知，巴赫拉可以捕杀比山羊速度更快的猎物。"

所以他摇动着翅膀，双脚并拢，等待时机。

这时，巴洛和巴赫拉正无比愤怒和悲伤。巴赫拉之前从未这样爬树，树枝因他的体重被折断，他滑

climbed before, but the branches broke beneath his weight, and he slipped down, his claws full of bark.

"Why didst thou not warn the man-cub!" he roared to poor Baloo, who had set off at a clumsy trot in the hope of overtaking the monkeys. "What was the use of half slaying him with blows if thou didst not warn him?"

"Haste! O haste! We – we may catch them yet!" Baloo panted.

"At that speed! It would not tire a wounded cow. Teacher of the Law, cub-beater – a mile of that rolling to and fro would burst thee open. Sit still and think! Make a plan. This is no time for chasing. They may drop him if we follow too close."

"Arrula! Whoo! They may have dropped him already, being tired of carrying him. Who can trust the Bandar-log? Put dead bats on my head! Give me black bones to eat! Roll me into the hives of the wild bees that I may be stung to death, and bury me with the hyena; for I am the most miserable of bears! Arulala! Wahooa! O Mowgli, Mowgli! Why did I not warn thee against the Monkey Folk instead of breaking thy head? Now perhaps I

倒了，爪子里都是树皮。

"怎么没有警告过人类幼崽呢？"巴赫拉对着可怜巴巴的巴洛大吼。巴洛迈着笨拙的步子追赶，希望能追上猴子。"把他打个半死又有什么用？你都没有警告他这些。"

"快跑！快跑！我们——我们或许能赶得上！"巴洛累得气喘吁吁。

"以这样的速度啊！这都追不上一头受伤的母牛，法则教师，打崽子的家伙——你这样圆球一样骨碌一英里就会把你自己炸开。静静地坐下想想！制定个计划。现在不是追赶的时候。如果我们追得太近，他们没准儿就把他抛下来了。"

"哎呀！呜呼！他们没准已经把他扔下来了，他们厌倦了带着他。班达尔-洛格谁能相信？他们往我头上扔死蝙蝠，还有发黑的骨头！让我滚进野蜂的蜂巢吧，我可能就被蜇死了！将我和鬣狗葬在一起吧，因为我是最可怜的熊，哎呀！哇啊！莫格里，莫格里！为什么我不警告你远离猴群，却打伤你的脑袋呢？现在我可能已经把一天的功课从他脑袋里敲出去了，不会主

may have knocked the day's lesson out of his mind, and he will be alone in the jungle without the Master Words!"

Baloo clasped his paws over his ears and rolled to and fro, moaning.

"At least he gave me all the Words correctly a little time ago," said Bagheera, impatiently. "Baloo, thou hast neither memory nor respect. What would the jungle think if I, the Black Panther, curled myself up like Ikki, the Porcupine, and howled?"

"What do I care what the jungle thinks? He may be dead by now."

"Unless and until they drop him from the branches in sport, or kill him out of idleness, I have no fear for the man-cub. He is wise and well-taught, and, above all, he has the eyes that make the Jungle People afraid. But (and it is a great evil) he is in the power of the Bandar-log, and they, because they live in trees, have no fear of any of our people." Bagheera licked his one fore paw thoughtfully.

"Fool that I am! Oh fat, brown, root-digging fool that I am!" said Baloo, uncoiling himself with a jerk. "It is true what Hathi, the Wild Elephant, says: 'To each his own fear'; and they, the Bandar-log, fear Kaa, the

人的话语，他在丛林里就会孤立无援的。

巴洛用爪子揪着耳朵，滚来滚去，不断呻吟着。

"起码片刻之前他跟我准确地背诵了全部的话语，"巴赫拉显得很不耐烦，"巴洛，你不长记性，也没有自尊。倘若我，黑豹，卷曲着身体，像豪猪伊基似的号叫，丛林大众会怎么想我？"

"我还介意什么丛林大众的想法？莫格里此刻都没命了。"

"除非是猴子们为了好玩把他从树枝上甩下来，或者是懒得再带着他就把他杀掉。我不担心这个人类幼崽。他那么聪明，又跟你学了很多，最最重要的一点，他的双眼让所有丛林居民都感到恐惧。但是（很不祥的）他现在被班达尔-洛格控制了，因为他们是生活在树上的，我们之中他们谁都不怕。"巴赫拉舔了舔他的一只前爪，若有所思。

"我是个傻瓜！哦，我就是一个胖乎乎的、周身棕色的、只晓得挖块根的大傻子，"巴洛说的时候，突然站直了，"野象哈提说得没错，他说，'谁都有自己的恐惧。'而他们，班达尔-洛格害怕那条岩石蟒

Rock Snake. He can climb as well as they can. He steals the young monkeys in the night. The mere whisper of his name makes their wicked tails cold. Let us go to Kaa."

"What will he do for us? He is not of our tribe, being footless and with most evil eyes," said Bagheera.

"He is very old and very cunning. Above all, he is always hungry," said Baloo, hopefully. "Promise him many goats."

"He sleeps for a full month after he has once eaten. He may be asleep now, and even were he awake, what if he would rather kill his own goats?" Bagheera, who did not know much about Kaa, was naturally suspicious.

"Then in that case, thou and I together, old hunter, may make him see reason." Here Baloo rubbed his faded brown shoulder against the panther, and they went off to look for Kaa, the Rock Python.

They found him stretched out on a warm ledge in the afternoon sun, admiring his beautiful new coat, for he had been in retirement for the last ten days changing his skin, and now he was very splendid – darting his big blunt-nosed head along the ground, and

蛇卡阿。卡阿爬树的本领和他们一样好。他可以在夜晚偷走小猴子。只要在他们面前轻轻地提到卡阿的名字，他们邪恶的尾巴都会吓得拔凉。咱们去找卡阿吧。"

"他能为我们做什么？他不是我们族群的成员，没有脚，长着最邪恶的双眼的家伙。"巴赫拉说。

"他老谋深算。不过最关键的是他总是饿肚子，"巴洛充满希望地说，"我们答应给他很多很多的山羊。"

"他要是吃饱了，能睡上一整月。他现在都可能睡着呢，就算是他清醒着，倘若他宁愿自己猎杀山羊呢，那怎么办？"对卡阿不是很了解的巴赫拉，当然会有疑惑。

"如果真的是那样的话，你和我一起去找他，老猎手，你或许能成为他动心的理由。"巴洛以他已经褪色的棕色肩膀擦着巴赫拉，他们一起出发去寻找岩石之蟒卡阿了。

他们找到他的时候，卡阿正在午后的阳光下舒展着身子，欣赏着他美丽的新皮肤，因为过去的十天他为了蜕皮，一直在休息。此时他确实光芒耀眼，他的钝头贴在地面上，三十英尺的身子蜷曲着绕成让人惊奇的结。他一直在舔着嘴唇，

twisting the thirty feet of his body into fantastic knots and curves, and licking his lips as he thought of his dinner to come.

"He has not eaten," said Baloo, with a grunt of relief, as soon as he saw the beautifully mottled brown and yellow jacket. "Be careful, Bagheera! He is always a little blind after he has changed his skin, and very quick to strike."

Kaa was not a poison snake – in fact he rather despised the Poison Snakes for cowards; but his strength lay in his hug, and when he had once lapped his huge coils round anybody there was no more to be said. "Good hunting!" cried Baloo, sitting up on his haunches. Like all snakes of his breed Kaa was rather deaf, and did not hear the call at first. Then he curled up ready for any accident, his head lowered.

"Good hunting for us all," he answered. "Oho, Baloo, what dost thou do here? Good hunting, Bagheera. One of us at least needs food. Is there any news of game afoot? A doe now, or even a young buck? I am as empty as a dried well."

"We are hunting," said Baloo, carelessly. He knew that you must not

想着要到嘴的晚餐。

"他还没有进食，"巴洛说，当他看到卡阿漂亮的褐黄相间的新皮肤，咕噜着吐出一口气，"要小心，巴赫拉！他刚换过皮肤之后，总是有点莽撞的，出击也非常迅速。"

卡阿不是什么毒蛇，事实上他非常瞧不起毒蛇，在他眼里那就是懦夫。卡阿的力量体现在他的拥抱之中，只要被他庞大的身躯缠绕住以后，就没什么必要挣扎了。"狩猎顺利！"巴洛坐下来喊道。就像同族的蛇一样，卡阿也有点耳背，开始的时候没有听到声音。然后他蜷曲着身子应对意外情况，脑袋也低下了。

"愿我们都狩猎顺利，"他回应道，"哦，巴洛，你在这儿是干什么？狩猎顺利，巴赫拉，我们当中至少一位需要食物，有关于猎物的消息吗？一只母鹿，甚至是关于一只小公鹿的？我都饿扁了，像枯井一般。"

"我们恰巧在捕猎。"巴洛漫不经心地说。他清楚你不能急于求

hurry Kaa. He is too big.

"Give me permission to come with you," said Kaa. "A blow more or less is nothing to thee, Bagheera or Baloo, but I – I have to wait and wait for days in a wood path and climb half a night on the mere chance of a young ape. Psshaw! The branches are not what they were when I was young. Rotten twigs and dry boughs are they all."

"Maybe thy great weight has something to do with the matter," said Baloo.

"I am a fair length – a fair length," said Kaa, with a little pride. "But for all that, it is the fault of this new-grown timber. I came very near to falling on my last hunt, – very near indeed, – and the noise of my slipping, for my tail was not tight wrapped round the tree, waked the Bandar-log, and they called me most evil names."

"Footless, yellow earthworm," said Bagheera under his whiskers, as though he were trying to remember something.

"Sssss! Have they ever called me that?" said Kaa.

"Something of that kind it was that they shouted to us last moon, but we never noticed them. They will say anything – even that thou hast lost all

成，卡阿太过于庞大。

"让我跟着你们一起捕猎吧，"卡阿说，"对于巴赫拉或者巴洛你们来说，捕猎一次多点儿少点儿没什么关系，可是我，我必须在木道上等待好几天，再爬上半夜，也只是有个逮住小猿猴的机会。噗哈！树枝也不像我年轻时候的样子了。现在都是烂树条和枯树枝。"

"或者一部分原因是你太重了。"巴洛说。

"我的身长刚刚好，刚刚好，"卡阿口气中透着小小的骄傲，"都要怪新长出的林木，上次捕猎的时候，我几乎就要，真的马上就要掉下来了。因为我的尾巴那时候没有缠紧在树上，我滑动时候的声响让班达尔-洛格惊醒了。他们就给我起最恶毒的外号。"

"没长脚的大虫，黄色的蚯蚓。"巴赫拉胡须下面的嘴巴说，好像在试图回忆什么。

"嘶嘶！他们曾那样说我？"卡阿说。

"这是他们上个月跟我们叫嚷着说的，不过我们从未注意他们。他们没有什么话不说，他们甚至说你掉光了所有牙齿，不能面对

thy teeth, and dare not face anything bigger than a kid, because (they are indeed shameless, these Bandar-log) – because thou art afraid of the he-goats' horns," Bagheera went on sweetly.

Now a snake, especially a wary old python like Kaa, very seldom shows that he is angry; but Baloo and Bagheera could see the big swallowing muscles on either side of Kaa's throat ripple and bulge.

"The Bandar-log have shifted their grounds," he said, quietly. "When I came up into the sun today I heard them whooping among the tree-tops."

"It – it is the Bandar-log that we follow now," said Baloo; but the words stuck in his throat, for this was the first time in his memory that one of the Jungle People had owned to being interested in the doings of the monkeys.

"Beyond doubt, then, it is no small thing that takes two such hunters – leaders in their own jungle, I am certain – on the trail of the Bandar-log," Kaa replied, courteously, as he swelled with curiosity.

"Indeed," Baloo began, "I am no more than the old, and sometimes very foolish, Teacher of the Law to the Seeonee

任何一个比山羊大的动物，因为你害怕山羊的那个角（他们真的非常无耻，这群班达尔-洛格）。"巴赫拉亲切地说。

对于一条蛇而言，尤其是谨慎的老蟒，就像卡阿这样的是很少会表现出生气的。可是此时巴洛与巴赫拉能够看到，卡阿的喉咙两边的大大的吞咽肌凸起来了。

"班达尔-洛格已经转换领地了，"卡阿平静地说着，"当我今天出来晒太阳的时候，我听到他们在树尖上大声地叫喊着。"

"我们正在追赶的就是，就是班达尔-洛格。"巴洛说的时候，话卡在喉咙里一样，这是他记忆中第一次，一个丛林居民承认对猴子的事情有兴趣。

"毫无疑问，我相信能让你们两位这种——丛林首领级别猎手出动的事情，绝非小事。"卡阿礼貌地回应，同时也充满好奇。

"的确如此，"巴洛说，"我只不过是已经年老的，有时甚至是非常愚蠢的，西奥尼狼崽的法则老师

wolf-cubs, and Bagheera here –"

"Is Bagheera," said the Black Panther, and his jaws shut with a snap, for he did not believe in being humble. "The trouble is this, Kaa. Those nut-stealers and pickers of palm-leaves have stolen away our man-cub, of whom thou hast perhaps heard."

"I heard some news from Ikki (his quills make him presumptuous) of a man-thing that was entered into a wolf-pack, but I did not believe. Ikki is full of stories half heard and very badly told."

"But it is true. He is such a man-cub as never was," said Baloo. "The best and wisest and boldest of man-cubs. My own pupil, who shall make the name of Baloo famous through all the jungles; and besides, I – we – love him, Kaa."

"Ts! Ts!" said Kaa, shaking his head to and fro. "I also have known what love is. There are tales I could tell that –"

"That need a clear night when we are all well fed to praise properly," said Bagheera, quickly. "Our man-cub is in the hands of the Bandar-log now, and we know that of all the Jungle People they fear Kaa alone."

"They fear me alone. They have

而已。这是巴赫拉……"

"就是巴赫拉。"黑豹本想谦虚一下，可又下巴一抬把嘴巴合上了，因为他觉得谦虚也没什么意义。"这就是麻烦所在，卡阿。那群坚果大盗和棕榈叶的采摘者，偷走了我们的人类幼崽，或许你也听说过这个幼崽。"

"我在伊基（他身上的刺让他很是放肆）那里听到了一些，他说有个像人的东西进入了狼群，我没信。伊基总是说些道听途说的故事，而且还胡说八道。"

"不过这确实是真的。他是以前从未有过的人类幼崽，"巴洛说，"他是最优秀的、最聪慧的、最大胆的人类幼崽。我亲自教的学生，他会让巴洛的名字在整个丛林声名鹊起。另外，我，我们，很爱他，卡阿。"

"呲！呲！"卡阿来回摇晃着头说，"我也知道爱是什么。有些故事我可以讲一讲……"

"那要找一个明亮的夜晚，我们可以饱餐之后，再好好地赞美吧，"巴赫拉语速很快，"我们的人类幼崽在班达尔-洛格手中，我们清楚，这群班达尔-洛格不惧怕任何丛林居民，他们只怕卡阿。"

"他们就怕我！他们有理由这

good reason," said Kaa. "Chattering, foolish, vain – vain, foolish, and chattering – are the monkeys. But a man-thing in their hands is in no good luck. They grow tired of the nuts they pick, and throw them down. They carry a branch half a day, meaning to do great things with it, and then they snap it in two. That man-thing is not to be envied. They called me also – 'yellow fish,' was it not?"

"Worm – worm – earthworm," said Bagheera; "as well as other things which I cannot now say for shame."

"We must remind them to speak well of their master. Aaa-sssh! We must help their wandering memories. Now, whither went they with thy cub?"

"The jungle alone knows. Toward the sunset, I believe," said Baloo. "We had thought that thou wouldst know, Kaa."

"I? How? I take them when they come in my way, but I do not hunt the Bandar-log – or frogs – or green scum on a water-hole, for that matter."

"Up, up! Up, up! Hillo! Illo! Illo! Look up, Baloo of the Seeonee Wolf Pack!"

Baloo looked up to see where the voice came from, and there was Rann,

样，"卡阿说，"猴子就是喋喋不休、愚笨、虚荣——虚荣、愚笨、喋喋不休——猴子就是这样。可是人那样的东西被他们架走可没什么好结果。他们摘下坚果，腻了就扔了。他们扛着一根树枝半天，是打算要拿它做点大事的，可接着就撅成两段。那个人一样的东西没什么好羡慕的。他们也把我叫作——'黄鱼'，是不是？"

"蠕虫，蠕虫，蚯蚓，"巴赫拉说，"还有别的外号，我都羞于说出口。"

"我们必须要提醒这群猴子，他们在谈论主人时要好好说话。啊，嘶！我们得帮助他们纠正一下错乱的记忆。现在，他们把那个人类幼崽带到哪儿了？"

"这个只有丛林才知晓。我相信，一定是朝着日落的方向走了，"巴洛说，"我们原本想着你清楚的，卡阿。"

"我吗？我怎么知道？他们和我狭路相逢的时候，我会干掉他们，可我不会搜寻班达尔-洛格或是青蛙，或是水坑里的绿色浮渣。"

"向上看，向上看！向上看，向上看！嗨咯！嗨咯！嗨咯！西奥密狼群的巴洛，抬头看看！"

巴洛抬头看，想找寻声音从哪

the Kite, sweeping down with the sun shining on the upturned flanges of his wings. It was near Rann's bedtime, but he had ranged all over the jungle looking for the bear, and missed him in the thick foliage.

"What is it?" said Baloo.

"I have seen Mowgli among the Bandar-log. He bade me tell you. I watched. The Bandar-log have taken him beyond the river to the Monkey City – to the Cold Lairs. They may stay there for a night, or ten nights, or an hour. I have told the bats to watch through the dark time. That is my message. Good hunting, all you below!"

"Full gorge and a deep sleep to you, Rann!" cried Bagheera. "I will remember thee in my next kill, and put aside the head for thee alone, O best of kites!"

"It is nothing. It is nothing. The boy held the Master Word. I could have done no less," and Rann circled up again to his roost.

"He has not forgotten to use his tongue," said Baloo, with a chuckle of pride. "To think of one so young remembering the Master Word for the birds while he was being pulled across

里来的。是兰恩，那只雄鹰，正向下飞来，阳光照在他的翅膀上，熠熠生辉。兰恩的睡觉时间就要到了，可他一直在丛林各处寻找着棕熊，茂密的树叶遮挡了他的视线。

"怎么了？"巴洛说。

"我在班达尔-洛格中看见莫格里了，他恳求我告诉你，我就一直盯着他们，班达尔-洛格把他带到了河对岸的猴子城——冷巢。他们可能在那里住一晚，或者十晚，或者一个小时。我叮嘱蝙蝠在夜晚盯着他们。这就是我要捎的信儿。狩猎顺利，下面的各位！"

"愿你吃得爽，睡得美，兰恩，"巴赫拉喊着，"下次捕猎的时候，我一定记得你，我把捕猎到的猎物头都放在一边留给你，你真是绝世好鹰。"

"这不算什么，真的不算什么。男孩会使用主人话语，我只略尽绵力而已。"兰恩再次盘旋而去，飞回他的巢穴。

"他还记得用自己的舌头，"巴洛笑着骄傲地说，"想想那么点的小东西，被猴子们架着在树林间穿行的时候，还能想着用对鸟族使用主人话语啊！"

trees!"

"It was most firmly driven into him," said Bagheera. "But I am proud of him, and now we must go to the Cold Lairs."

They all knew where that place was, but few of the Jungle People ever went there, because what they called the Cold Lairs was an old deserted city, lost and buried in the jungle, and beasts seldom use a place that men have once used. The wild boar will, but the hunting-tribes do not. Besides, the monkeys lived there as much as they could be said to live anywhere, and no self-respecting animal would come within eye-shot of it except in times of drouth, when the half-ruined tanks and reservoirs held a little water.

"It is half a night's journey – at full speed," said Bagheera. Baloo looked very serious. "I will go as fast as I can," he said, anxiously.

"We dare not wait for thee. Follow, Baloo. We must go on the quick-foot – Kaa and I."

"Feet or no feet, I can keep abreast of all thy four," said Kaa, shortly.

Baloo made one effort to hurry, but had to sit down panting, and so they left him to come on later, while

"那可是最结实的巴掌拍到他脑子里的，"巴赫拉说，"他让我自豪，我们此刻必须得赶到冷巢那里。"

他们都知道冷巢在什么方位，只是很少有丛林居民去过那里的丛林。他们所谓的冷巢，是一座被废弃的旧城，被埋没在了丛林之中。野兽很少会使用人类曾占据的地方。野猪会去，可狩猎族们是不会踏访的。除此之外，猴子会住在那里，因为他们什么地方都住。没有一个有自尊的动物会到视线之内能看到冷巢的地方，除了久旱之后，半损坏的水槽和水库里能有一点点水。

"这得走上半个晚上，还得全速前行。"巴赫拉说。巴洛看起来很严肃，担忧地说，"我会使出全身力气奔跑。"

"我们不敢等着你一起了。巴洛，你就跟着跑吧，我和卡阿必须快速前进了。"

"不管有没有脚，我也能追上你的四条腿儿。"卡阿简洁地说。

巴洛试图冲刺一下，最后却被追坐下来大口地喘气。所以他们就让他留下来，后面再追他们。巴赫

Bagheera hurried forward, at the rocking panther-canter. Kaa said nothing, but, strive as Bagheera might, the huge Rock Python held level with him. When they came to a hill-stream, Bagheera gained, because he bounded across while Kaa swam, his head and two feet of his neck clearing the water, but on level ground Kaa made up the distance.

"By the Broken Lock that freed me," said Bagheera, when twilight had fallen, "thou art no slow-goer."

"I am hungry," said Kaa. "Besides, they called me speckled frog."

"Worm – earthworm, and yellow to boot."

"All one. Let us go on," and Kaa seemed to pour himself along the ground, finding the shortest road with his steady eyes, and keeping to it.

In the Cold Lairs the Monkey People were not thinking of Mowgli's friends at all. They had brought the boy to the Lost City, and were very pleased with themselves for the time. Mowgli had never seen an Indian city before, and though this was almost a heap of ruins it seemed very wonderful and splendid. Some king had built it long ago on a little hill. You could still trace the stone

拉匆忙地快步向前，卡阿什么也没说，不过他尽可能像巴赫拉一样，全力爬行，和巴赫拉保持着相同的速度。他们来到一条山间的小溪时，巴赫拉抢先一步，因为他可以跳过去，卡阿将头和两英尺的脖子划着水游了过去。到了同一地面，卡阿弥补了差距。

"以我获得自由所砸坏的那把锁头起誓，"巴赫拉在夜幕降临的时候说，"你爬得一点都不慢！"

"我肚子已经饿了，"卡阿说，"此外，他们叫我斑点青蛙。"

"蠕虫——蚯蚓，该踢的黄蚯蚓。"

"一回事。我们赶路吧，"卡阿就像是地面上流动一样，用他坚定的眼睛搜寻最短的路径，拾径而行。

到了冷巢，猴子们根本不认为莫格里是他们的朋友。他们将那个男孩带到了败落的城市里，对当前的状况非常满意。莫格里之前从未见过印度城市，虽然这几乎是一堆废墟了，但是看起来还是很美好很辉煌。很久之前，有位国王在小山上建造了它。你仍然可以沿着石堤道走向损坏的大门，那些大门剩下了一些碎片，挂在锈迹斑斑的链子

causeways that led up to the ruined gates where the last splinters of wood hung to the worn, rusted hinges. Trees had grown into and out of the walls; the battlements were tumbled down and decayed, and wild creepers hung out of the windows of the towers on the walls in bushy hanging clumps.

A great roofless palace crowned the hill, and the marble of the courtyards and the fountains was split and stained with red and green, and the very cobblestones in the courtyard where the king's elephants used to live had been thrust up and apart by grasses and young trees. From the palace you could see the rows and rows of roofless houses that made up the city, looking like empty honeycombs filled with blackness; the shapeless block of stone that had been an idol in the square where four roads met; the pits and dimples at street corners where the public wells once stood, and the shattered domes of temples with wild figs sprouting on their sides.

The monkeys called the place their city, and pretended to despise the Jungle People because they lived in the forest. And yet they never knew what the buildings were made for nor how to

上。树木已经从墙内长到了墙外，城垛不是倒塌就是腐烂掉了；野藤蔓挂在塔楼的窗户上，浓密的灌木悬倒在墙面上。

一座了不起的没有屋顶的宫殿在山顶上屹立，庭院跟喷泉的大理石裂开了，上面浸满红色和绿色。国王曾经养过大象的院子，野草和新长的小树已经将原来的鹅卵石拱起。从宫殿里可以看到，组成整个城市的一排排没有屋顶的房屋，看起来就像是黑色的空蜂巢。四条路相汇的广场上，曾经是神像的石头如今也乱得不成样子；往日的公共水井边的街角也都已经坑坑洼洼，两侧散落着掉落的寺庙破碎的屋顶，上面都已经长了野生的无花果的枝条。

猴子们将此处叫作他们的城市，并假装蔑视丛林里的居民，因为他们生活在森林之中。然而猴民们从来都不知晓这些建筑因什么而建，也不知道如何物尽其用。他们

use them. They would sit in circles on the hall of the king's council-chamber, and scratch for fleas and pretend to be men; or they would run in and out of the roofless houses and collect pieces of plaster and old bricks in a corner, and forget where they had hidden them, and fight and cry in scuffling crowds, and then break off to play up and down the terraces of the king's garden, where they would shake the rose-trees and the oranges in sport to see the fruit and flowers fall. They explored all the passages and dark tunnels in the palace and the hundreds of little dark rooms; but they never remembered what they had seen and what they had not, and so drifted about in ones and twos or crowds, telling one another that they were doing as men did. They drank at the tanks and made the water all muddy, and then they fought over it, and then they would all rush together in mobs and shout: "There are none in the jungle so wise and good and clever and strong and gentle as the Bandar-log." Then all would begin again till they grew tired of the city and went back to the tree-tops, hoping the Jungle People would notice them.

Mowgli, who had been trained under

会坐在国会议事厅中围坐在一起，假扮成人的样子挠痒痒抓跳蚤。或者跑进跑出在没有屋顶的房子，捡拾石膏碎片和角落里的旧砖块，接着又会忘记将它们藏在哪里了，混战在一起，乱打乱叫；然后再分散开来，在国王花园的露台那里上蹿下跳，摇动着玫瑰和橘子树，就是因为看果实和花朵落下很好玩。他们在宫殿中探索了所有的通道和黑暗的隧道，钻遍了数以百计的小而黑的房间，但是他们从不记得什么看见过，什么没看见过。他们或是单独一只，或是两只，或是成群结队来回游荡，彼此告诉对方，说自己在像人一样做事。他们在水池中喝水之后，把水搅浑，然后在水池上方打斗，一窝蜂似的乱作一团，吼叫着："丛林里没有谁可以如同班达尔-洛格一般聪慧、善良、灵巧、强壮、义雅。" 接下来，一切都会再重新开始，一直到他们厌倦了在城市里的生活，他们会再回到树顶，心里期盼着丛林居民会注意到他们。

受过丛林法则训练的莫格里，

the Law of the Jungle, did not like or understand this kind of life. The monkeys dragged him into the Cold Lairs late in the afternoon, and instead of going to sleep, as Mowgli would have done after a long journey, they joined hands and danced about and sang their foolish songs.

One of the monkeys made a speech, and told his companions that Mowgli's capture marked a new thing in the history of the Bandar-log, for Mowgli was going to show them how to weave sticks and canes together as a protection against rain and cold. Mowgli picked up some creepers and began to work them in and out, and the monkeys tried to imitate; but in a very few minutes they lost interest and began to pull their friends' tails or jump up and down on all fours, coughing.

"I wish to eat," said Mowgli. "I am a stranger in this part of the jungle. Bring me food, or give me leave to hunt here."

Twenty or thirty monkeys bounded away to bring him nuts and wild pawpaws; but they fell to fighting on the road, and it was too much trouble to go buck with what was left of the fruit. Mowgli was sore and angry as well as

不喜欢也不理解这种生活。猴子们把他拖到冷巢的时候，已经是下午了。到了冷巢之后，他们手拉手跳舞，唱着很傻的歌，不像一般动物长途跋涉之后，会睡一觉休息。

其中有只猴子发表了一段讲话，他对同伴说，莫格里的捕获对班达尔-洛格的历史来说，具有里程碑一般的意义。莫格里会告诉他们如何将树枝藤条编起来防雨防寒。莫格里拿起一些藤蔓一进一出地编起来，猴子们也试图模仿。可是几分钟的时间，他们就觉得索然无味，转而去玩朋友的尾巴，跳上跳去地，咳嗽声不断。

"我希望有口吃的，"莫格里说，"在你们的地盘，我是外人，给我吃的，或者让我出去捕猎。"

有二三十只猴子蹦蹦跶跶走了，打算给莫格里带回来一些坚果和野木瓜。可是他们半道上开始掐架，抱怨太麻烦了，把瓜果什么的就地扔了。莫格里浑身疼痛，又十分饥饿，感到十分恼火。他在空

hungry, and he roamed through the empty city giving the Strangers' Hunting Call from time to time, but no one answered him, and Mowgli felt that he had reached a very bad place indeed.

"All that Baloo has said about the Bandar-log is true," he thought to himself. "They have no Law, no Hunting Call, and no leaders – nothing but foolish words and little picking, thievish hands. So if I am starved or killed here, it will be all my own fault. But I must try to return to my own jungle. Baloo will surely beat me, but that is better than chasing silly rose-leaves with the Bandar-log."

No sooner had he walked to the city wall than the monkeys pulled him back, telling him that he did not know how happy he was, and pinching him to make him grateful. He set his teeth and said nothing, but went with the shouting monkeys to a terrace above the red sandstone reservoirs that were half full of rain-water. There was a ruined summer-house of white marble in the center of the terrace, built for queens dead a hundred years ago. The domed roof had half fallen in and blocked up the underground passage

荡荡的城中逛荡，不时地发出外来人要捕猎的信息，可是没有得到任何回应。莫格里感到他确实到了相当糟糕的地方。

"所有那些巴洛说班达尔-洛格的话都是真的，"他对自己说，"他们不遵循法则，没有狩猎招呼，没有头领，除了说着愚蠢的话，用他们贼手小偷小摸，什么都没有。所以说我要是饿死在这儿或者被杀了，都怪我自己。可是我必须努力回到我自己的丛林。巴洛一定会打我的，不过那总好过傻傻地跟着班达尔-洛格追寻玫瑰的落叶。"

莫格里才走到城墙处，就被猴子们拉回来了。猴子跟他讲，不要身在福中不知福，还掐他，让他表示感激。他咬着牙，没吭一声，只是跟着那些吱哇乱叫的猴子走到了一个平台上，这个平台下面是一个红砂岩围成的蓄水池，还有半池雨水在里面。在平台的中央位置，有一座白色大理石的亭子，是一百年前为王妃们建造，用来避暑的。如今圆的屋顶有一半已经塌了，将宫殿到此处的地下通道都堵住了。凉亭的墙是用大理石做成的花纹屏风，乳白色的浮雕，玛瑙、玉髓、

from the palace by which the queens used to enter; but the walls were made of screens of marble tracery – beautiful, milk-white fretwork, set with agates and cornelians and jasper and lapis lazuli, and as the moon came up behind the hill it shone through the openwork, casting shadows on the ground like black-velvet embroidery.

Sore, sleepy, and hungry as he was, Mowgli could not help laughing when the Bandar-log began, twenty at a time, to tell him how great and wise and strong and gentle they were, and how foolish he was to wish to leave them. "We are great. We are free. We are wonderful. We are the most wonderful people in all the jungle! We all say so, and so it must be true," they shouted. "Now as you are a new listener and can carry our words back to the Jungle People so that they may notice us in future, we will tell you all about our most excellent selves."

Mowgli made no objection, and the monkeys gathered by hundreds and hundreds on the terrace to listen to their own speakers singing the praises of the Bandar-log, and whenever a speaker stopped for want of breath they would all shout together: "This is true; we all

碧玉和青金石镶嵌在上面,非常漂亮。当月亮的光线从山丘后面穿过镂空的格子,就像在地上投影似的,印出黑色的天鹅绒刺绣图案。

疼痛、困乏、饥饿折磨着莫格里,但是班达尔-洛格的话还是让他忍不住大笑。同一个时间里有二十只猴子告诉他,他们有多么了不起,多么聪明、强壮又文雅,他要是想离开他们是相当愚蠢的。"我们是了不起的。我们是自由的。我们非常棒。我们是丛林中最棒的居民!我们都这么说,所以这必定不假,"他们喊着,"既然你是头次听说,那你可以把我们的话带回丛林中。以便丛林居民日后会注意到我们,我们会告诉你我们最优秀的一切。"

莫格里没有反驳。猴子们数以百计地聚集到露台上面,听他们自己的演讲者赞颂班达尔-洛格。当演讲者停下歇口气的空档,他们都会一起喊道:"千真万确,我们都这么说。"

say so."

Mowgli nodded and blinked, and said "Yes" when they asked him a question, and his head spun with the noise. "Tabaqui, the Jackal, must have bitten all these people," he said to himself, "and now they have the madness. Certainly this is dewanee – the madness. Do they never go to sleep? Now there is a cloud coming to cover that moon. If it were only a big enough cloud I might try to run away in the darkness. But I am tired."

That same cloud was being watched by two good friends in the ruined ditch below the city wall, for Bagheera and Kaa, knowing well how dangerous the Monkey People were in large numbers, did not wish to run any risks. The monkeys never fight unless they are a hundred to one, and few in the jungle care for those odds.

"I will go to the west wall," Kaa whispered, "and come down swiftly with the slope of the ground in my favor. They will not throw themselves upon my back in their hundreds, but –"

"I know it," said Bagheera. "Would that Baloo were here; but we must do what we can. When that cloud covers the moon I shall go to the terrace. They

当猴子们问莫格里问题的时候，莫格里就点点头，眨眨眼，说一声"是"。他被吵得头昏脑涨的。"塔巴克，那条豺狗，一定是咬过这帮家伙，"他自言自语道，"现在他们是疯了，这肯定是'地瓦泥'，就是那种疯病。他们从不睡觉吗？此刻一片云遮住了月亮，如果这片云足够大，我或者就能试着在黑暗中逃脱了。可是我现在太累了。"

被损毁的城墙根下，两个好友也在仰望着这片云彩。是巴赫和卡阿，他们两个深知猴子们聚众是十分危险的，他们不想冒任何风险。猴子们从不打架，除非是占有绝对优势的情况下，在丛林中很少有居民愿意面对这种战斗。

"我去西墙那边，"卡阿低声说，"在那边可以借助斜坡，用我的优势迅速地滑到地面，他们不会一下子几百个跳到我背上，但是……"

"我明白，"巴赫拉说，"真希望巴洛此刻在这儿，但我们必须竭尽所能。当乌云覆盖上月亮，我会到平台上面去。猴子们在那上面围

hold some sort of council there over the boy."

"Good hunting," said Kaa, grimly, and glided away to the west wall. That happened to be the least ruined of any, and the big snake was delayed a while before he could find a way up the stones.

The cloud hid the moon, and as Mowgli wondered what would come next he heard Bagheera's light feet on the terrace. The Black Panther had raced up the slope almost without a sound, and was striking – he knew better than to waste time in biting – right and left among the monkeys, who were seated round Mowgli in circles fifty and sixty deep. There was a howl of fright and rage, and then as Bagheera tripped on the rolling, kicking bodies beneath him, a monkey shouted: "There is only one here! Kill him! Kill!" A scuffling mass of monkeys, biting, scratching, tearing, and pulling, closed over Bagheera, while five or six laid hold of Mowgli, dragged him up the wall of the summer-house, and pushed him through the hole of the broken dome. A man-trained boy would have been badly bruised, the fall was a good

着那孩子商议着什么。"

"狩猎顺利。"卡阿严肃地说。他顺着西墙爬走了，西墙是损毁最少的部分，耽误了大蟒的进度，过了一会儿他才找到石头上的路。

月亮被乌云遮住，莫格里正想着接下来会怎么样的时候，他听到了平台上巴赫拉轻轻的脚步声。黑豹冲上斜坡的一刹那，几乎没有任何动静，他迅速发起进攻。他知道不要浪费时间去咬他们为妙，便在猴子中间左右开弓，这些猴子们围在莫格里周围有五六十圈那么多。平台上充满了惊恐和愤怒的咆哮声，巴赫拉落脚之处，猴子们七翻八滚。此刻，一只猴子大喊："只有一个！杀了他！杀啊！"乌泱泱一群猴子咬、抓、撕、拉，围住了巴赫拉；而其中五六只猴子抓着莫格里，把他拖到了凉亭的墙上，将他从一个破圆顶的洞推了下去。这要是人类训练的男孩，必定会伤得周身瘀青，这一摔起码十多英尺，可是莫格里掉下去的时候，是按照巴洛曾教他的方法，轻轻地落地。

ten feet, but Mowgli fell as Baloo had taught him to fall, and landed light.

"Stay there," shouted the monkeys, "till we have killed thy friend. Later we will play with thee, if the Poison People leave thee alive."

"We be of one blood, ye and I," said Mowgli, quickly giving the Snake's Call. He could hear rustling and hissing in the rubbish all round him, and gave the Call a second time to make sure.

"Down hoods all," said half a dozen low voices. Every old ruin in India becomes sooner or later a dwelling-place of snakes, and the old summer-house was alive with cobras. "Stand still, Little Brother, lest thy feet do us harm."

Mowgli stood as quietly as he could, peering through the openwork and listening to the furious din of the fight round the Black Panther – the yells and chatterings and scufflings, and Bagheera's deep, hoarse cough as he backed and bucked and twisted and plunged under the heaps of his enemies. For the first time since he was born, Bagheera was fighting for his life.

"Baloo must be at hand; Bagheera would not have come alone," Mowgli

"好好待在那里，"猴子们喊道，"直到我们把你的朋友解决了。然后我们再跟你玩，如果毒民还留你性命的话。"

"我们血脉相通，你和我。"莫格里立马给蛇族发出信号。他可以听到在他周围有沙沙嘶嘶的声音，他又说了一遍以确保他们听见。

"大家都放松吧！"有六个声音低声说道。在印度，每一座废墟早晚有一天会成为蛇的栖息地，而这个古老的凉亭里到处都是眼镜蛇。"站住，小兄弟。免得你的脚伤到我们。"

莫格里尽他可能安静地站在那里，透过镂空处凝视着外面。他听到了黑豹周围激烈打斗的喧闹声——猴子们乱喊乱叫，喋喋不休，巴赫拉深沉而嘶哑的咳嗽。在黑压压的敌人紧逼之下，黑豹向后退着，弓起背瞬间跳起，扭着身子，向前猛攻。这是巴赫拉出生后，第一次为自己的生命而战。

"巴洛肯定就在不远处。巴赫拉是不会独自过来的，"莫格里想，

thought; and then he called aloud: "To the tank, Bagheera! Roll to the water-tanks! Roll and plunge! Get to the water!"

Bagheera heard, and the cry that told him Mowgli was safe gave him new courage. He worked his way desperately, inch by inch, straight for the reservoirs, hitting in silence.

Then from the ruined wall nearest the jungle rose up the rumbling war-shout of Baloo. The old bear had done his best, but he could not come before. "Bagheera," he shouted, "I am here! I climb! I haste! Ahuwora! The stones slip under my feet! Wait my coming, O most infamous Bandar log!"

He panted up the terrace only to disappear to the head in a wave of monkeys, but he threw himself squarely on his haunches, and spreading out his fore paws, hugged as many as he could hold, and then began to hit with a regularbat-bat-bat, like the flipping strokes of a paddle-wheel.

A crash and a splash told Mowgli that Bagheera had fought his way to the tank, where the monkeys could not follow. The panther lay gasping for breath, his head just out of water, while the monkeys stood three deep on the

然后他大声喊道，"去蓄水池，巴赫拉！滚到蓄水池！滚到那里跳进去！到水里去！"

巴赫拉听到了莫格里的喊声，这喊声告诉他莫格里是安全的，巴赫拉因此获得了勇气。他拼命地，一步一步地向水库冲去，默默战斗着。

就在这时，从倒塌的城墙附近的丛林里，响起了巴洛隆隆的开战之声。这只老熊竭尽全力，也不能更快一步了。"巴赫拉，"他喊道，"我在这儿！我爬上来了！我拼命往这儿赶！啊呜啦！石头都在我的脚底下打滑！我来了，你们等着，最臭名昭著的班达尔-洛格！"

他气喘吁吁地爬上露台，一大波猴子就将他淹没了。不过他一屁股坐下来，用他的前爪抱住尽可能多的猴子，啪啪一顿开打，就像翻转的桨轮。

噼里啪啦的声音让莫格里知道，巴赫拉已经冲开一条路进到了蓄水池。猴子们不会跟着跳下去的。黑豹就躺在水池里大口喘气，脑袋刚刚露出水面；而猴子们围站在红色的石阶上，多达三层。他们

red stone steps, dancing up and down with rage, ready to spring upon him from all sides if he came out to help Baloo. It was then that Bagheera lifted up his dripping chin, and in despair gave the Snake's Call for protection, – "We be of one blood, ye and I," – for he believed that Kaa had turned tail at the last minute. Even Baloo, half smothered under the monkeys on the edge of the terrace, could not help chuckling as he heard the big Black Panther asking for help.

Kaa had only just worked his way over the west wall, landing with a wrench that dislodged a coping-stone into the ditch. He had no intention of losing any advantage of the ground, and coiled and uncoiled himself once or twice, to be sure that every foot of his long body was in working order.

All that while the fight with Baloo went on, and the monkeys yelled in the tank round Bagheera, and Mang, the Bat, flying to and fro, carried the news of the great battle over the jungle, till even Hathi, the Wild Elephant, trumpeted, and, far away, scattered bands of the Monkey Folk woke and came leaping along the tree-roads to help their comrades in the Cold Lairs,

上蹿下跳，气得不行。他们时刻准备着，如果巴赫拉出来去帮巴洛，他们就从各个方向跳到他身上。就在这时，巴赫拉仰起滴水的下巴，在绝望中向蛇类发出求救的信号，"我们血脉相通，你和我，"他料定卡阿在最后一刻逃了。即使巴洛已经在露台边缘的猴子们中间快要窒息了，听到求救也忍不住咯咯大笑。

卡阿刚刚翻越西城墙，落地时扭了下身子，将墙头上的石头带进了沟里。他不想失去地面优势，盘绕起来又伸展开一两次，就为了确保他长长的身躯的每一寸都能正常运转。

巴洛的战斗仍在继续，围着巴赫拉的蓄水池的猴子们号叫着；蝙蝠芒恩在上空盘旋，在丛林中散播着大战的消息，就连野象哈提也在大肆宣扬；散落在远处的猴子们也被唤醒，沿着树林跳跃奔向冷巢，给自己的同伴助力。战斗的喧闹声吵醒了周围几只白天才能见到的鸟。

and the noise of the fight roused all the day-birds for miles round.

Then Kaa came straight, quickly, and anxious to kill. The fighting strength of a python is in the driving blow of his head, backed by all the strength and weight of his body. If you can imagine a lance, or a battering-ram, or a hammer, weighing nearly half a ton driven by a cool, quiet mind living in the handle of it, you can imagine roughly what Kaa was like when he fought. A python four or five feet long can knock a man down if he hits him fairly in the chest, and Kaa was thirty feet long, as you know. His first stroke was delivered into the heart of the crowd round Baloo – was sent home with shut mouth in silence, and there was no need of a second. The monkeys scattered with cries of "Kaa! It is Kaa! Run! Run!"

Generations of monkeys had been scared into good behavior by the stories their elders told them of Kaa, the night-thief, who could slip along the branches as quietly as moss grows, and steal away the strongest monkey that ever lived; of old Kaa, who could make himself look so like a dead branch or a rotten stump that the wisest were

接着卡阿就直接快速、焦急地展开厮杀。巨蟒的战斗力是他头部的推动，这股力量以他身体的力量和重量为后盾。倘若你能想象着，一根长矛，或者攻城槌，一个锤子，有半吨那么重，一个冷静、沉着的头脑的动物手里握着它猛然出击的场景，你或许可以在知道卡阿战斗时是什么样子。四五英尺长的一条蟒蛇直击一个人的胸口位置，可以将人打到；而你清楚卡阿有三十英尺长。卡阿的第一下出击就正中围困巴洛的猴子们的中心。他们没等开口就直接被"送回老家"了，都不用来第二下。猴子们大喊着逃散开来："卡阿！是卡阿！跑啊！快跑！"

一代又一代的猴子们听到长辈们告诉他们卡阿的故事时，都被吓得非常听话。在长辈的口中，卡阿是个夜贼，滑行的时候就像悄悄生长的苔藓，无声无息，能够偷走最强壮的猴子。老卡阿可以使自己看起来像一根枯死的树枝或者是一段烂了的树桩，最有智慧的猴子也会被骗，直到伪装成树枝的卡阿

deceived till the branch caught them.

Kaa was everything that the monkeys feared in the jungle, for none of them knew the limits of his power, none of them could look him in the face, and none had ever come alive out of his hug. And so they ran, stammering with terror, to the walls and the roofs of the houses, and Baloo drew a deep breath of relief. His fur was much thicker than Bagheera's, but he had suffered sorely in the fight. Then Kaa opened his mouth for the first time and spoke one long hissing word, and the far-away monkeys, hurrying to the defense of the Cold Lairs, stayed where they were, cowering, till the loaded branches bent and crackled under them. The monkeys on the walls and the empty houses stopped their cries, and in the stillness that fell upon the city Mowgli heard Bagheera shaking his wet sides as he came up from the tank.

Then the clamor broke out again. The monkeys leaped higher up the walls; they clung round the necks of the big stone idols and shrieked as they skipped along the battlements; while Mowgli, dancing in the summer-house, put his eye to the screen-work and

捕获他们。

在丛林中只有卡阿能让猴子们惧怕，因为没有任何一只猴子能够清楚卡阿的力量到底有多强大，没有任何一只猴子能看清卡阿的脸长什么样，没有任何一只猴子能够从他的怀抱中存活下来。于是他们惊恐地跑到房子的墙壁和屋顶上去。巴洛深吸了一口气，虽然他的皮毛跟巴赫拉相比更加厚实，可是在战斗中也被打得不轻。接着，卡阿第一次开口嘶嘶地讲了不少话。远道而来的助威的猴子们也都蜷缩在一边，直到树枝承受不住了，响起咔嚓咔嚓的断裂声。城墙上面还有空房子里面的猴子们停止了哭喊。城区中的寂静下，莫格里听到了巴赫拉从蓄水池中上岸，抖动身上湿漉漉的水滴的声音。

喧闹声随即再次爆发。有些猴子跳到城墙找个更高的落脚点，有些猴子紧紧地抱住大石像的脖子，有些猴子在城垛上蹦蹦跳跳，嘴里尖叫着。而莫格里，此时在凉亭内跳舞欢呼，眼睛盯着屏风的镂空处，门牙间发出猫头鹰一样的声

hooted owl-fashion between his front teeth, to show his derision and contempt.

"Get the man-cub out of that trap; I can do no more," Bagheera gasped. "Let us take the man-cub and go. They may attack again."

"They will not move till I order them. Stay you sssso!" Kaa hissed, and the city was silent once more. "I could not come before, Brother, but I think I heard thee call" – this was to Bagheera.

"I – I may have cried out in the battle," Bagheera answered. "Baloo, art thou hurt?"

"I am not sure that they have not pulled me into a hundred little bearlings," said Baloo, gravely shaking one leg after the other. "Wow! I am sore. Kaa, we owe thee, I think, our lives – Bagheera and I."

"No matter. Where is the manling?"

"Here, in a trap. I cannot climb out," cried Mowgli. The curve of the broken dome was above his head.

"Take him away. He dances like Mao, the Peacock. He will crush our young," said the cobras inside.

"Hah!" said Kaa, with a chuckle, "he has friends everywhere, this manling. Stand back, manling; and hide you, O

音，以示他的嘲讽。

"将那个人类幼崽从陷阱里拽出来，我没劲儿了，"巴赫拉喘着粗气说，"咱们带着人类幼崽赶紧走，他们或许会再次进攻。"

"除非我开口，否则他们是不会动的。你歇会儿吧！"卡阿嘶嘶地说，城区再次安静了，"我做不到更快一些了，兄弟，但我觉得我听到了你的呼救。"这是对巴赫拉说的。

"我——我或许是在战斗中大喊了，"巴赫拉回答，"巴洛，你受伤了吗？"

"我不确定我有没有被他们撕得七零八碎的，"巴洛说这话的时候，沉重地挨个抖了抖几条腿儿，"哇！好疼！卡阿，我们欠你的，我想，我和巴赫拉都欠你一命。"

"这没什么，人类幼崽在哪里？"

"这儿呢，陷阱里，我没法爬出去，"莫格里大喊。破碎的穹顶的弯曲处正在他的头顶上方。

"将他带走。他跳起舞来像孔雀莫奥。他会踩碎我们的小崽儿。"这话来自里面的眼镜蛇。

"哈！"卡阿笑着说，"哪里都

Poison People. I break down the wall."

Kaa looked carefully till he found a discolored crack in the marble tracery showing a weak spot, made two or three light taps with his head to get the distance, and then lifting up six feet of his body clear of the ground, sent home half a dozen full-power, smashing blows, nose-first. The screen-work broke and fell away in a cloud of dust and rubbish, and Mowgli leaped through the opening and flung himself between Baloo and Bagheera – an arm round each big neck.

"Art thou hurt?" said Baloo, hugging him softly.

"I am sore, hungry, and not a little bruised; but, oh, they have handled ye grievously, my Brothers! Ye bleed."

"Others also," said Bagheera, licking his lips and looking at the monkey-dead on the terrace and round the tank.

"It is nothing, it is nothing if thou art safe, O my pride of all little frogs!" whimpered Baloo.

"Of that we shall judge later," said Bagheera, in a dry voice that Mowgli did not at all like. "But here is Kaa, to whom we owe the battle and thou owest thy life. Thank him according to

有他的朋友,这个人类幼崽。退后,人类幼崽,毒族们,你们也藏好,我要撞到这面墙。"

卡阿仔细地看了看,发现了大理石花纹上有一条褪色的裂纹,这里是个漏洞。他用头试探了两下,估摸出距离,然后将自己的身体举起六英尺那么高,鼻子在前,全力出击,狠狠地撞击五六下。屏风墙被撞塌,消失在尘土和垃圾之中,莫格里从缺口中跳了出来,向着巴洛和巴赫拉之间飞扑过去,一只胳膊搂住一个大脖子。

"你受伤了吗?"巴洛轻轻地拥抱他,问道。

"我浑身都疼,肚子也饿扁了,身上青的可不是一块两块。但是,哦,他们让你们受了不少苦头,我的兄弟们,你们都挂彩了。"

"他们也很惨。"巴赫拉舔着嘴唇,看着平台上和蓄水池边死掉的猴子说。

"没什么,只要你安然无恙,一切都没关系。哦,我的骄傲,在所有的小青蛙中,只有你是!"巴洛哽咽道。

"我们以后再来评说这个,"巴赫拉用莫格里一点也不喜欢的干巴巴的声音说道,"但是这是卡阿,我们这场战斗多亏他帮忙,尤

our customs, Mowgli."

Mowgli turned and saw the great python's head swaying a foot above his own.

"So this is the manling," said Kaa. "Very soft is his skin, and he is not so unlike the Bandar-log. Have a care, manling, that I do not mistake thee for a monkey some twilight when I have newly changed my coat."

"We be of one blood, thou and I," Mowgli answered. "I take my life from thee, to-night. My kill shall be thy kill if ever thou art hungry, O Kaa."

"All thanks, Little Brother," said Kaa, though his eyes twinkled. "And what may so bold a hunter kill? I ask that I may follow when next he goes abroad."

"I kill nothing – I am too little, – but I drive goats toward such as can use them. When thou art empty come to me and see if I speak the truth. I have some skill in these (he held out his hands), and if ever thou art in a trap, I may pay the debt which I owe to thee, to Bagheera, and to Baloo, here. Good hunting to ye all, my masters."

"Well said," growled Baloo, for Mowgli had returned thanks very prettily. The python dropped his head

其是你欠他一条命。根据我们的习俗，快感谢他，莫格里。"

莫格里转身，看见巨蟒的脑袋就在自己头部上面一英尺的距离。

"这就是你们说的人类幼崽了，"卡阿说，"他的皮肤好软，和班达尔-洛格有些相像。你要当心，人类幼崽，当我换新皮肤的时候，不要让我在视线不清的时候将你误认为猴子。"

"我们血脉相通，你和我，"莫格里回应道，"今晚你救了我的命。卡阿，日后若是你饿了，我捕杀的猎物就是你的猎物。"

"谢谢你，小兄弟，"卡阿说，但是他眨了眨眼睛，"如此勇敢的猎手，能捕杀到什么呢？我先问好，下次他去捕猎的时候，我就可以跟着他了。"

"我什么也杀不了，我太小了。不过我会把山羊赶到可以一下子抓到他们的地方。你要是肚子饿了，来找我，看我的话是真是假。我在这方面是有些办法的（说着的同时，莫格里伸出他的手），如果你们也困在陷阱，我就能偿还欠你们，巴赫拉和巴洛的债。祝你们狩猎顺利，我的老师们。"

"说得不错！"巴洛低声吼道，因为莫格里的感谢之情表达得非常完美。巨蟒低下他的头，轻轻地

222

lightly for a minute on Mowgli's shoulder. "A brave heart and a courteous tongue," said he. "They shall carry thee far through the jungle, manling. But now go hence quickly with thy friends. Go and sleep, for the moon sets, and what follows it is not well that thou shouldst see."

The moon was sinking behind the hills and the lines of trembling monkeys huddled together on the walls and battlements looked like ragged, shaky fringes of things. Baloo went down to the tank for a drink, and Bagheera began to put his fur in order, as Kaa glided out into the center of the terrace and brought his jaws together with a ringing snap that drew all the monkeys' eyes upon him.

"The moon sets," he said. "Is there yet light to see?"

From the walls came a moan like the wind in the tree-tops: "We see, O Kaa!"

"Good! Begins now the Dance – the Dance of the Hunger of Kaa. Sit still and watch."

He turned twice or thrice in a big circle, weaving his head from right to left. Then he began making loops and figures of eight with his body, and soft, oozy triangles that melted into squares

靠在莫格里的肩上待了一分钟。"你有勇敢的心灵,谦恭的舌头,"卡阿说,"它们会让你在丛林中走得很远,人类幼崽。现在你和你的朋友们赶紧走吧。好好睡上一觉,月亮要落下了。后面就没什么好事情了,你不应该看到。"

月亮正从山丘后面沉落而下,那些颤抖的猴子们在城墙上蜷缩在一起,使得城垛看起来就像破烂不齐的流苏一般。巴洛下到蓄水池喝了些水,巴赫着手整理他的皮毛,卡阿滑到平台的中央位置,合上嘴巴,发出响亮的声音,吸引了所有猴子的目光。

"月亮落下去了,"卡阿说,"你们还能见到亮光吗?"

墙边传来像树尖的风声一般的呻吟:"我们能看见,哦卡阿。"

"很好!马上开始跳舞——卡阿饥饿之舞。老实坐着,注意看。"

他在一个大圈里又转了两三圈,左右摇晃着他的脑袋。接着他开始绕成一个环形,再把身体拧成八字,然后变成软软的三角形,转眼又变成了正方形、五边形,接下

and five-sided figures, and coiled mounds, never resting, never hurrying, and never stopping his low, humming song. It grew darker and darker, till at last the dragging, shifting coils disappeared, but they could hear the rustle of the scales.

Baloo and Bagheera stood still as stone, growling in their throats, their neck-hair bristling, and Mowgli watched and wondered.

"Bandar-log," said the voice of Kaa at last, "can ye stir foot or hand without my order? Speak!"

"Without thy order we cannot stir foot or hand, O Kaa!"

"Good! Come all one pace nearer to me."

The lines of the monkeys swayed forward helplessly, and Baloo and Bagheera took one stiff step forward with them.

"Nearer!" hissed Kaa, and they all moved again.

Mowgli laid his hands on Baloo and Bagheera to get them away, and the two great beasts started as though they had been waked from a dream.

"Keep thy hand on my shoulder," Bagheera whispered. "Keep it there, or I must go back – must go back to Kaa.

去又是小山丘的形状，一点都没有空档，但也不疾不徐，慢慢地跳着他的舞，哼着歌。天色越来越黑，直到最后不断移动的蛇身看不见了，不过他们还是可以听到沙沙的摩擦声。

巴洛和巴赫拉静静地站着，仿佛石头一般，喉咙咆哮着，颈部的毛发竖起，莫格里看到这一切感到很惊讶。

"班达尔-洛格，"卡阿最终说道，"没有我的允许，你们手脚可以动吗？说！"

"没有您的命令，我们不敢动手动脚，哦，卡阿。"

"很好！全部向我走近一步。"

一排排的猴子们无助地摇晃着往前走了一步，巴洛和巴赫拉跟着向前走了一步。

"再近点儿！"卡阿嘶声道，他们集体向前再次移动。

莫格里拍打着巴洛和巴赫拉，提醒他们离开，两头大兽仿佛从梦中惊醒，赶紧起身离开。

"你的手就放在我肩上，"巴赫拉低声说，"就放在那儿，要不然我一定得回去，回到卡阿那里，

Aah!"

"It is only old Kaa making circles on the dust," said Mowgli; "let us go"; and the three slipped off through a gap in the walls to the jungle.

"Whoof!" said Baloo, when he stood under the still trees again. "Never more will I make an ally of Kaa," and he shook himself all over.

"He knows more than we," said Bagheera, trembling. "In a little time, had I stayed, I should have walked down his throat."

"Many will walk that road before the moon rises again," said Baloo. "He will have good hunting – after his own fashion."

"But what was the meaning of it all?" said Mowgli, who did not know anything of a python's powers of fascination. "I saw no more than a big snake making foolish circles till the dark came. And his nose was all sore. Ho! Ho!"

"Mowgli," said Bagheera, angrily, "his nose was sore on thy account; as my ears and sides and paws, and Baloo's neck and shoulders are bitten on thy account. Neither Baloo nor Bagheera will be able to hunt with pleasure for many days."

啊!"

"就是老卡阿在尘土上画圈圈而已,"莫格里说,"咱们走。"他们三个通过城墙的一个间隙进入了丛林。

"呼!"当巴洛再次站在寂静的树下,不禁感叹,"我再也不跟卡阿联手了。"他全身颤抖着。

"他比我们知道的还多,"巴赫拉也颤抖了,"再多留一刻,我就自己溜到卡阿的喉咙里去了。"

"很多猴子会在月亮再次升起前,走上那条路的,"巴洛说,"他这次狩猎一定大有所获,以他自己的方式。"

"不过这都是什么意思?"莫格里说,他一点也不了解蟒蛇的迷惑力,"我只看到了一条大蛇一直在那里傻傻地画圈,一直画到了天黑。他的鼻子都疼了。嗬!嗬!"

"莫格里,"巴赫拉很恼火地说,"他的鼻子疼也是怪你,就跟我耳朵、肋骨和爪子,还有巴洛的脖子、肩膀被咬都一样,全都怪你。巴洛和巴赫拉好些个日子没法高高兴兴地狩猎了。"

"It is nothing," said Baloo; "we have the man-cub again."

"True; but he has cost us most heavily in time which might have been spent in good hunting, in wounds, in hair, – I am half plucked along my back, – and last of all, in honor. For, remember, Mowgli, I, who am the Black Panther, was forced to call upon Kaa for protection, and Baloo and I were both made stupid as little birds by the Hunger-Dance. All this, Man-cub, came of thy playing with the Bandar-log."

"True; it is true," said Mowgli, sorrowfully. "I am an evil man-cub, and my stomach is sad in me."

"Mf! What says the Law of the Jungle, Baloo?"

Baloo did not wish to bring Mowgli into any more trouble, but he could not tamper with the Law, so he mumbled, "Sorrow never stays punishment. But remember, Bagheera, he is very little."

"I will remember; but he has done mischief; and blows must be dealt now. Mowgli, hast thou anything to say?"

"Nothing. I did wrong. Baloo and thou art wounded. It is just."

Bagheera gave him half a dozen love-taps from a panther's point of

"没关系，"巴洛说，"人类幼崽回到了我们身边。"

"是这么回事，不过他严重浪费了我们的时光，我们本可以用这些时间好好狩猎，我们周身是伤口，毛发被扯掉，我背部一半的毛都没了，还有最严重的，是我们的名誉。因此，莫格里你记住，我，黑豹，被迫求救于卡阿。而且，巴洛和我被卡阿的饥饿之舞弄得像只傻鸟。所有这些，人类的幼崽，都是因为你和班达尔-洛格一起玩耍。"

"对的，就是因为这个，"莫格里悲伤地说，"我是一个恶人，我真的很后悔。"

"唔！丛林法则如何规定的，巴洛？"

巴洛不想让莫格里再受什么折磨，但他不能篡改法则，于是他嘟囔着："悔恨不能代替惩罚。不过请记得，巴赫拉，他那么小。"

"我会记得。可是他做了错事，现在就得受罚。莫格里，你要说什么吗？"

"没什么要说的，我确实错了。害巴洛和你受伤，我就该受罚。"

以一个黑豹的角度来看，巴赫

view (they would hardly have waked one of his own cubs), but for a seven year-old boy they amounted to as severe a beating as you could wish to avoid. When it was all over Mowgli sneezed, and picked himself up without a word.

"Now," said Bagheera, "jump on my back, Little Brother, and we will go home."

One of the beauties of Jungle Law is that punishment settles all scores. There is no nagging afterward.

Mowgli laid his head down on Bagheera's back and slept so deeply that he never waked when he was put down by Mother Wolf's side in the home-cave.

拉就是给了莫格里五六下爱抚一样的几巴掌(这样的力度打他们自己的崽子的话,恐怕连叫醒他们都困难)。不过对一个七岁的小男孩来说,这几下子已经严重到希望能躲就躲的地步。挨完了打,莫格里打了个喷嚏,爬起来,一句话都没说。

"现在,"巴赫拉说,"跳到我的背上,小兄弟,我们要回家了。"

丛林法则的一大优点就是,惩罚结束问题也结束,事后不会旧账重提。

莫格里一头倒在巴赫拉的背上,睡着了。他睡得太沉,一直到他自家的洞口,巴赫拉把他放到他的狼妈身边,他都没有醒过来。

ROAD-SONG OF THE BANDAR-LOG

班达尔-洛格的行路歌

HERE we go in a flung festoon,
Half-way up to the jealous moon!
Don't you envy our pranceful bands?
Don't you wish you had extra hands?
Wouldn't you like if your tails were –
so –
Curved in the shape of a Cupid's
bow?
Now you're angry, but – never mind,
Brother, thy tail hangs down behind!

Here we sit in a branchy row,
Thinking of beautiful things we
know;
Dreaming of deeds that we mean to
do,
All complete, in a minute or two –
Something noble and grand and
good,
Done by merely wishing we could.
We've forgotten, but – never mind,
Brother, thy tail hangs down behind!

All the talk we ever have heard

我们如彩旗一般飘动，
半路撞见嫉妒的明月！
难道你就不羡慕我们欢腾的乐队？
难道你就不盼望再有一双手掌？
难道你就不希望自己的尾巴也弯曲成丘比特的爱弓？
现在生气了吧，不过请别在意，
兄弟，你的尾巴垂在身后！

我们成排坐在这树枝上，
思索着我们熟悉的美好事物，
梦想着我们打算要做的事儿，

一两分钟就能全部完成，
高贵、宏伟又美好的事儿，

心有所想，我们就能做到。
我们忘记了，不过，请别在意，
兄弟，你的尾巴垂在身后！

那些我们曾听过的所有话语，

Uttered by bat or beast or bird –
Hide or fin or scale or feather –
Jabber it quickly and all together!
Excellent! Wonderful! Once again!
Now we are talking just like men.
Let's pretend we are ... never mind,
Brother, thy tail hangs down behind!
This is the way of the Monkey-kind.

Then join our leaping lines that scum fish through the pines,

That rocket by where, light and high, the wild-grape swings.

By the rubbish in our wake, and the noble noise we make,

Be sure, be sure, we're going to do some splendid things!

来自蝙蝠、野兽或者是什么鸟，

长着皮的，还是长着鳍的，又或者带鳞片的，有羽毛的，

通通过来，叽叽喳喳痛快说！

厉害！漂亮！再来啊！

我们现在说话就跟人一样！

就让我们假装……请别在意，

兄弟，你的尾巴垂在身后！

这就是所谓的猴民之道！

跟我们的队伍一起跳跃吧，犹如鱼儿在水中一般在松林中穿梭，

犹如火箭一般，轻巧升高，在野葡萄摇摆的天际。

就凭我们清醒时制造的垃圾，

就凭我们清醒时发出的噪声，

确信，确信，我们必定要做一番不同凡响的大事。

CHAPTER 3   "TIGER! TIGER!"

第三章　"老虎！老虎！"

WHAT of the hunting, hunter bold?

Brother, the watch was long and cold.

What of the quarry ye went to kill?

Brother, he crops in the jungle still.

Where is the power that made your pride?

Brother, it ebbs from my flank and side.

Where is the haste that ye hurry by?

Brother, I go to my lair to die.

WHEN Mowgli left the wolf's cave after the fight with the Pack at the Council Rock, he went down to the plowed lands where the villagers lived, but he would not stop there because it was too near to the jungle, and he knew that he had made at least one bad enemy at the Council. So he hurried on, keeping to the rough road that ran down the valley, and followed it at a steady jog-trot for nearly twenty miles, till he came to a country that he did not

捕猎如何呀，英勇的猎手？

兄弟，狩猎时的观望又冷又长。

你要捕杀什么样的猎物呢？

兄弟，他还在丛林里吃着草。

给你骄傲的力量去哪儿了？

兄弟，它消失在我的肋骨边了。

你如此匆忙是要往哪里赶？

兄弟，我要去我的巢穴去死。

在会议岩石上与狼群之战结束之后，莫格里就离开了狼洞，朝山下走去，走到有村民的耕地那里。可他不会在此停留，因为这个地方太靠近丛林，并且他清楚，在狼族大会上，他起码是树立了一个恶毒的仇敌，于是他继续匆忙前行。莫格里沿着山谷的崎岖的路走着，慢跑了差不多有二十英里，来到了一个他不认识的村庄。山谷展开就是一块不小的草原。草原上有岩石点缀，还有一道道沟壑将其分

know. The valley opened out into a great plain dotted over with rocks and cut up by ravines. At one end stood a little village, and at the other the thick jungle came down in a sweep to the grazing-grounds, and stopped there as though it had been cut off with a hoe. All over the plain, cattle and buffaloes were grazing, and when the little boys in charge of the herds saw Mowgli they shouted and ran away, and the yellow pariah dogs that hang about every Indian village barked. Mowgli walked on, for he was feeling hungry, and when he came to the village gate he saw the big thorn-bush that was drawn up before the gate at twilight, pushed to one side.

"Umph!" he said, for he had come across more than one such barricade in his night rambles after things to eat. "So men are afraid of the People of the Jungle here also." He sat down by the gate, and when a man came out he stood up, opened his mouth, and pointed down it to show that he wanted food. The man stared, and ran back up the one street of the village shouting for the priest, who was a big, fat man dressed in white, with a red and yellow mark on his forehead. The priest came to the gate, and with him at least a hundred people, who stared and talked and shouted and pointed at Mowgli.

"They have no manners, these Men Folk," said Mowgli to himself. "Only the gray ape would behave as they do." So he threw back his long hair and frowned at the crowd.

"What is there to be afraid of?" said the priest. "Look at the marks on his arms and legs. They are the bites of wolves. He is but a wolf-child run away from the jungle."

Of course, in playing together, the cubs had often nipped Mowgli harder than they intended, and there were white scars all over his arms and legs. But he would have been the last person in the world to call these bites; for he knew what real biting meant.

"Arré! Arré!" said two or three women together. "To be bitten by wolves, poor child! He is a handsome boy. He has eyes like red fire. By my honor, Messua, he is not unlike thy boy that was taken by the tiger."

"Let me look," said a woman with heavy copper rings on her wrists and ankles, and she peered at Mowgli under the palm of her hand. "Indeed he is not. He is thinner, but he has the very look

"他们可真没礼貌，这些人啊，"莫格里自言自语，"只有灰猿是这个样子的。"所以他将长长的头发向后甩去，皱起眉头看着人群。

"怕什么？"祭司说，"看看他胳膊腿上的伤疤。那是被狼咬过的痕迹。他不过是个逃出丛林的狼孩。"

确实，在一起玩耍的时候，狼崽们常常不经意地将他咬得很重，于是他的胳膊腿上满是白色的伤疤。不过他绝对不会认为这是咬伤，因为他清楚什么是真正的咬。

"啊！啊！"两三个妇人一起说，"他被狼咬了，可怜的小孩子！他长得真帅气。他的眼睛就像红色的火焰。以我的名誉起誓，梅苏阿，他跟你那个被老虎叼走的孩子很像。"

"我来看看。"一个女人说，她的手腕和脚踝上戴着沉重的铜环。他仔细注视着莫格里，手掌搭在眼眶上。"真的很像。他更瘦，不过和我的孩子非常像。"

of my boy."

The priest was a clever man, and he knew that Messua was wife to the richest villager in the place. So he looked up at the sky for a minute, and said solemnly: "What the jungle has taken the jungle has restored. Take the boy into thy house, my sister, and forget not to honor the priest who sees so far into the lives of men."

"By the bull that bought me," said Mowgli to himself, "but all this talking is like another looking-over by the Pack! Well, if I am a man, a man I must be."

The crowd parted as the woman beckoned Mowgli to her hut, where there was a red lacquered bedstead, a great earthen grain-chest with funny raised patterns on it, half a dozen copper cooking-pots, an image of a Hindu god in a little alcove, and on the wall a real looking-glass, such as they sell at the country fairs for eight cents.

She gave him a long drink of milk and some bread, and then she laid her hand on his head and looked into his eyes; for she thought perhaps that he might be her real son come back from the jungle where the tiger had taken him. So she said: "Nathoo, O Nathoo!"

祭司非常聪明，他了解梅苏阿是这个地方最富裕的村民的妻子，于是他抬头望了一眼天空，严肃地说："丛林从这里拿走的东西，如今又送还回来。将这个孩子带到你的家里，我的姐妹。不要忘记给祭司以敬意，他对人的一生看得通透。"

"以赎我的那头公牛起誓，"莫格里自言自语道，"他们说的这一切就像是狼群再一次接纳的过程！好吧，倘若我真的是一个人，我就一定要像个人一样。"

人们都散开了，女人示意莫格里去她的小屋子。屋内有一个红漆的床架、一个有着有趣的凸起图案的大粮柜、五六个铜制的锅、一个印度教神像、一面真正的镜子挂在墙上，就是乡村集市上卖八分钱一枚的那种。

她给了莫格里一大杯牛奶和一些面包，然后把手放在他头上，打量着他的眼睛，因为她想或许他真的就是被老虎叼走的儿子，现在从丛林回来了。于是她说："纳苏，哦，纳苏！"莫格里没有表现出他知道这个名字，"你不记得我给你

Mowgli did not show that he knew the name. "Dost thou not remember the day when I gave thee thy new shoes?" She touched his foot, and it was almost as hard as horn. "No," she said, sorrowfully; "those feet have never worn shoes, but thou art very like my Nathoo, and thou shalt be my son."

Mowgli was uneasy, because he had never been under a roof before; but as he looked at the thatch, he saw that he could tear it out any time if he wanted to get away, and that the window had no fastenings. "What is the good of a man," he said to himself at last, "if he does not understand man's talk? Now I am as silly and dumb as a man would be with us in the jungle. I must learn their talk."

He had not learned while he was with the wolves to imitate the challenge of bucks in the jungle and the grunt of the little wild pig. So as soon as Messua pronounced a word Mowgli would imitate it almost perfectly, and before dark he had learned the names of many things in the hut.

There was a difficulty at bedtime, because Mowgli would not sleep under anything that looked so like a panther-trap as that hut, and when they

买新鞋的那一天吗？"她摸了摸他的脚，他的脚硬得跟牛角似的。"不，"她悲伤地说，"这双脚从未穿过鞋，不过你真的很像我的纳苏，你就是我的儿子。"

莫格里感到不安，因为他之前从未在有屋顶的房子待过。不过当他望着茅草屋顶的时候，他清楚地知道若是他想逃离这里，随时就可以掀翻屋顶，况且窗口也没有闩紧。"成为一个人有什么好处，"他最后对自己说，"如果我不懂人类的语言。那我就跟人在丛林里同我们在一起时一样又傻又哑。我必须学会他们的语言。"

他和狼在一起时，学会了模仿公鹿发起挑战的叫声和小野猪睡觉的呼噜声。可不是因为有趣。所以，梅苏阿一旦说出一个字，莫格里就可以模仿得近乎完美，天黑没黑，莫格里已经知道了小屋子里很多东西的名字。

睡觉的时候出现了难题，莫格里不想睡在像捕杀黑豹的陷阱一样的屋子里。就在他们关门的时候，他从窗户跳出去了。"让他随

shut the door he went through the window. "Give him his will," said Messua's husband. "Remember he can never till now have slept on a bed. If he is indeed sent in the place of our son he will not run away."

So Mowgli stretched himself in some long, clean grass at the edge of the field, but before he had closed his eyes a soft gray nose poked him under the chin.

"Phew!" said Gray Brother (he was the eldest of Mother Wolf's cubs). "This is a poor reward for following thee twenty miles. Thou smellest of wood-smoke and cattle – altogether like a man already. Wake, Little Brother; I bring news."

"Are all well in the jungle?" said Mowgli, hugging him.

"All except the wolves that were burned with the Red Flower. Now, listen. Shere Khan has gone away to hunt far off till his coat grows again, for he is badly singed. When he returns he swears that he will lay thy bones in the Wainganga."

"There are two words to that. I also have made a little promise. But news is always good. I am tired to-night, – very tired with new things, Gray Brother, –

意，"梅苏阿的丈夫说，"记住，他或许从来都没躺在床上睡过觉。倘若他真的是来做我们儿子的，他不会逃跑的。"

莫格里伸展着四肢，躺在田边干净的草地上。可是在他闭上眼睛之前，一个灰色的鼻子就开始戳他的下巴。

"哟！"灰兄弟说（他是狼妈妈的长子），"跟你跑了二十英里，就获得这个奖励，真可怜。你身上的炊烟和牛的气味已经让你很像一个人了。醒醒，小兄弟，我带着消息来的。"

"丛林里什么都好吗？"莫格里抱住他说。

"那些被红色的花朵烧伤的狼除外都很好。现在，听好，谢尔可汗已经到非常选的地方狩猎了，他的皮毛不长好，他是不会回来的，因为他烧伤很严重。他发誓说回来的时候要将你的骨头扔在韦恩根格河。"

"这可要有两种说法了。我也做出了小小的承诺。但是有消息终归是好的。我今晚上很累，新事物让我很疲倦。灰兄弟，请经常带消

but bring me the news always."

"Thou wilt not forget that thou art a wolf? Men will not make thee forget?" said Gray Brother, anxiously.

"Never. I will always remember that I love thee and all in our cave; but also I will always remember that I have been cast out of the Pack."

"And that thou mayest be cast out of another pack. Men are only men, Little Brother, and their talk is like the talk of frogs in a pond. When I come down here again, I will wait for thee in the bamboos at the edge of the grazing-ground."

For three months after that night Mowgli hardly ever left the village gate, he was so busy learning the ways and customs of men. First he had to wear a cloth round him, which annoyed him horribly; and then he had to learn about money, which he did not in the least understand, and about plowing, of which he did not see the use. Then the little children in the village made him very angry. Luckily, the Law of the Jungle had taught him to keep his temper, for in the jungle, life and food depend on keeping your temper; but when they made fun of him because he would not play games or fly kites, or

息给我。"

"你不会忘记自己是一只狼吧？人们不会让你忘记这一点吧？"灰兄弟担忧地说。

"一定不会。我会永远记得我爱你，还有我们洞穴里的所有狼，不过我也会永远记得，我被赶出了狼群。"

"也许别的族群也会赶你走。人就是人，小兄弟，他们说的就跟池塘里的青蛙叫一样。等我再到这里来的时候，我就在草场边的竹林里等候你。"

在那晚之后的三个月，莫格里甚至没有走出过村门。他要学习人类的习俗和行为举止，忙得焦头烂额。首先，他必须在身上披一块布，这令他非常生气。接着他不得不学习他一点也不了解的钱的使用。还有怎么耕地，他没看出用处是什么。再有村子里的小孩子们让他很恼火。庆幸的是，丛林法则教会他控制自己的脾气。在丛林中，生命和食物都依赖于你控制住自己的脾气。但是当他不会玩游戏或者放风筝，或者因为他说错了某个词的时候，孩子们就取笑他。只是知道杀掉光溜溜的小崽子算不上光明正大，莫格里才忍住没有把他们举

because he mispronounced some word, only the knowledge that it was unsportsmanlike to kill little naked cubs kept him from picking them up and breaking them in two.

He did not know his own strength in the least. In the jungle he knew he was weak compared with the beasts, but in the village, people said he was as strong as a bull.

And Mowgli had not the faintest idea of the difference that caste makes between man and man. When the potter's donkey slipped in the clay-pit, Mowgli hauled it out by the tail, and helped to stack the pots for their journey to the market at Khanhiwara. That was very shocking, too, for the potter is a low-caste man, and his donkey is worse. When the priest scolded him, Mowgli threatened to put him on the donkey, too, and the priest told Messua's husband that Mowgli had better be set to work as soon as possible; and the village head-man told Mowgli that he would have to go out with the buffaloes next day, and herd them while they grazed. No one was more pleased than Mowgli; and that night, because he had been appointed a servant of the village, as it were, he

起来撕成两半。

他对自己的力量丝毫都不了解。在丛林里，他知道和野兽相比，自己是弱小的，可是在村子里，人们说他像公牛一样强壮。

莫格里不了解人与人之间的等级差别。当陶工的驴掉进了泥坑里，莫格里拽住了它的尾巴将其拉了上来，并且帮助整理好陶盆，让他们拉到可汗希瓦拉市场上去卖。这件事情非常令人震惊，因为陶工是一个低种姓的人，他的驴子更是低贱。当祭司因此责备他的时候，莫格里威胁祭司要将他放到驴背上。祭司告诉梅苏阿的丈夫，最好让他尽快出去干活。然后村长告诉莫格里，让他第二天出去放牛，并且让它们吃草。这让莫格里比任何人都高兴。那天晚上，他在某种程度上受命成为村子里的一个仆人。他去了村里的集会，就跟每晚见到的那样，人们围坐在一颗大无花果树下的石头台上。这是乡村俱乐部，村长、守夜人、理发师（他知道村里所有的八卦）、村里的猎手老布迪奥，他有一只塔式步枪，他

went off to a circle that met every evening on a masonry platform under a great fig-tree. It was the village club, and the head-man and the watchman and the barber (who knew all the gossip of the village), and old Buldeo, the village hunter, who had a Tower musket, met and smoked. The monkeys sat and talked in the upper branches, and there was a hole under the platform where a cobra lived, and he had his little platter of milk every night because he was sacred; and the old men sat around the tree and talked, and pulled at the bighuqas(the water-pipes) till far into the night. They told wonderful tales of gods and men and ghosts; and Buldeo told even more wonderful ones of the ways of beasts in the jungle, till the eyes of the children sitting outside the circle bulged out of their heads. Most of the tales were about animals, for the jungle was always at their door. The deer and the wild pig grubbed up their crops, and now and again the tiger carried off a man at twilight, within sight of the village gates.

Mowgli, who naturally knew something about what they were talking of, had to cover his face not to

们聚在一起，抽着烟，聊着天。头顶的树枝上有猴子们坐在一起叽里呱啦；平台下面的洞里有一条眼镜蛇，每天晚上他都能喝到一盘牛奶，因为人们认为他是神圣的；老人们围坐在树边一边说着话，一边抽着大水烟枪，直到深夜。他们讲着神奇的关于神、人和鬼的故事，布迪奥会讲述丛林中更加精彩的野兽的生活方式。坐在圈子外面的孩子们听得眼珠子都要掉出来了。大部分的故事都是关于动物的，因为丛林就在家的门口跟前。有鹿和野猪啃食他们的庄稼的，老虎在暮色中一次又一次地在村口把人叼走。

莫格里自然知道他们讲的这些，为了不被察觉他在偷笑，他只好捂住脸。而布迪奥，膝盖上放着

show that he was laughing, while Buldeo, the Tower musket across his knees, climbed on from one wonderful story to another, and Mowgli's shoulders shook.

Buldeo was explaining how the tiger that had carried away Messua's son was a ghost-tiger, and his body was inhabited by the ghost of a wicked old money-lender, who had died some years ago. "And I know that this is true," he said, "because Bhagat always limped from the blow that he got in a riot when his account-books were burned, and the tiger that I speak of he limps, too, for the tracks of his pads are unequal."

"True, true; that must be the truth," said the graybeards, nodding together.

"Are all these tales such cobwebs and moon-talk?" said Mowgli. "That tiger limps because he was born lame, as every one knows. To talk of the soul of a money-lender in a beast that never had the courage of a jackal is child's talk."

Buldeo was speechless with surprise for a moment, and the head-man stared.

"Oho! It is the jungle brat, is it?" said Buldeo. "If thou art so wise, better bring his hide to Khanhiwara, for the

他的塔式步枪，讲完一个精彩的故事，接着再讲一个，听得莫格里肩膀都在打战。

布迪奥此时正在解说，那只把梅苏阿的儿子叼走的老虎是一只幽灵老虎，他是被几年前死去的邪恶的老放债者的鬼混附体了。"我知道的确如此，"他说，"因为一次暴乱中。巴加特的账本被烧，还挨了一顿打，在那之后他就瘸了。我提到的那只老虎腿也是瘸的，他的掌印都不是一样的深浅。"

"的确，的确！事实一定是这样。"灰胡子的老人们一起点头呼应。

"这些故事都是你吞云吐雾一般瞎编出来的吧？"莫格里说，"那只老虎出生的时候就是个跛脚，这一点在丛林里谁都知道。说一个放债人的鬼魂附体到一个胆子不如豺狼的野兽身上，只有小孩子才会那么说。"

布迪奥一时惊讶得没说出话来，村长也瞪大了眼睛。

"哦吼！这是那个丛林小子，对吗？"布迪奥说，"如果你那么

Government has set a hundred rupees on his life. Better still, do not talk when thy elders speak."

Mowgli rose to go. "All the evening I have lain here listening," he called back over his shoulder, "and, except once or twice, Buldeo has not said one word of truth concerning the jungle, which is at his very doors. How, then, shall I believe the tales of ghosts and gods and goblins which he says he has seen?"

"It is full time that boy went to herding," said the head-man, while Buldeo puffed and snorted at Mowgli's impertinence.

The custom of most Indian villages is for a few boys to take the cattle and buffaloes out to graze in the early morning, and bring them back at night; and the very cattle that would trample a white man to death allow themselves to be banged and bullied and shouted at by children that hardly come up to their noses. So long as the boys keep with the herds they are safe, for not even the tiger will charge a mob of cattle. But if they straggle to pick flowers or hunt lizards, they are sometimes carried off. Mowgli went through the village street in the dawn, sitting on the back of

厉害，最好剥下他的皮送到卡尼瓦拉去，政府出价一百卢比索买他的命。最好安静一些，当长辈说话时，不要讲话。"

莫格里起身要走。"我躺在这里听了一个晚上，"他回头说，"不过，除了一两处之外，布迪奥说的丛林的那些故事都不是事实，这丛林可就在他的家门口。那么，我该如何相信他说亲眼所见的鬼神传说呢？"

"到了让这个男孩去放牧的时间了。"村长说。而布迪奥则吐了一口烟，对莫格里的无礼嗤之以鼻。

大多数印度的村庄都有个习俗，清晨时分让几个男孩将黄牛和水牛赶去吃草，夜晚来临时再把牛赶回。那些能把白人踩死的牛却任凭甚至没有他们鼻子高的孩子们敲打，吼叫。只要男孩们跟着牛群就可以确保安全，就算是一只老虎，也没有胆量进攻一大群牛。可是要是有人走开去摘花或者捕蜥蜴，他们有时就会被叼走。莫格里在清晨骑在大公牛拉玛的背上，穿过乡间的街道。那群长着向后弯的犄角的带着凶神恶煞的眼睛的灰蓝色水牛，跟在他身后，一头头走出牛棚。莫格里和孩子们说得很清

Rama, the great herd bull; and the slaty-blue buffaloes, with their long, backward-sweeping horns and savage eyes, rose out of their byres, one by one, and followed him, and Mowgli made it very clear to the children with him that he was the master. He beat the buffaloes with a long, polished bamboo, and told Kamya, one of the boys, to graze the cattle by themselves, while he went on with the buffaloes, and to be very careful not to stray away from the herd.

An Indian grazing-ground is all rocks and scrub and tussocks and little ravines, among which the herds scatter and disappear. The buffaloes generally keep to the pools and muddy places, where they lie wallowing or basking in the warm mud for hours. Mowgli drove them on to the edge of the plain where the Wainganga River came out of the jungle; then he dropped from Rama's neck, trotted off to a bamboo clump, and found Gray Brother. "Ah," said Gray Brother, "I have waited here very many days. What is the meaning of this cattle-herding work?"

"It is an order," said Mowgli. "I am a village herd for a while. What news of Shere Khan?"

楚，他是老大。他用一根长长的光滑的竹竿驱赶着水牛，对一个名叫卡姆亚的男孩说，让他们自己放牧，要小心，不要离开牛群，自己骑着水牛继续向前了。

印度放牧地布满石头、灌木丛、草丛和小水沟，牛群是分开就看不见了。水牛基本上会待在池塘和泥泞的地方，他们就躺在那里打滚或者沐浴着温暖的阳光待上几个小时。莫格里将他们赶到韦恩根格河流出丛林地带平原的边缘。然后他跳下拉玛的后背，小跑到竹林处，看到了灰兄弟。"啊，"灰兄弟说，"这些天我一直在此处等你。你这放牛的活计，有什么劲啊？"

"这是个命令，"莫格里说，"我要做一段时间村里的放牧人了。谢尔可汗有什么消息吗？"

"He has come back to this country, and has waited here a long time for thee. Now he has gone off again, for the game is scarce. But he means to kill thee."

"Very good," said Mowgli. "So long as he is away do thou or one of the brothers sit on that rock, so that I can see thee as I come out of the village. When he comes back wait for me in the ravine by the dhâk-tree in the center of the plain. We need not walk into Shere Khan's mouth."

Then Mowgli picked out a shady place, and lay down and slept while the buffaloes grazed round him. Herding in India is one of the laziest things in the world. The cattle move and crunch, and lie down, and move on again, and they do not even low. They only grunt, and the buffaloes very seldom say anything, but get down into the muddy pools one after another, and work their way into the mud till only their noses and staring china-blue eyes show above the surface, and there they lie like logs. The sun makes the rocks dance in the heat, and the herd-children hear one kite (never any more) whistling almost out of sight overhead, and they know that if they died, or a cow died, that

"他已经返回这个地方，还在此处守候你很长时间。现在他又离开了，是因为这里没什么猎物。但是他计划着要杀掉你。"

"非常好，"莫格里说，"只要他不在，你或者兄弟中的任何一个，就在那块石头上坐着，那样的话我走出村子就能看见你们。当他回来等我时，你们就在平原中心达哈树下的沟壑里等我。我们不必把自己送进谢尔可汗的嘴里。"

接着，莫格里选了一个有阴凉的地方，躺下睡觉了。而水牛就在周边吃草。在印度，放牧是世界上最懒散的事情之一。黄牛慢慢挪着脚步，嘎吱嘎吱嚼着草，吃着吃着就躺下了，然后再继续往前走，他们甚至叫都不叫，就哼哼两下。水牛更是没什么声音，他们陆续地下到泥塘里，只有鼻子和瞪着的蓝眼睛露出水面，他们躺在那里就像圆木头一样。岩石在太阳的炙烤下开始跳舞，放牧的孩子们听到一只老鹰（永远不会有更多）在他们头顶几乎看不清的地方鸣叫着。而且他们知道，倘若他们死了，或者一头母牛死了，那只老鹰会飞扑下来。远处的老鹰看到他飞扑下来，就会跟在后面，一只接着一只，在他们

kite would sweep down, and the next kite miles away would see him drop and follow, and the next, and the next, and almost before they were dead there would be a score of hungry kites come out of nowhere. Then they sleep and wake and sleep again, and weave little baskets of dried grass and put grasshoppers in them; or catch two praying-mantises and make them fight; or string a necklace of red and black jungle-nuts; or watch a lizard basking on a rock, or a snake hunting a frog near the wallows. Then they sing long, long songs with odd native quavers at the end of them, and the day seems longer than most people's whole lives, and perhaps they make a mud castle with mud figures of men and horses and buffaloes, and put reeds into the men's hands, and pretend that they are kings and the figures are their armies, or that they are gods to be worshiped. Then evening comes, and the children call, and the buffaloes lumber up out of the sticky mud with noises like gunshots going off one after the other, and they all string across the gray plain back to the twinkling village lights.

Day after day Mowgli would lead the buffaloes out to their wallows, and

没死之前，会有一堆老鹰不知道从哪里冒出来。看过老鹰之后，放牧的孩子们就睡觉了，一会儿醒过来，接着再睡。他们将干草编成小筐，里面放蚱蜢；或者抓两只螳螂让他们打斗；或者用红的黑的丛林坚果做一串项链；或者观察在岩石上晒太阳的蜥蜴，在泥坑旁边捕杀青蛙的蛇。然后他们会唱长长的歌曲，长歌的结尾还会带着奇怪的本地的颤音。这一天似乎比大多数的一生还要长久。或许他们会用泥人、泥马、泥水牛筑一座泥城，泥人的手里还会放上芦苇，假装他们就是君王，而泥人就是他们的军队，或者假装是受人敬仰的神。夜幕降临的时候，孩子们开始呼喊着。从黏黏的泥土中爬出来的水牛，一声接着一声弄出枪响一般的啪啪声。他们排成排穿过灰色的平原，回到灯火闪烁的村庄。

一天又一天，莫格里领着水牛去往泥塘；一天又一天，他瞧着一

day after day he would see Gray Brother's back a mile and a half away across the plain (so he knew that Shere Khan had not come back), and day after day he would lie on the grass listening to the noise round him, and dreaming of old days in the jungle. If Shere Khan had made a false step with his lame paw up in the jungles by the Wainganga, Mowgli would have heard him in those long still mornings.

At last a day came when he did not see Gray Brother at the signal place, and he laughed and headed the buffaloes for the ravine by thedhâk-tree, which was all covered with golden-red flowers. There sat Gray Brother, every bristle on his back lifted.

"He has hidden for a month to throw thee off thy guard. He crossed the ranges last night with Tabaqui, hot-foot on thy trail," said the wolf, panting.

Mowgli frowned. "I am not afraid of Shere Khan, but Tabaqui is very cunning."

"Have no fear," said Gray Brother, licking his lips a little. "I met Tabaqui in the dawn. Now he is telling all his wisdom to the kites, but he told me everything before I broke his back.

英里半之外的平原上灰兄弟的背部（他因此知道谢尔可汗没有回来）；一天又一天，他躺在草地上，身边各种噪声响起，使他重温在丛林中的旧日时光。在那些长久而宁静的清晨里，若是谢尔可汗在韦恩根格河河畔迈着他的跛脚走错一步，莫格里都会听到。

最终等来了这一天，莫格里没有在约定的信号地看到灰兄弟。他笑了，把水牛向前赶到达哈树旁的沟壑，上面满是金红的花朵。灰兄弟就坐在那儿，他背上的鬃毛都直立着。

"为了消除你的警惕，他已经在此藏身一个月了。他和塔巴克昨天晚上循着你的足迹，穿过了你们的放牧区。"灰兄弟气喘吁吁地说。

莫格里皱了皱眉。"谢尔可汗我倒不怕，可是塔巴克太奸诈了。"

"不要怕，"灰兄弟舔了舔嘴唇说，"我在黎明时分见到了塔巴克，估计他现在正在跟老鹰们显摆他的聪明机智。但是，我还没打断他的脊梁骨，他就告诉了我所有的

Shere Khan's plan is to wait for thee at the village gate this evening – for thee and for no one else. He is lying up now in the big dry ravine of the Wainganga."

"Has he eaten to-day, or does he hunt empty?" said Mowgli, for the answer meant life or death to him.

"He killed at dawn – a pig– and he has drunk too. Remember, Shere Khan could never fast even for the sake of revenge."

"Oh! Fool, fool! What a cub's cub it is! Eaten and drunk too, and he thinks that I shall wait till he has slept! Now, where does he lie up? If there were but ten of us we might pull him down as he lies. These buffaloes will not charge unless they wind him, and I cannot speak their language. Can we get behind his track so that they may smell it?"

"He swam far down the Wainganga to cut that off," said Gray Brother.

"Tabaqui told him that, I know. He would never have thought of it alone." Mowgli stood with his finger in his mouth, thinking. "The big ravine of the Wainganga. That opens out on the plain not half a mile from here. I can take the herd round through the jungle to the

事情。谢尔可汗打算今晚在村口等你，就等你，不等别人。这个时间他正在韦恩根格河干涸的沟渠中藏身。"

"他今天有没有吃什么？还是什么都没猎着？"莫格里问，因为答案关乎他的生死。

"拂晓时刻他杀死了一头猪，水也喝了。要记得，谢尔可汗就算是为了复仇，也绝不会禁食的。"

"哦！蠢货！蠢货！他就是个幼崽的崽子！不仅吃了，还喝了。他觉得我会等他美美地睡上一觉吧！现在，他是躺在哪里？倘若我们有十个弟兄，我们就能抓住机会，在他躺在那儿的时候直接控制住他，这些水牛一定得闻到他的气味，要不然他们不会对他进行攻击的，可我不会说他们的话。我们可以走到他的后面，好让水牛闻到他的气味吗？"

"他在韦恩根格河里远远游去，就为了把气味切断。"灰兄弟说。

"塔巴克告诉他那样做的，我了解。他自己绝不会想到这个办法，"莫格里站起来，嘴里含着手指，思索着，"韦恩根格河的沟壑，半英里之外的平原就是出口。我就

head of the ravine and then sweep down – but he would slink out at the foot. We must block that end. Gray Brother, canst thou cut the herd in two for me?"

"Not I, perhaps – but I have brought a wise helper." Gray Brother trotted off and dropped into a hole. Then there lifted up a huge gray head that Mowgli knew well, and the hot air was filled with the most desolate cry of all the jungle – the hunting-howl of a wolf at midday.

"Akela! Akela!" said Mowgli, clapping his hands. "I might have known that thou wouldst not forget me. We have a big work in hand. Cut the herd in two, Akela. Keep the cows and calves together, and the bulls and the plow-buffaloes by themselves."

The two wolves ran, ladies'-chain fashion, in and out of the herd, which snorted and threw up its head, and separated into two clumps. In one the cow-buffaloes stood, with their calves in the center, and glared and pawed, ready, if a wolf would only stay still, to charge down and trample the life out of him. In the other the bulls and the young bulls snorted and stamped; but, though they looked more imposing,

带着牛群从丛林绕到沟壑的出口，将他围堵。不过他可以从沟壑的这一个口子偷偷溜走，我们必须这头也堵上。灰兄弟，你可以帮我将牛群分为两拨吗？"

"我，可能不行，不过我带来了一个聪明的帮手。"灰兄弟小跑跳进一个洞中。然后，一个灰色的头露了出来，这可是莫格里非常熟悉的，热热的空气中立刻充斥着整个丛林中最凄凉的号叫——这是正午时刻，一只狼狩猎的号叫声。

"阿克拉！阿克拉！"莫格里边鼓掌边说，"我就知道，你不会把我忘掉的。我们手头有大任务，阿克拉，把牛一分为二。母牛和牛犊分为一拨，公牛和犁地的水牛分为一拨。"

两只狼开始跑起来，在牛群里进进出出，踩着女士链子一样的步子。那些牛鼻子哼哼着，抬起头，被分成了两拨。一拨牛是母水牛，他们站立着，小水牛被围在中间，都瞪着眼睛刨着爪子，蓄势待发，一只狼要是站那儿不动，他们就冲上去踩死他；另一拨牛是大公牛和少年公牛，他们鼻子哼哼着踩着蹄子，尽管他们看起来更有气势，实际上威胁性更小。因为他们不需要

they were much less dangerous, for they had no calves to protect. No six men could have divided the herd so neatly.

"What orders!" panted Akela. "They are trying to join again."

Mowgli slipped on to Rama's back. "Drive the bulls away to the left, Akela. Gray Brother, when we are gone hold the cows together, and drive them into the foot of the ravine."

"How far?" said Gray Brother, panting and snapping.

"Till the sides are higher than Shere Khan can jump," shouted Mowgli. "Keep them there till we come down." The bulls swept off as Akela bayed, and Gray Brother stopped in front of the cows. They charged down on him, and he ran just before them to the foot of the ravine, as Akela drove the bulls far to the left.

"Well done! Another charge and they are fairly started. Careful, now – careful, Akela. A snap too much, and the bulls will charge. Hujah! This is wilder work than driving black-buck. Didst thou think these creatures could move so swiftly?" Mowgli called.

"I have – have hunted these too in my time," gasped Akela in the dust.

保护小牛。即使是六个大男人也不能把牛群分得如此整齐。

"下命令啊！"阿克苏喘着粗气说，"他们又想合起来呢。"

莫格里一下子滑到拉玛的背上。"将公牛赶到左边去，阿卡拉。灰兄弟，我们出发以后，你将母牛赶到一起，把她们赶到沟壑的这头儿去。"

"要赶到多远？"灰兄弟气喘吁吁，边说，边对着母牛撕叫着。

"一直到沟壑的两侧高到谢尔可汗跳不上去为止，"莫格里喊道，"就让她们留在那里，直到我们从另一头赶到这儿。"公牛在阿克拉的吠叫声中疾驰而去 而灰兄弟就停在母牛的前方。母牛冲着他跑去，他就再往前跑，一直保持在他们前方不远处，将她们带到沟壑的出口，阿卡拉把公牛赶往左边很远的地方了。

"棒极了！接着再赶，他们就真的要跑了。当心点，这时候要当心了，阿克拉。你再来一嗓子，公牛们就冲得更猛了。嘿呀！这比驱赶黑鹿狂野多了。这些牛能跑这么快，你没想到吧？"

"我正当盛年的时候，曾经，也曾经捕杀过他们，"阿卡拉在尘

"Shall I turn them into the jungle?"

"Aye! Turn! Swiftly turn them. Rama is mad with rage. Oh, if I could only tell him what I need of him to-day!"

The bulls were turned to the right this time, and crashed into the standing thicket. The other herd-children, watching with the cattle half a mile away, hurried to the village as fast as their legs could carry them, crying that the buffaloes had gone mad and run away.

But Mowgli's plan was simple enough. All he wanted to do was to make a big circle uphill and get at the head of the ravine, and then take the bulls down it and catch Shere Khan between the bulls and the cows, for he knew that after a meal and a full drink Shere Khan would not be in any condition to fight or to clamber up the sides of the ravine. He was soothing the buffaloes now by voice, and Akela had dropped far to the rear, only whimpering once or twice to hurry the rear-guard. It was a long, long circle, for they did not wish to get too near the ravine and give Shere Khan warning. At last Mowgli rounded up the bewildered herd at the head of the

土飞扬中喘着粗气说，"我要把他们往丛林里面赶吗？"

"是呀！往丛林里赶！快点赶！拉玛要发气疯了。哦，若是我能让他知晓他今天需要怎么配合就好了。"

公牛这回被赶往右边，撞到了直直的灌木丛。其他放牧的孩子，半英里外就看见牛群，匆忙地往村子里跑，能跑多快就跑多快，边跑边喊着水牛疯了，都跑了。

不过莫格里原本的打算其实很简单。他就想在山上围成一个大圈，赶到沟壑的另一个出口，再将公牛赶到沟壑里，在公牛和母牛围成的圈中抓住谢尔可汗。因为他清楚吃饱喝足之后的谢尔可汗没什么战斗力，也爬不上沟壑的两侧。此时他用声音让水牛得到安抚，阿克拉已经被落下很远，只发出一两声悲鸣，催促着最后面的水牛。这是一个很长很长的圈子，因为他们不想太靠近沟壑，让谢尔可汗有所警觉。最后，莫格里把晕头转向的牛群驱赶到沟壑的另一个出口，在一片延伸到沟壑的草坡上聚到了一起。在这个高度，你可以从树尖一直看到下面的平原。可是出现在莫格里视线中的，只是沟壑的两

ravine on a grassy patch that sloped steeply down to the ravine itself. From that height you could see across the tops of the trees down to the plain below; but what Mowgli looked at was the sides of the ravine, and he saw with a great deal of satisfaction that they ran nearly straight up and down, and the vines and creepers that hung over them would give no foothold to a tiger who wanted to get out.

"Let them breathe, Akela," he said, holding up his hand. "They have not winded him yet. Let them breathe. I must tell Shere Khan who comes. We have him in the trap."

He put his hands to his mouth and shouted down the ravine, – it was almost like shouting down a tunnel, – and the echoes jumped from rock to rock.

After a long time there came back the drawling, sleepy snarl of a full-fed tiger just awakened.

"Who calls?" said Shere Khan, and a splendid peacock fluttered up out of the ravine, screeching.

"I, Mowgli. Cattle-thief, it is time to come to the Council Rock! Down – hurry them down, Akela. Down, Rama, down!"

沿，他非常满意地发现沟壑的两边可以说是直上直下的，并且到处都长着藤蔓植物，一只老虎想要出去的话，连落脚的地儿都没有。

"让他们歇口气，阿克拉，"莫格里举起手说，"他们还没有闻到他的气味，让他们先喘口气。我必须让谢尔可汗知道是谁来了，我们已经把他困在陷阱里了。"

他把手放在嘴边拢起，顺着沟壑大喊，听起来就好像在隧道下面喊一样，回声在岩石间传荡着。

好一会儿之后，才有一声咆哮声传回，这咆哮声来自一只吃饱喝足的刚刚醒来的还带着困意的老虎。

"是谁在叫唤？"谢尔可汗说。一只色彩斑斓的孔雀飞出沟壑，尖叫着。

"我是莫格里。窃牛贼。到了去会议岩石的时候了！下去，赶快把他们往下赶，阿克拉。下去，拉

The herd paused for an instant at the edge of the slope, but Akela gave tongue in the full hunting-yell, and they pitched over one after the other just as steamers shoot rapids, the sand and stones spurting up round them. Once started, there was no chance of stopping, and before they were fairly in the bed of the ravine Rama winded Shere Khan and bellowed.

"Ha! Ha!" said Mowgli, on his back. "Now thou knowest!" and the torrent of black horns, foaming muzzles, and staring eyes whirled down the ravine like boulders in flood-time; the weaker buffaloes being shouldered out to the sides of the ravine where they tore through the creepers. They knew what the business was before them – the terrible charge of the buffalo-herd, against which no tiger can hope to stand. Shere Khan heard the thunder of their hoofs, picked himself up, and lumbered down the ravine, looking from side to side for some way of escape, but the walls of the ravine were straight, and he had to keep on, heavy with his dinner and his drink, willing to do anything rather than fight. The herd splashed through the pool he had just left, bellowing till the narrow cut rang.

玛，下去！"

牛群在山坡上暂停了一小会儿，不过阿克拉扯着嗓子大喊狩猎号角，他们就像汽船在急流中奔腾一般一头头地向下冲去，沙子石子都飞溅起来。一旦开了头，就没有停下的机会了，在他们赶到沟壑的河床之前，拉玛就闻到了谢尔可汗的气味，大声咆哮起来。

"哈！哈！"莫格里在拉玛的背上说，"现在你知道怎么回事了！"牛群的黑牛角、吐出白沫的牛嘴、睁大的牛眼睛飞流一般顺着沟壑翻卷而下，就像洪水迸发那一刻，巨石从山上滚落。弱一些的水牛被顶到山沟的两侧，他们就势穿过藤蔓。他们清楚自己接下来要怎么做——水牛的疯狂冲锋，没有一只老虎可以抵挡住这个。谢尔可汗听到了隆隆的蹄声，站了起来，脚步沉重地顺着沟壑跑，一边跑一边左右打量着，看是否有逃跑的出口。可是沟壑的两侧都是直上直下的，他不得不继续跑着。肚子里装了太多的食物和水，身体重得他干什么都可以，就是不想战斗。牛群从他刚趟过的水塘经过，水花四起。牛群吼叫着直到狭窄的谷口轰隆直响。莫格里听见沟壑底部传来呼应声，他看见谢尔可汗转了身。

Mowgli heard an answering bellow from the foot of the ravine, saw ShereKhan turn (the tiger knew if the worst came to the worst it was better to meet the bulls than the cows with their calves), and then Rama tripped, stumbled, and went on again over something soft, and, with the bulls at his heels, crashed full into the other herd, while the weaker buffaloes were lifted clean off their feet by the shock of the meeting. That charge carried both herds out into the plain, goring and stamping and snorting. Mowgli watched his time, and slipped off Rama's neck, laying about him right and left with his stick.

"Quick, Akela! Break them up. Scatter them, or they will be fighting one another. Drive them away, Akela. Hai, Rama! Hai! hai! hai! my children. Softly now, softly! It is all over."

Akela and Gray Brother ran to and fro nipping the buffaloes' legs, and though the herd wheeled once to charge up the ravine again, Mowgli managed to turn Rama, and the others followed him to the wallows.

Shere Khan needed no more trampling. He was dead, and the kites were coming for him already.

老虎明白,倘若是火上浇油,面对公牛要比迎战护着小牛的母牛要强。拉玛这时候绊了下,趔趄着踏过一个软软的东西,继续向前了。跟在他身后的公牛,一下子撞入了另一群牛中,弱一些的水牛在冲击中完全四脚离地了。两群水牛冲出了沟壑,到了平原上,他们互相顶着,跺着脚,鼻子哼哼着。莫格里抓住时机,从拉玛脖子上滑下来,用棍子左右挥舞着。

"快点,阿克拉,将他们驱散开。驱散开,要不然他们将互相攻击。赶走他们,阿克拉。嗨,拉玛!嗨!嗨!嗨!我的孩子们。轻轻地,轻轻地!一切都结束了。"

阿克拉和灰兄弟跑去咬着牛的腿。尽管牛群转身要再次往沟壑里冲去,但是莫格里设法让拉玛转回身,其余的牛就跟着他去了泥塘。

谢尔可汗不需要更多的践踏,他已经死了,老鹰们正向他飞来。

"Brothers, that was a dog's death," said Mowgli, feeling for the knife he always carried in a sheath round his neck now that he lived with men. "But he would never have shown fight. Wallah! His hide will look well on the Council Rock. We must get to work swiftly."

A boy trained among men would never have dreamed of skinning a ten-foot tiger alone, but Mowgli knew better than any one else how an animal's skin is fitted on, and how it can be taken off. But it was hard work, and Mowgli slashed and tore and grunted for an hour, while the wolves lolled out their tongues, or came forward and tugged as he ordered them.

Presently a hand fell on his shoulder, and looking up he saw Buldeo with the Tower musket. The children had told the village about the buffalo stampede, and Buldeo went out angrily, only too anxious to correct Mowgli for not taking better care of the herd. The wolves dropped out of sight as soon as they saw the man coming.

"What is this folly?" said Buldeo, angrily. "To think that thou canst skin a tiger! Where did the buffaloes kill him? It is the Lame Tiger, too, and there is a

"兄弟们，他死得像条狗一样。"莫格里说，摸起刀来。因为现在和人生活在一起，所以他也在脖子上的刀鞘里放着刀。"不过，他从来也不想要真的打斗。把他的皮往会议岩石上一放，肯定漂亮，我们必须立马忙活起来。"

一个在人类当中培养长大的男孩，是无法想象他可以单独剥下一张十英尺长的虎皮的。但是莫格里可比其他人更清楚动物的皮是怎么长的，也更清楚要怎么剥皮。不过这真是个难干的活儿，莫格里撕扯了一个小时，狼就吐着舌头在一旁看着，莫格里让他们帮忙的时候，他们就走上前一起用力拉。

就在莫格里忙活的时候，他的肩膀搭上了一只手，莫格里抬头一看是带着塔式步枪的布迪奥。是那群小孩子告诉了村民水牛的踩踏事件，布迪奥很愤怒地冲出来，只是为了急于纠正莫格里没有好好照顾牛群的错误。一看到有人来了，两只狼就立刻消失不见了。

"你做了什么傻事？布迪奥气愤地说，"你觉得你自己可以剥下老虎的皮！水牛在哪里将他弄死的？这是那只瘸老虎，他的头值一

hundred rupees on his head. Well, well, we will overlook thy letting the herd run off, and perhaps I will give thee one of the rupees of the reward when I have taken the skin to Khanhiwara." He fumbled in his waist-cloth for flint and steel, and stooped down to singe Shere Khan's whiskers. Most native hunters singe a tiger's whiskers to prevent his ghost haunting them.

"Hum!" said Mowgli, half to himself as he ripped back the skin of a fore paw. "So thou wilt take the hide to Khanhiwara for the reward, and perhaps give me one rupee? Now it is in my mind that I need the skin for my own use. Heh! Old man, take away that fire!"

"What talk is this to the chief hunter of the village? Thy luck and the stupidity of thy buffaloes have helped thee to this kill. The tiger has just fed, or he would have gone twenty miles by this time. Thou canst not even skin him properly, little beggar-brat, and forsooth I, Buldeo, must be told not to singe his whiskers. Mowgli, I will not give thee one anna of the reward, but only a very big beating. Leave the carcass!"

"By the Bull that bought me," said

百卢比。好了，好了，我们不计较你让牛群跑了这件事了，也许我将虎皮拿去给可汗席瓦拉换回赏金，还能从中给你一个卢比。"他在围在腰间的布里拿出燧石和打火镰，弯下腰，想要把谢尔可汗的胡须烧掉。大多数的本地人会把死掉的老虎的胡须烧掉，以防止被他的鬼魂纠缠。

"哼！"莫格里说着，一半是说给自己的，他撕开了老虎前爪子上的皮，"所以说你要拿着虎皮去换赏金，还有可能给我一个卢比？可是我的想法是这张皮我要自己用。呵！老家伙，把火拿走！"

"怎么能这样跟村子里的猎手头领说话呢？是你的运气和愚蠢的水牛帮你杀死了这只老虎。老虎刚刚吃饱，不然他现在已经跑出有二十英里了。你甚至都不会好好地剥老虎皮，小乞丐崽子。我，布迪奥，还得被你叮嘱不能烧老虎胡须。莫格里，赏金的一个子儿我都不会给你，不过我会大揍你一顿，不要动老虎尸体！"

"以赎买我的公牛起誓，"正

Mowgli, who was trying to get at the shoulder, "must I stay babbling to an old ape all noon? Here, Akela, this man plagues me."

Buldeo, who was still stooping over Shere Khan's head, found himself sprawling on the grass, with a gray wolf standing over him, while Mowgli went on skinning as though he were alone in all India.

"Ye-es," he said, between his teeth. "Thou art altogether right, Buldeo. Thou wilt never give me one anna of the reward. There is an old war between this lame tiger and myself – a very old war, and – I have won."

To do Buldeo justice, if he had been ten years younger he would have taken his chance with Akela had he met the wolf in the woods, but a wolf who obeyed the orders of this boy who had private wars with man-eating tigers was not a common animal. It was sorcery, magic of the worst kind, thought Buldeo, and he wondered whether the amulet round his neck would protect him. He lay as still as still, expecting every minute to see Mowgli turn into a tiger, too.

"Maharaj! Great King," he said at last, in a husky whisper.

试图剥老虎肩上的皮的莫格里说，"我一个中午都必须要在这里与一个老猿唠唠叨叨吗？这儿，阿克拉，这个人太烦了。"

布迪奥还俯身探究着谢尔可汗的脑袋，突然间惊觉自己躺在了草地上，他的身上站着一只灰狼俯视着。这时候的莫格里还继续剥着老虎皮，好像全印度只有他一个人。

"是的，"话从莫格里的牙缝中挤出来，"你一点没错，布迪奥，你绝不会给我一个赏钱，不过这只跛脚老虎与我之间的战争很早之前就开始了，非常非常久远，并且这场战争是以我的胜利结束了。"

为布迪奥说句公道话的话，如果他年轻十岁，在森林中遇见阿克拉，他会搏上一搏。可是这只狼只听一个男孩的指令，这个男孩与吃人的老虎之间还有着个人恩怨，所以这只狼就不是一只普通的狼了。这是巫术，最坏的一种，布迪奥想着，他想知道脖子上的护身符是否能保护他。他躺在那里非常非常老实，时刻期待着莫格里也变成一只老虎。

"马哈拉杰！伟大的王啊！"他最后用沙哑的声音说。

"Yes," said Mowgli, without turning his head, chuckling a little.

"I am an old man. I did not know that thou wast anything more than a herd-boy. May I rise up and go away, or will thy servant tear me to pieces?"

"Go, and peace go with thee. Only, another time do not meddle with my game. Let him go, Akela."

Buldeo hobbled away to the village as fast as he could, looking back over his shoulder in case Mowgli should change into something terrible. When he got to the village he told a tale of magic and enchantment and sorcery that made the priest look very grave.

Mowgli went on with his work, but it was nearly twilight before he and the wolves had drawn the great gay skin clear of the body.

"Now we must hide this and take the buffaloes home! Help me to herd them, Akela."

The herd rounded up in the misty twilight, and when they got near the village Mowgli saw lights, and heard the conches and bells in the temple blowing and banging. Half the village seemed to be waiting for him by the gate. "That is because I have killed Shere Khan," he said to himself; but a

"是的。"莫格里说，他没有回头，只是咯咯地笑了几声。

"我是一个老头儿了，我原本就知道你是个放牧娃娃。我可以起身离开吗？还是你的仆人要把我撕碎？"

"走吧，愿安宁永伴。只是，别再对我的猎物动心思了。让他走吧，阿克拉。"

布迪奥尽可能快速地蹒跚着走向村子，同时还不忘回头看看，就怕莫格里变成什么可怕的东西。布迪奥回到村子里，讲了一个魔法和巫术的故事，使得祭司表情非常严肃。

莫格里继续剥着老虎皮，当他和两只狼将那张艳丽的老虎皮从老虎尸身上剥下来，都已经是夜幕降临的时候了。

"现在我们必须藏起这张老虎皮，把水牛赶回家去！帮我将他们聚到一起，阿克拉。"

牛群在暮雾中聚到了一起，他们要到村子的时候，莫格里看见了亮光，听见庙里的海螺号角还有当当的钟声。看起来村子里一半的人都站在大门口等他。"那是因为我杀了谢尔可汗。"他自言自语道。可是在他的耳边响起一阵呼呼的石子雨一般的声音，村民们喊道：

shower of stones whistled about his ears, and the villagers shouted: "Sorcerer! Wolf's brat! Jungle-demon! Go away! Get hence quickly, or the priest will turn thee into a wolf again. Shoot, Buldeo, shoot!"

The old Tower musket went off with a bang, and a young buffalo bellowed in pain.

"More sorcery!" shouted the villagers. "He can turn bullets. Buldeo, that wasthybuffalo."

"Now what is this?" said Mowgli, bewildered, as the stones flew thicker.

"They are not unlike the Pack, these brothers of thine," said Akela, sitting down composedly. "It is in my head that, if bullets mean anything, they would cast thee out."

"Wolf! Wolf's cub! Go away!" shouted the priest, waving a sprig of the sacredtulsiplant.

"Again? Last time it was because I was a man. This time it is because I am a wolf. Let us go, Akela."

A woman – it was Messua – ran across to the herd, and cried: "Oh, my son, my son! They say thou art a sorcerer who can turn himself into a beast at will. I do not believe, but go away or they will kill thee. Buldeo says

"巫师！狼崽子！丛林里的恶魔！滚快！快滚开，不然祭司会把你变成狼的。开枪，布迪奥，开枪！"

老塔步枪砰地响起，一头青年水牛痛苦地吼了以来。

"又使用巫术了！"村民们喊道，"他能掉转子弹方向。布迪奥，你的水牛被打中了。"

"现在这是什么情况？"莫格里困惑地说。飞过来的石头更多了。

"他们和狼群没什么差别，你这些人类的兄弟，"阿克拉说着，从容地坐了下来，"我脑子里想的是，要是子弹意味着什么，那就是他们要赶你走。"

"狼！狼崽子！滚开！"祭司喊道，手里挥舞着神圣的树枝。

"又被驱逐？上次是因为我是个人，这次是因为我是只狼。我们走吧，阿克拉。"

有个女人——是梅苏阿——向牛群方向跑来，她大喊着："哦，我的儿子，我的儿子！他们将你说成巫师，他们说你可以任意将自己变成野兽。我不信他们说的，不过你走吧，要不然他们会杀了你的。

thou art a wizard, but I know thou hast avenged Nathoo's death."

"Come back, Messua!" shouted the crowd. "Come back, or we will stone thee."

Mowgli laughed a little short ugly laugh, for a stone had hit him in the mouth. "Run back, Messua. This is one of the foolish tales they tell under the big tree at dusk. I have at least paid for thy son's life. Farewell; and run quickly, for I shall send the herd in more swiftly than their brickbats. I am no wizard, Messua. Farewell!"

"Now, once more, Akela," he cried. "Bring the herd in."

The buffaloes were anxious enough to get to the village. They hardly needed Akela's yell, but charged through the gate like a whirlwind, scattering the crowd right and left.

"Keep count!" shouted Mowgli, scornfully. "It may be that I have stolen one of them. Keep count, for I will do your herding no more. Fare you well, children of men, and thank Messua that I do not come in with my wolves and hunt you up and down your street."

He turned on his heel and walked away with the Lone Wolf; and as he looked up at the stars he felt happy.

布迪奥说你是巫师，但是我清楚你为纳索的死报仇了。"

"回来吧，梅苏阿！"人群喊道，"回来，不然我们会拿石头打你。"

莫格里简短地笑了笑，不过笑声很奇怪，因为一个石子正砸到了他的嘴巴。"梅苏阿，跑回去吧。这是黄昏时他们在大树下讲述的愚蠢的故事之一。我反正已经给你儿子报了仇。再见吧，快跑吧，我还要将牛群赶过去，他们可比砖头的速度快多了。我不是巫师，梅苏阿，告辞了！"

"那就再来一回，阿克拉，"他喊道，"将牛群赶进村子。"

水牛都非常急迫地跑回村子，甚至都不用阿克拉号叫，他们就旋风一般冲过大门，也冲散了人群。

"数清楚一些！"莫格里不屑地喊道，"没准我偷了一头牛呢，数清楚喽，我不会再给你们放牧了。孩子们，你们要感激梅苏阿，我是因为她才不会与我的狼伴儿在大街上追逐你们。"

莫格里转身与孤狼一起离开了。当他抬头望着天空的时候，他感到很高兴。"阿克拉，我再也不

"No more sleeping in traps for me, Akela. Let us get Shere Khan's skin and go away. No; we will not hurt the village, for Messua was kind to me."

When the moon rose over the plain, making it look all milky, the horrified villagers saw Mowgli, with two wolves at his heels and a bundle on his head, trotting across at the steady wolf's trot that eats up the long miles like fire. Then they banged the temple bells and blew the conches louder than ever; and Messua cried, and Buldeo embroidered the story of his adventures in the jungle, till he ended by saying that Akela stood up on his hind legs and talked like a man.

The moon was just going down when Mowgli and the two wolves came to the hill of the Council Rock, and they stopped at Mother Wolf's cave.

"They have cast me out from the Man Pack, Mother," shouted Mowgli, "but I come with the hide of Shere Khan to keep my word."

Mother Wolf walked stiffly from the cave with the cubs behind her, and her eyes glowed as she saw the skin.

"I told him on that day, when he crammed his head and shoulders into this cave, hunting for thy life, Little

用睡在陷阱一样的地方了,我们把谢尔可汗的皮带上走吧。不,我们不能伤害到村民,因为梅苏阿一直善待我。"

当月亮升起来的时候,月光将整个平原映照得一片乳白色,吓破胆的村民看见两只狼跟在莫格里身后,他的头顶上顶着虎皮,以狼一样稳定的步伐小跑着,如火焰一般掠过数英里远后消失了。接着村民们将神庙里的钟撞响,海螺的号角声也越来越高。梅苏阿哭喊着,布迪奥将丛林中的冒险经历添油加醋了一番。最后他说,阿克拉能够像人一样后腿站直,开口说话。

月亮正要落下的时候,莫格里和两只狼来到了会议岩石所在的山上,他们停在了狼妈妈的洞穴口。

"我被他们从人群中赶出来了,妈妈,"莫格里喊着,"不过我把谢尔可汗的皮带回来了,我遵守了我的诺言。"

狼妈妈踉跄地跑出洞口,身后跟着狼崽们。当她看到那张虎皮的时候,眼睛一亮。

"那天他把头和肩膀塞进洞口的时候,我就告诉过他,要猎杀你的性命,最终会被你猎杀,小青

Frog – I told him that the hunter would be the hunted. It is well done."

"Little Brother, it is well done," said a deep voice in the thicket. "We were lonely in the jungle without thee," and Bagheera came running to Mowgli's bare feet. They clambered up the Council Rock together, and Mowgli spread the skin out on the flat stone where Akela used to sit, and pegged it down with four slivers of bamboo, and Akela lay down upon it, and called the old call to the Council, "Look – look well, O Wolves!" exactly as he had called when Mowgli was first brought there.

Ever since Akela had been deposed, the Pack had been without a leader, hunting and fighting at their own pleasure. But they answered the call from habit, and some of them were lame from the traps they had fallen into, and some limped from shot-wounds, and some were mangy from eating bad food, and many were missing; but they came to the Council Rock, all that were left of them, and saw Shere Khan's striped hide on the rock, and the huge claws dangling at the end of the empty, dangling feet. It was then that Mowgli made up a song

蛙, 你做得太棒了。"

"小兄弟, 做得真好," 灌木丛中响起一个低沉的声音, "你不在这里, 我们觉得很孤单。" 巴赫拉跑到莫格里赤裸的脚掌边。他们都爬上了会议岩石, 莫格里将虎皮平铺在阿克拉之前常坐的扁平的石头上, 四个竹条钉在上面固定住, 阿克拉躺在上面, 如往日召开狼群大会一般发出旧时的呼叫: "瞧瞧吧, 认真地瞧一瞧, 狼伙计们!" 就像当年莫格里被首次带到这个地方一样呼喊着。

从阿克拉被罢黜到现在, 狼群一直是没有首领的, 狼伙计们全凭自己高兴决定打猎和打斗, 不过他们还是习惯性地回应了阿克拉的呼唤。他们当中的一部分狼掉进陷阱摔断了腿, 一部分狼挨了枪子成了瘸子, 一部分食用了腐坏的食物长了疥癣, 还有些狼失踪不见了。不过他们来到了会议岩石, 幸免于难的狼都来了, 他们看见了岩石上平铺的谢尔可汗的条纹皮, 巨大的爪子空荡荡地耷拉着, 四只脚悬空。莫格里这时候唱起了自己创造的歌曲, 没有韵律, 自然而然无需准备就唱出来。他大声地唱着, 在

without any rhymes, a song that came up into his throat all by itself, and he shouted it aloud, leaping up and down on the rattling skin, and beating time with his heels till he had no more breath left, while Gray Brother and Akela howled between the verses.

"Look well, O Wolves. Have I kept my word?" said Mowgli when he had finished; and the wolves bayed "Yes," and one tattered wolf howled:

"Lead us again, O Akela. Lead us again, O Man-cub, for we be sick of this lawlessness, and we would be the Free People once more."

"Nay," purred Bagheera, "that may not be. When ye are full-fed, the madness may come upon ye again. Not for nothing are ye called the Free People. Ye fought for freedom, and it is yours. Eat it, O Wolves."

"Man Pack and Wolf Pack have cast me out," said Mowgli. "Now I will hunt alone in the jungle."

"And we will hunt with thee," said the four cubs.

So Mowgli went away and hunted with the four cubs in the jungle from that day on. But he was not always alone, because years afterward he became a man and married.

虎皮上来回上蹿下跳，脚跟还不忘打着拍子，直到气都喘不过来。每到两句歌词的空档，就会有灰兄弟和阿克拉的号叫伴唱。

"狼伙计们，仔细瞧一瞧吧。我是否遵守了诺言？"莫格里说，当他讲话结束的时候，狼群回应道："是。"一只毛皮破烂的狼号叫着：

"再次做我们的首领吧，哦，阿克拉。再次做我们的首领吧，哦，人类幼崽。我们对这种无法无天的状况感到厌烦，我们想要再次做自由民。"

"不行，"巴赫拉轻声地说，"那不可能。你们要是吃饱了以后，又会发疯的。把你们称为自由民，不是毫无根据的。你们为自由而战，你们拥有自由。将自由吃掉吧，狼伙计们。"

"人群与狼群都将我赶出群体了，"莫格里说，"我现在要独自在丛林中打猎。"

"我们要跟着你一同捕猎。"四个小狼崽说。

自此，莫格里就离开了，那一天开始，他就带着四只狼崽在丛林中一同捕猎。不过他并不是一直孤

But that is a story for grown-ups.

身一人，因为几年后他从男孩变成男人，结了婚。不过那个故事是说给大人们听的了。

MOWGLI'S SONG

莫格里之歌

THAT HE SANG AT THE COUNCIL ROCK WHEN HE DANCED ON SHERE KHAN'S HIDE

下面是莫格里在会议岩石谢尔可汗的皮上跳舞的时候哼唱的歌曲。

The Song of Mowgli – I, Mowgli, am singing. Let the jungle listen to the things I have done.

Shere Khan said he would kill – would kill! At the gates in the twilight he would kill Mowgli, the Frog!

He ate and he drank. Drink deep, Shere Khan, for when wilt thou drink again? Sleep and dream of the kill.

I am alone on the grazing-grounds. Gray Brother, come to me! Come to me, Lone Wolf, for there is big game afoot.

Bring up the great bull-buffaloes, the blue-skinned herd-bulls with the angry eyes. Drive them to and fro as I order.

Sleepest thou still, Shere Khan? Wake, O wake! Here come I, and the bulls are behind.

Rama, the King of the Buffaloes,

莫格里之歌——我，莫格里在歌唱。让丛林聆听我做过的事。

谢尔可汗曾扬言要捕杀——要捕杀！在黄昏时分的村口，他要杀掉莫格里，小青蛙！

他吃了，也喝了。喝那么多，谢尔可汗，你什么时候还能再喝？睡吧，去梦里捕杀吧。

我一人在牧场上。灰兄弟，来找我！来吧，孤狼，因为这里即将爆发一场大战。

将公牛驱赶过来，蓝皮的牛群怒目圆睁，依我的指令，来回驱赶他们。

谢尔可汗，你还睡着？醒醒吧，醒醒！我来了，公牛就跟在我的身后。

拉玛，水牛之王跺着脚。韦恩

stamped with his foot. Waters of the Wainganga, whither went Shere Khan?

He is not Ikki to dig holes, nor Mao, the Peacock, that he should fly. He is not Mang, the Bat, to hang in the branches. Little bamboos that creak together, tell me where he ran?

Ow! He is there.Ahoo! He is there. Under the feet of Rama lies the Lame One! Up, Shere Khan! Up and kill! Here is meat; break the necks of the bulls!

Hsh! He is asleep. We will not wake him, for his strength is very great. The kites have come down to see it. The black ants have come up to know it. There is a great assembly in his honor.

Alala! I have no cloth to wrap me. The kites will see that I am naked. I am ashamed to meet all these people.

Lend me thy coat, Shere Khan. Lend me thy gay striped coat that I may go to the Council Rock.

By the Bull that bought me I have made a promise – a little promise. Only thy coat is lacking before I keep my word.

With the knife – with the knife that men use – with the knife of the hunter, the man, I will stoop down for my gift.

Waters of the Wainganga, bear

根格河之水呀，谢尔可汗去了哪里？

他不是会挖洞的伊基，也不是会飞的孔雀莫奥。他不是能挂在树枝上的蝙蝠芒恩。一起吱吱响的细竹子，告诉我他跑哪儿去了？

哦！他在那里！啊！他在那里！躺在拉玛脚下的跛子！站起来，谢尔可汗！站起来捕杀！肉在这里，来咬断公牛的脖子啊！

嘘！他睡着了。我们不要叫醒他，他的力量太强大。老鹰都下来看他了。黑色蚂蚁前来见识一下他。因他的名誉展开了盛大集会。

啊啦啦！我没有用布包裹自己，老鹰会看见我光溜溜的。我如此羞愧这样见到所有居民。

借给我你的外套吧，谢尔可汗。将你艳丽的条纹外套借给我披上，我才能去会议岩石。

以赎买我的公牛，我立下过一个誓言——一个小小的誓言。在我履行誓言之前，只缺了你的外套。

用刀——用人类使用的刀——用猎人使用的刀，为了我的礼物，我要弯腰取之。

韦恩根格河之水见证了谢尔

witness that Shere Khan gives me his coat for the love that he bears me. Pull, Gray Brother! Pull, Akela! Heavy is the hide of Shere Khan. Heavy is the hide of Shere Khan.

The Man Pack are angry. They throw stones and talk child's talk. My mouth is bleeding. Let us run away.

Through the night, through the hot night, run swiftly with me, my brothers. We will leave the lights of the village and go to the low moon.

Waters of the Wainganga, the Man Pack have cast me out. I did them no harm, but they were afraid of me. Why?

Wolf Pack, ye have cast me out too. The jungle is shut to me and the village gates are shut. Why?

As Mang flies between the beasts and the birds so fly I between the village and the jungle. Why?

I dance on the hide of Shere Khan, but my heart is very heavy. My mouth is cut and wounded with the stones from the village, but my heart is very light because I have come back to the jungle. Why?

These two things fight together in me as the snakes fight in the spring. The water comes out of my eyes; yet I

可汗对我的爱,他将自己的外套给了我。拉,灰兄弟!拉,阿克拉!谢尔可汗的皮好沉。

人们生气了。他们丢石子,讲小孩子一般幼稚的话。我的嘴流血了。我们逃离这个地方吧。

穿过夜晚,穿过炎热的夜晚,快和我一起跑,我的兄弟们。我们离开村子的光亮,去低悬的月亮那里。

韦恩根格河之水,人类将我驱赶出族群,我没有做过伤害他们的事,可是他们惧怕我。这是为什么?

狼群,你们也将我驱赶出族群。丛林在我面前关闭,村门也关闭了。这是为什么?

仿佛芒恩飞行在野兽和鸟类之间一样,我在村庄和丛林之间来回徘徊。这是为什么?

我在谢尔可汗的皮上跳着舞,心里却很沉重。我的嘴被村民扔的石头割伤,心里却很轻松,因为我回到了丛林。这是为什么?

这两件事情在我体内缠斗,犹如蛇在春天里战斗一样。泪水从我的眼里流出,可我却笑了。这是为

laugh while it falls. Why?

I am two Mowglis, but the hide of Shere Khan is under my feet.

All the jungle knows that I have killed Shere Khan. Look – look well, O Wolves!

Ahae! My heart is heavy with the things that I do not understand.

什么？

我是两个莫格里，不过谢尔可汗的皮在我的足下，千真万确。

丛林里无人不知我杀掉了谢尔可汗。瞧一瞧，好好地瞧一瞧，狼伙计们！

哎呀！我的心很沉重，里面有好多我无法理解的事。

CHAPTER 4   THE WHITE SEAL

第四章　白海豹

OH! hush thee, my baby, the night is behind us,

And black are the waters that sparkled so green.

The moon, o'er the combers, looks downward to find us

At rest in the hollows that rustle between.

Where billow meets billow, there soft be thy pillow;

Ah, weary wee flipperling, curl at thy ease!

The storm shall not wake thee, nor shark overtake thee,

Asleep in the arms of the slow-swinging seas.

Seal Lullaby

ALL these things happened several years ago at a place called Novastoshnah, or North East Point, on the Island of St. Paul, away and away in the Bering Sea. Limmershin, the Winter Wren, told me

　　哦！轻轻地，我的宝贝，黑夜在我们身后，

　　黝黑的是海水，闪耀着绿色的光芒。

　　月亮在卷浪之上，低头俯看着我们，

　　在沙沙作响的浪窝之间休息。

　　浪涛满天的地方，有你柔软的枕头，

　　小小鳍足折腾不动了，蜷起身子好好睡吧！

　　暴风雨不会叫醒你，鲨鱼也不会追上你，

　　安睡在缓缓摆动的大海的臂弯里吧。

　　《海豹的摇篮曲》

　　这一切都发生在几年前，在遥远的白令海峡的圣保罗岛上的一个名为诺瓦斯托什纳的地方，也叫作东北岬。冬鹪鹩利莫辛告诉了我这个故事。那时候，

the tale when he was blown on to the rigging of a steamer going to Japan, and I took him down into my cabin and warmed and fed him for a couple of days till he was fit to fly back to St. Paul's again. Limmershin is a very odd little bird, but he knows how to tell the truth.

Nobody comes to Novastoshnah except on business, and the only people who have regular business there are the seals. They come in the summer months by hundreds and hundreds of thousands out of the cold gray sea; for Novastoshnah Beach has the finest accommodation for seals of any place in all the world.

Sea Catch knew that, and every spring would swim from whatever place he happened to be in – would swim like a torpedo-boat straight for Novastoshnah, and spend a month fighting with his companions for a good place on the rocks as close to the sea as possible. Sea Catch was fifteen years old, a huge gray fur-seal with almost a mane on his shoulders, and long, wicked dog-teeth. When he heaved himself up on his front flippers he stood more than four feet clear of the ground, and his weight, if any one had been bold enough to weigh

利莫辛被风吹到开往日本的一艘蒸汽轮船上，我救下了他，把他带进我的小屋，并且喂食了几天，一直到他恢复体力能够再次飞回圣保罗。利莫辛这只小鸟很奇怪，不过他知道如何说出真相。

除非有什么事要办，否则谁都不会来诺瓦斯托纳，而经常要到此处办事的族类只有海豹。在夏季的时候，几十甚至上百万只海豹游过冰冷的灰蒙蒙的海水聚集此处，因为诺瓦斯托什纳海滩对于海豹来说，是世界上最好的栖息地。

大海捕手清楚这一点。每到春季，不管他恰巧在什么地方，他都会像鱼雷快艇一般径直游向诺瓦斯托什纳，他要花上一个月的时间与同伴打斗，就为了尽可能靠近海边的岩石上占个好地方。大海捕手是一只巨大的灰皮海豹，已经十五岁了，他的肩上有鬃毛一样的毛，还有长长的、凶狠的犬牙。当他前鳍肢站直的时候，距离地面有四英尺那么高。他的体重，要是谁够胆称一下的话，差不多要有七百磅[1]那么沉。他的全身上下都是野蛮战

---

[1] 重量单位，1 磅等于 453 克。

him, was nearly seven hundred pounds. He was scarred all over with the marks of savage fights, but he was always ready for just one fight more. He would put his head on one side, as though he were afraid to look his enemy in the face; then he would shoot it out like lightning, and when the big teeth were firmly fixed on the other seal's neck, the other seal might get away if he could, but Sea Catch would not help him.

Yet Sea Catch never chased a beaten seal, for that was against the Rules of the Beach. He only wanted room by the sea for his nursery; but as there were forty or fifty thousand other seals hunting for the same thing each spring, the whistling, bellowing, roaring, and blowing on the beach was something frightful.

From a little hill called Hutchinson's Hill you could look over three and a half miles of ground covered with fighting seals; and the surf was dotted all over with the heads of seals hurrying to land and begin their share of the fighting. They fought in the breakers, they fought in the sand, and they fought on the smooth-worn basalt rocks of the nurseries; for they were just as stupid and unaccommodating as men. Their wives never came to the island until late in May or early in June, for they

斗的伤痕，不过他总是做好准备再战一场。他将头往一边歪着，好像没有胆量看对手的脸，然后像闪电一般突然射出脑袋，长长的犬牙牢牢地咬住另一只海豹的脖子。那只海豚这时候若是能够逃走的话就会逃走，不过大海捕手不会帮他。

但大海捕手不会追赶被击败的海豹，因为那样做会违反海滩法则。他只想在海边找个地方，繁衍后代。但是因为每年春季，有四五万只海豹抱着同样的想法争夺地盘。海滩上的呼啸声、吼叫声、咆哮声就会非常吓人。

从一个名叫哈钦森山的小山上，你可以看到周边三英里半的海滩上充满了在打斗的海豹。海浪中也到处是海豹的脑袋，他们急匆匆赶往岸边，要开始战斗。他们在浪涛中打斗，在沙滩上打斗，在繁衍后代的岩石上打斗，他们如同人类一般愚蠢，不肯与他人方便。他们的妻子不到五月末或者六月初，一定不会来到岛上，因为她们不想自己被撕得粉碎。年少的两岁、三岁、四

did not care to be torn to pieces; and the young two-, three-, and four-year-old seals who had not begun housekeeping went inland about half a mile through the ranks of the fighters and played about on the sand-dunes in droves and legions, and rubbed off every single green thing that grew. They were called the holluschickie, – the bachelors, – and there were perhaps two or three hundred thousand of them at Novastoshnah alone.

Sea Catch had just finished his forty-fifth fight one spring when Matkah, his soft, sleek, gentle-eyed wife came up out of the sea, and he caught her by the scruff of the neck and dumped her down on his reservation, saying gruffly: "Late, as usual. Where have you been?"

It was not the fashion for Sea Catch to eat anything during the four months he stayed on the beaches, and so his temper was generally bad. Matkah knew better than to answer back. She looked around and cooed: "How thoughtful of you. You've taken the old place again."

"I should think I had," said Sea Catch. "Look at me!"

He was scratched and bleeding in twenty places; one eye was almost blind, and his sides were torn to ribbons.

"Oh, you men, you men!" Matkah

岁的小海豹还无需开始维持家庭，他们穿过正在打斗的行列，去往陆地大约半英里的地方，在沙丘上成群结队地玩耍着，并且蹭光陆地上长出来的每一片绿植。他们被叫作霍鲁斯奇基，意思就是单身汉。单单在诺瓦斯托什纳这里，就有大概二三十万只霍鲁斯奇基。

一年春天，大海捕手刚刚结束他的第四十五场战斗的时候，他皮肤柔软、细嫩光滑。眼神温和的妻子玛特卡从海中上来。大海捕手叼起她的颈背，将她扔进自己的地盘，粗暴地说："又来迟了，年年如此，你到哪儿去了？"

在海滩上的四个月时间里，大海捕手不吃任何东西，因此他的脾气一向很差。玛特卡清楚最好还是不要回应。她环顾四周，柔声柔气地说："你考虑得真周详，你又占领了老地方。"

"就要想着抢到老地方，"大海捕手说，"看看我！"

他身上被抓伤的地方有二十处，都流血了，一只眼睛甚至要瞎了，两侧的皮毛上也被抓出一道道伤痕。

said, fanning herself with her hind flipper. "Why can't you be sensible and settle your places quietly? You look as though you had been fighting with the Killer Whale."

"I haven't been doing anything but fight since the middle of May. The beach is disgracefully crowded this season. I've met at least a hundred seals from Lukannon Beach, house-hunting. Why can't people stay where they belong?"

"I've often thought we should be much happier if we hauled out at Otter Island instead of this crowded place," said Matkah.

"Bah! Only the holluschickie go to Otter Island. If we went there they would say we were afraid. We must preserve appearances, my dear."

Sea Catch sunk his head proudly between his fat shoulders and pretended to go to sleep for a few minutes, but all the time he was keeping a sharp lookout for a fight. Now that all the seals and their wives were on the land you could hear their clamor miles out to sea above the loudest gales. At the lowest counting there were over a million seals on the beach, – old seals, mother seals, tiny babies, and holluschickie, fighting, scuffling, bleating, crawling, and playing

"哦，你是汉子，你是汉子，"玛特卡说着，扇着后鳍肢，"你们为什么不能理智平和地解决地盘之争呢？你看起来好像刚和虎鲸打了一场。"

"从五月中旬以来，我除了打斗，没有做任何其他的事。这个海滩在这个季节挤得有点像话。我碰到了至少一百只从鲁坎农海滩来这里抢地盘的海豹。为什么他们不能待在自己的地方呢？"

"我经常在想，如果我们脱离这个地方，到水獭岛上去，应该会比在这个拥挤的地方更快乐。"玛特卡说。

"呸！只有霍鲁斯奇基去水獭岛。倘若我们去那里，我们会被认为是害怕了。亲爱的，我们要维护颜面。"

大海捕手自豪地将头缩进肥肥的肩膀上，假装睡了一小会儿，实际上他一直密切关注准备应对一场打斗。此时所有的海豹及他们的妻子都到了海岛上，数英里之外你也能听得见他们的喧哗，最强烈的风声都掩盖不住。海滩上最少也有超过百万只的海豹，年老的海豹、海豹妈妈、小宝宝和霍鲁斯奇基。这些海豹打斗、混战、慢慢爬着、又玩耍

together, – going down to the sea and coming up from it in gangs and regiments, lying over every foot of ground as far as the eye could reach, and skirmishing about in brigades through the fog. It is nearly always foggy at Novastoshnah, except when the sun comes out and makes everything look all pearly and rainbow-colored for a little while.

Kotick, Matkah's baby, was born in the middle of that confusion, and he was all head and shoulders, with pale, watery blue eyes, as tiny seals must be; but there was something about his coat that made his mother look at him very closely.

"Sea Catch," she said, at last, "our baby's going to be white!"

"Empty clam-shells and dry seaweed!" snorted Sea Catch. "There never has been such a thing in the world as a white seal."

"I can't help that," said Matkah; "there's going to be now"; and she sang the low, crooning seal-song that all the mother seals sing to their babies:

You mustn't swim till you're six weeks old,

Or your head will be sunk by your heels;

在一起，他们成群结队地到海里去，又呼啦啦一帮上岸来。眼睛可以看到的每一寸地方，都躺满了海豹，迷雾中小的群体打斗一直没有停止。诺瓦斯托什纳几乎一直是雾蒙蒙的，只有当太阳出来的时候让一切片刻间显得如珍珠和彩虹一般色彩斑斓。

可迪克，玛特卡的宝宝在一片混乱之中降生了。如其他的小海豹宝宝一样，他的脑袋、肩膀发育得不错，淡蓝色的眼睛水汪汪的。不过他的皮肤却有点不一样，这引起了他妈妈的密切关注。

"大海捕手，"她最后说，"我们的宝宝会是个白海豹！"

"空蛤壳干海藻！"大海捕手哼了一下，"世上从未有过像白海豹这样的东西。"

"这个我也没辙，"玛特卡说，"现在开始要有了。"接着她低声轻柔唱起所有海豹妈妈都会唱给她们宝宝的海豹之歌。

六周之前，不允许你游泳，

否则你的大头朝上沉下去；

And summer gales and Killer Whales
Are bad for baby seals.

Are bad for baby seals, dear rat,
As bad as bad can be;
But splash and grow strong,
And you can't be wrong,
Child of the Open Sea!

Of course the little fellow did not understand the words at first. He paddled and scrambled about by his mother's side, and learned to scuffle out of the way when his father was fighting with another seal, and the two rolled and roared up and down the slippery rocks. Matkah used to go to sea to get things to eat, and the baby was fed only once in two days; but then he ate all he could, and throve upon it.

The first thing he did was to crawl inland, and there he met tens of thousands of babies of his own age, and they played together like puppies, went to sleep on the clean sand, and played again. The old people in the nurseries took no notice of them, and the holluschickie kept to their own grounds, so the babies had a beautiful playtime.

When Matkah came back from her deep-sea fishing she would go straight to

夏季的大风还有刽子手虎鲸，
都是海豹宝宝的敌人。

他们是海豹宝宝的敌人，亲爱的小老鼠，
他们坏到不能再坏；
去拍打水花吧，茁壮成长，
你不要犯错，
你是辽阔大海的孩子啊！

当然，这个小家伙起初并不明白这些话的意思。他在妈妈的身边划着圈圈。他的爸爸与另外一只海豚打斗的时候，两只海豹在光溜溜的岩石上翻滚咆哮的时候，他学会了在混战之中滚到一旁。玛特卡时常要到海里寻找食物，小宝宝两天喂食一次。吃的时候他会一直吃到没法再塞下去为止，这让他长得很健壮。

他做的第一件事就是爬到内陆。他在那里遇到了成千上万只年纪相仿的宝宝，他们仿佛小狗般一起打打闹闹，在干净的沙滩上小憩，醒了又玩在一起。海豹窝的老海豹不理会他们，霍鲁斯奇基在自己的地盘待着，因此海豹宝宝可以愉快地玩耍。

当玛特卡从深海捕鱼回来的时候，她会径直去他们玩耍的

their playground and call as a sheep calls for a lamb, and wait until she heard Kotick bleat. Then she would take the straightest of straight lines in his direction, striking out with her fore flippers and knocking the youngsters head over heels right and left. There were always a few hundred mothers hunting for their children through the playgrounds, and the babies were kept lively; but, as Matkah told Kotick, "So long as you don't lie in muddy water and get mange; or rub the hard sand into a cut or scratch; and so long as you never go swimming when there is a heavy sea, nothing will hurt you here."

Little seals can no more swim than little children, but they are unhappy till they learn. The first time that Kotick went down to the sea a wave carried him out beyond his depth, and his big head sank and his little hind flippers flew up exactly as his mother had told him in the song, and if the next wave had not thrown him back again he would have drowned.

After that he learned to lie in a beach-pool and let the wash of the waves just cover him and lift him up while he paddled, but he always kept his eye open for big waves that might hurt. He was

地方呼唤可迪克，就好像绵羊呼唤羊羔一样。她会一直等到可迪克发出咩咩的叫声。接着她顺着他那个方向，选择最短最直接的路线用前鳍开路，将左右的小海豹踢得四脚朝天。总是有几百个母亲在宝宝玩耍的地方寻找他们，宝宝们也一直活泼欢闹。但是，就像玛特卡告诉可迪克的，"只要你不躺在泥泞的水里染上疥癣，不将坚硬的沙子蹭进割伤或者划伤的口子里，只要你不在风暴来临时到海里游泳，这里不会有什么会伤害你。"

小海豹跟小孩子一样，出生的时候是不会游泳的。直到他们学会游泳，他们才会开心。可迪克来到海边，首次要下海的时候，一个浪花将他卷进了海里。正如他妈妈在歌里唱的那样，他的大头沉下去，小后鳍立起来了。倘若下一波浪没有将他推回来，他会被淹死。

之后，可迪克学会了躺在一个沙滩的水池，让海浪恰好能将自己淹没，他划水就能让自己浮起来。但是他一直睁大眼睛，盯着可能让自己受伤的大浪。两周

two weeks learning to use his flippers; and all that while he floundered in and out of the water, and coughed and grunted and crawled up the beach and took cat-naps on the sand, and went back again, until at last he found that he truly belonged to the water.

Then you can imagine the times that he had with his companions, ducking under the rollers; or coming in on top of a comber and landing with a swash and a splutter as the big wave went whirling far up the beach; or standing up on his tail and scratching his head as the old people did; or playing "I'm the King of the Castle" on slippery, weedy rocks that just stuck out of the wash. Now and then he would see a thin fin, like a big shark's fin, drifting along close to shore, and he knew that that was the Killer Whale, the Grampus, who eats young seals when he can get them; and Kotick would head for the beach like an arrow, and the fin would jig off slowly, as if it were looking for nothing at all.

Late in October the seals began to leave St. Paul's for the deep sea, by families and tribes, and there was no more fighting over the nurseries, and the holluschickie played anywhere they liked. "Next year," said Matkah to

的时间里他都在学习使用鳍肢，他在水中挣扎的时候，要么呛水咳嗽，要么咕噜咕噜喝下不少水。他爬到岸边，在海滩上小睡一下，接着又返回水里，一直到他最终发现自己真正属于海水了。

然后你就能够想象得出他和同伴们度过怎么样的时光了。他们在卷起的浪涛之下藏身，他们的脑袋从卷起的浪涛尖上露出来，顺着浪头冲到很远的沙滩之上，噼噼啪啪地作响；或者就如老海豹一般，尾巴支起让身子直立，抓自己的脑袋；或者在光滑的杂草丛生的岩石上玩"我是城堡之王"的游戏，而这些石头只是刚刚露出水面。他偶尔会看到一条像大鲨鱼鳍一样的细鳍，沿着岸边漂流。他清楚那是杀手虎鲸，格兰普斯，他要是抓到了小海豹会将其吃掉。可迪克看见他，会像箭头一样冲往海滩，那头鳍会缓缓离开，好像并没有在寻找什么。

十月末的时候，海豹们会以家族或者族群为单位离开圣保罗岛，前往深海。繁衍后代的地方不再有争斗，霍鲁斯奇基可以在他们喜欢的任何地方玩耍。"明年，"玛特卡对可迪克说，

Kotick, "you will be a holluschickie; but this year you must learn how to catch fish."

They set out together across the Pacific, and Matkah showed Kotick how to sleep on his back with his flippers tucked down by his side and his little nose just out of the water. No cradle is so comfortable as the long, rocking swell of the Pacific. When Kotick felt his skin tingle all over, Matkah told him he was learning the "feel of the water," and that tingly, prickly feelings meant bad weather coming, and he must swim hard and get away.

"In a little time," she said, "you'll know where to swim to, but just now we'll follow Sea Pig, the Porpoise, for he is very wise." A school of porpoises were ducking and tearing through the water, and little Kotick followed them as fast as he could. "How do you know where to go to?" he panted. The leader of the school rolled his white eyes, and ducked under. "My tail tingles, youngster," he said. "That means there's a gale behind me. Come along! When you're south of the Sticky Water (he meant the Equator), and your tail tingles, that means there's a gale in front of you and you must head north. Come along! The water feels bad

"你会成为霍鲁斯奇基了，不过今年你必须学会怎么抓鱼。"

他们一起出发穿越太平洋。玛特卡向可迪克展示如何在水中仰躺着，他的鳍肢在侧边收拢，小鼻子刚好从水面露出。没有什么摇篮比太平洋摇晃得更舒服了。当可迪克感觉他的皮肤刺痛的时候，玛特卡跟他讲，他在体会"水的感觉"，这种刺痛意味着恶劣天气的到来，他必须加把劲儿游出这里。

"在很短的时间内，"她说，"你会知道往哪里游，但是现在我们跟着海豚波帕斯吧，他是非常有智慧的。"一群波帕斯正低头潜在水里破浪前行，小可迪克尽可能快地跟着他们。"你们如何知晓要往哪里游？"他喘着气说。海豚的头领转动他的白眼珠，潜到了水下。"我的尾巴刺痛，小家伙，"他说，"那就是说我的后面有风暴。跟我来！倘若你在黏水（他指的是赤道海水）以南觉得尾巴刺痛，就说明风暴在你们的前面，你必须转过头朝北游。跟我来！此处的海水感觉更糟糕。"

here."

This was one of very many things that Kotick learned, and he was always learning. Matkah taught him how to follow the cod and the halibut along the under-sea banks, and wrench the rockling out of his hole among the weeds; how to skirt the wrecks lying a hundred fathoms below water, and dart like a rifle-bullet in at one porthole and out at another as the fishes ran; how to dance on the top of the waves when the lightning was racing all over the sky, and wave his flipper politely to the Stumpy-tailed Albatross and the Man-of-war Hawk as they went down the wind; how to jump three or four feet clear of the water, like a dolphin, flippers close to the side and tail curved; to leave the flying-fish alone because they are all bony; to take the shoulder-piece out of a cod at full speed ten fathoms deep; and never to stop and look at a boat or a ship, but particularly a row boat. At the end of six months, what Kotick did not know about deep-sea fishing was not worth the knowing, and all that time he never set flipper on dry ground.

One day, however, as he was lying half asleep in the warm water somewhere off the Island of Juan Fernández, he felt faint

这是可迪克学会的许许多多的事情当中的一件，他总在学习。玛特卡教他如何沿着水下的海岸跟随鳕鱼与大比目鱼，将三须鳕揪出杂草丛生的洞穴，教他如何避开百丈之下的沉船，在一个舷窗里像一个步枪子弹飞奔而入，再从另一个舷窗飞奔而出；教他闪电在天空飞驰的时候，如何在浪尖顶端跳舞，彬彬有礼地向顺风顺水的信天翁和军舰鹰挥舞着鳍肢；教他如何像海豚一样将鳍肢收起，尾巴弯着，跳离水面三四英尺；教他放过飞鱼，因为他们浑身除了骨头几乎没有肉；教他如何从十丈之下全速前行的鳕鱼肩胛上撕咬下肉；教他永远不要停下观看小船或者轮船，特别是划艇。六个月之后，可迪克还不知道的关于深海捕鱼的事情，就是没什么必要了解的事情了。在这段时间里，他从没让自己的鳍肢待在干爽的陆地上。

然而有一天，当可迪克半睡半醒地躺在胡安·费尔南德斯岛上某处温海中的时候，他感到身

and lazy all over, just as human people do when the spring is in their legs, and he remembered the good firm beaches of Novastoshnah seven thousand miles away; the games his companions played, the smell of the seaweed, the seal-roar, and the fighting. That very minute he turned north, swimming steadily, and as he went on he met scores of his mates, all bound for the same place, and they said: "Greeting, Kotick! This year we are all holluschickie, and we can dance the Fire-dance in the breakers off Lukannon and play on the new grass. But where did you get that coat?"

Kotick's fur was almost pure white now, and though he felt very proud of it, he only said: "Swim quickly! My bones are aching for the land." And so they all came to the beaches where they had been born and heard the old seals, their fathers, fighting in the rolling mist.

That night Kotick danced the Fire-dance with the yearling seals. The sea is full of fire on summer nights all the way down from Novastoshnah to Lukannon, and each seal leaves a wake like burning oil behind him, and a flaming flash when he jumps, and the waves break in great phosphorescent streaks and swirls. Then they went inland

体疲惫不堪，就像人类到了春季腿脚乏力那样。他想起了七千英里之外的诺瓦斯托什纳不错的海滩，还有与同伴们一起玩过的游戏、海草的气味、海豹们的咆哮和厮打。他立刻转身游向北方。他在路上遇到了很多同伴，他们都赶往同一个目的地。他们说："可迪克，你好啊！今天我们都变成霍鲁斯奇基了，我们能够在鲁坎农的浪涛中跳火焰舞了，我们还能在新鲜的草地上玩耍。不过，你的新外套是从哪里弄来的？"

可迪克的皮毛现在差不多纯白了，虽然这让他非常骄傲，但他只说："快点游吧，我的骨头很疼，我要上岸去。"于是他们都来到了他们出生的海滩之上，听到那些老海豹——他们的父辈正在缭绕的雾中战斗着。

那个夜晚，可迪克与满周岁的海豹们一起跳起了火焰舞。从诺瓦斯托什纳到鲁坎农的海面上，充满了夏季之夜的火焰。每个海豹在他的身后都留下了像燃烧着的油一样的尾流，跳起来的时候还有火红的闪光，海浪便破碎成巨大的磷光条纹和漩涡。接下来，他们前往内陆，那片属

to the holluschickie grounds, and rolled up and down in the new wild wheat, and told stories of what they had done while they had been at sea. They talked about the Pacific as boys would talk about a wood that they had been nutting in, and if any one had understood them, he could have gone away and made such a chart of that ocean as never was. The three- and four-year-old holluschickie romped down from Hutchinson's Hill, crying: "Out of the way, youngsters! The sea is deep, and you don't know all that's in it yet. Wait till you've rounded the Horn. Hi, you yearling, where did you get that white coat?"

"I didn't get it," said Kotick; "it grew." And just as he was going to roll the speaker over, a couple of black-haired men with flat red faces came from behind a sand-dune, and Kotick, who never seen a man before, coughed and lowered his head. The holluschickie just bundled off a few yards and sat staring stupidly. The men were no less than Kerick Booterin, the chief of the seal-hunters on the island, and Patalamon, his son. They came from the little village not half a mile from the seal nurseries, and they were deciding what seals they would drive up to the

于霍鲁斯奇基的地方，新长出的野麦田上到处是他们翻滚的身影，他们互相讲述着各自在海洋之中都做过什么。他们谈论太平洋的时候，就跟男孩子谈起他们曾经采摘坚果的树林一样。如果有人理解他们在说什么，他可能在离开之后可以创造出从未有过的太平洋海图。三四岁的霍鲁斯奇基跳下哈钦森山，叫嚷道："滚开，小家伙！大海深不可测，你们所知甚少。等到你们绕着何恩角游一圈回来吧。嗨！一岁的小子，那身白色的外套你从哪里弄到的？"

"我没有弄，"可迪克说，"它自己长出来的。"正当他想掀翻讲话的家伙的时候，两个扁平红脸的黑发男人从沙丘后面走了出来。可迪克之前从未见过人类，咳了一声赶紧低下了头。霍鲁斯奇基们只是退后了几码，呆呆地坐在那里。这两个男人就是克里克·布特林，岛上的海豹猎人首领，和他的儿子帕塔拉蒙。他们来自距离海豹繁衍窝半英里之外的小村庄。他们正筹划把什么样的海豹驱赶到屠宰栏，因为赶海豹就像赶绵羊一样，最后将他们变成海豹皮夹克。

killing-pens – for the seals were driven just like sheep– to be turned into sealskin jackets later on.

"Ho!" said Patalamon. "Look! There's a white seal!"

Kerick Booterin turned nearly white under his oil and smoke, for he was an Aleut, and Aleuts are not clean people. Then he began to mutter a prayer. "Don't touch him, Patalamon. There has never been a white seal since – since I was born. Perhaps it is old Zaharrof's ghost. He was lost last year in the big gale."

"I'm not going near him," said Patalamon. "He's unlucky. Do you really think he is old Zaharrof come back? I owe him for some gulls' eggs."

"Don't look at him," said Kerick. "Head off that drove of four-year-olds. The men ought to skin two hundred to-day, but it's the beginning of the season, and they are new to the work. A hundred will do. Quick!"

Patalamon rattled a pair of seal's shoulder-bones in front of a herd of holluschickie and they stopped dead, puffing and blowing. Then he stepped near, and the seals began to move, and Kerick headed them inland, and they never tried to get back to their companions. Hundreds and hundreds of

"嗨!"帕塔拉蒙说,"看!这儿有只白海豹。"

克里克·布特林蒙了一层油烟的脸几乎是煞白的,因为他是阿留申人,而阿留申人就是不太干净的。接下来,他开始低声祈祷:"不要碰他,帕塔拉蒙。自从,自从我出生以来,从未有白海豹出现过。没准这是老扎哈罗夫的鬼魂。去年在一场大风中他消失了。"

"我不去接近他,"帕塔拉蒙说,"他不吉祥。你真的觉得他是老扎哈罗夫附体了?我欠着他几个海鸥蛋呢。"

"别看他,"克里克说,"把四岁的海豹赶走。今天大家应该剥下两百张海豹皮,不过现在是季首,他们也刚接触这个工作,也就能剥一百张。快点赶!"

帕塔拉蒙在一群霍鲁斯奇基面前,拿着一堆海豹的肩胛骨敲打着。这群霍鲁斯奇基都愣愣地停下来了,喘着粗气。然后他走上前来,海豹也跟着移动,克里克在前面开路,带领他们前往内陆。他们从来没有试图回到同伴身边。几十万只海豹就看着它

thousands of seals watched them being driven, but they went on playing just the same. Kotick was the only one who asked questions, and none of his companions could tell him anything, except that the men always drove seals in that way for six weeks or two months of every year.

"I am going to follow," he said, and his eyes nearly popped out of his head as he shuffled along in the wake of the herd.

"The white seal is coming after us," cried Patalamon. "That's the first time a seal has ever come to the killing-grounds alone."

"Hsh! Don't look behind you," said Kerick. "It is Zaharrof's ghost! I must speak to the priest about this."

The distance to the killing-grounds was only half a mile, but it took an hour to cover, because if the seals went too fast Kerick knew that they would get heated and then their fur would come off in patches when they were skinned. So they went on very slowly, past Sea-Lion's Neck, past Webster House, till they came to the Salt House just beyond the sight of the seals on the beach. Kotick followed, panting and wondering. He thought that he was at the world's end, but the roar of the seal

们被驱赶,继续玩着刚刚的游戏。可迪克是唯一有疑问的,可是没有一个同伴能跟他解释什么,只是说每年有六周或者两个月的时间,人们总是用这样的方式驱赶海豹。

"我要跟着看个究竟。"他说着,便拖着鳍肢,跟着海豹的足迹走,眼珠子几乎要从头顶冒出来了。

"白色海豹跟我们来了,"帕塔拉蒙喊道,"这是第一次,一只海豹独自走向屠宰场。"

"嘘!别看你的后面,"克里克说,"它是扎哈罗夫的鬼魂!这个我一定要跟祭司说。"

到屠宰场的距离只有半英里,但是却走了一个小时。因为克里克清楚如果海豹走得太快,使得身体发热,剥他们皮的时候上面的毛会成片掉下来。于是他们慢慢地走着,经过海狮颈,经过韦伯斯特宅邸,最后来到海滩上的海豹看不见的盐宅。可迪克跟在后面,喘着粗气,充满了好奇。他觉得自己到了世界尽头,但是身后的海豹繁衍窝里的吼叫声,就仿佛隧道里的火车在轰鸣一样响亮。接着,克里克坐在

nurseries behind him sounded as loud as the roar of a train in a tunnel. Then Kerick sat down on the moss and pulled out a heavy pewter watch and let the drove cool off for thirty minutes, and Kotick could hear the fog-dew dripping from the brim of his cap. Then ten or twelve men, each with an iron-bound club three or four feet long, came up, and Kerick pointed out one or two of the drove that were bitten by their companions or were too hot, and the men kicked those aside with their heavy boots made of the skin of a walrus's throat, and then Kerick said: "Let go!" and then the men clubbed the seals on the head as fast as they could.

Ten minutes later little Kotick did not recognize his friends any more, for their skins were ripped off from the nose to the hind flippers – whipped off and thrown down on the ground in a pile.

That was enough for Kotick. He turned and galloped (a seal can gallop very swiftly for a short time) back to the sea, his little new mustache bristling with horror. At Sea-Lion's Neck, where the great sea-lions sit on the edge of the surf, he flung himself flipper over-head into the cool water, and rocked there, gasping miserably. "What's here?" said a

苔藓上，掏出一块沉甸甸的锡制手表看看时间，决定让赶路的队伍停下冷却三十分钟。可迪克可以听见他帽檐滴下了雾露。然后，有十到十二个人过来，每个人手里都拿着一根铁棍，有三四英尺长。克里克指出那些被同伴咬伤的，或者身体太热的一两只海豹，这些人用海象脖颈皮做成的沉重的靴子踢开他们。克里克接着说："动手吧！"这些人就用最快的速度拿着铁棍敲击海豹的脑袋。

十分钟以后，小可迪克再也无法认出他的朋友们了，因为他们从鼻子一直到后鳍肢的皮都被扯下，扔成了一堆。

可迪克挺不住了，他转身飞奔回到大海（海豹在很短的时间内可以跑得非常快）。他被吓得新长出的鬈须都直立着。在海狮颈，大海狮们坐在海浪边缘，他把自己的鳍肢举过头顶，猛地扎进清凉的水中，摇晃着，喘着粗气。"这是什么东西？"一只海狮粗声粗气地说。因为海狮有条

sea-lion, gruffly; for as a rule the sea-lions keep themselves to themselves.

"*Scoochnie! Ochen Scoochnie!*" said Kotick. "They're killing all the holluschickie on all the beaches!"

The sealion turned his head inshore. "Nonsense," he said; "your friends are making as much noise as ever. You must have seen old Kerick polishing off a drove. He's done that for thirty years."

"It's horrible," said Kotick, backing water as a wave went over him, and steadying himself with a screw-stroke of his flippers that brought him up all standing within three inches of a jagged edge of rock.

"Well done for a yearling!" said the sea-lion, who could appreciate good swimming. "I suppose itisrather awful from your way of looking at it; but if you seals will come here year after year, of course the men get to know of it, and unless you can find an island where no men ever come, you will always be driven."

"Isn't there any such island?" began Kotick.

"I've followed the poltoos for twenty

规则，他们的地盘上只有海狮存在。

"斯库切尼！欧沁斯库切尼！"[1]可迪克说，"他们此刻正杀死海滩上所有的霍鲁斯奇基。"

海狮转过头来，朝内陆望去。"乱讲！"他说，"你的朋友们正在那里吵吵闹闹，和平常一样。你肯定是见着老克里克剥光了一群海豹的皮，他这样做已经三十年了。"

"这太可怕了！"可迪克说。一阵浪潮将他淹没，他倒划在水中，在急流中用鳍肢让自己稳住，在离一块岩石的锯齿状边缘三英寸[2]的地方停下了。

"一岁就能做到这样真不错！"海狮说，他很欣赏不俗的泳技。"我觉得从你的角度看待这件事情，确实是相当恐怖的。可如果你们海豹每年都来这里，人们当然会了解这一点。除非你能找到一个岛，人类从不曾涉足的地方，要不然你们总是会被驱赶的。"

"难道没有这样的岛吗？"可迪克开始问道。

"我已经跟随波尔图[3]二十

---

1 我是孤独的！特别孤独！
2 英制长度单位，1 英寸等于 2.54 厘米。
3 大比目鱼

years, and I can't say I've found it yet. But look here – you seem to have a fondness for talking to your betters; suppose you go to Walrus Islet and talk to Sea Vitch. He may know something. Don't flounce off like that. It's a six-mile swim, and if I were you I should haul out and take a nap first, little one."

Kotick thought that that was good advice, so he swam round to his own beach, hauled out, and slept for half an hour, twitching all over, as seals will. Then he headed straight for Walrus Islet, a little low sheet of rocky island almost due northeast from Novastoshnah, all ledges of rock and gulls' nests, where the walrus herded by themselves.

He landed close to old Sea Vitch – the big, ugly, bloated, pimpled, fat-necked, long-tusked walrus of the North Pacific, who has no manners except when he is asleep – as he was then– with his hind flippers half in and half out of the surf.

"Wake up!" barked Kotick, for the gulls were making a great noise.

"Hah! Ho! Hmph! What's that?" said Sea Vitch, and he struck the next walrus a blow with his tusks and waked him up, and the next struck the next, and so on till they were all awake and staring in every direction but the right one.

年之久，我不能说我找到了这样的地方。不过看起来——你好像很愿意跟比自己优秀的族类交流，那你就去海象岛询问一下海威兹吧，他可能知道些什么。不要着急上路，要游上六英里才能找到他。如果我是你，我会上岸小睡一会儿，小家伙。"

可迪克认为这是很好的建议，所以他游到自己的海滩，上了岸，睡了半个小时。他的全身一直抽搐，海豹就是这个样子。醒来后，可迪克直奔海象岛。这是一片低矮的岩石岛，位置几乎是诺瓦斯托什纳的正东北，上面布满了岩石和海鸥巢穴。海象岛上只有成群的海象。

在老海威兹的附近，可迪克上了岸。老海威兹长得又大又丑，很臃肿，身上有很多疙瘩，肥肥的脖颈，长长的牙齿。这只北太平洋的海象除非是睡着了，否则一直都很无礼。此刻他正睡着，后鳍肢有一半在浪花之中，一半露在水面。

"醒醒！"可迪克叫道。实在是因为海鸥太吵了。

"哈！嗬！哼！那是什么？"海威兹说。他用象牙敲击身旁的海象将他敲醒，被敲醒的海象又敲另一个，直到所有的海象都被

"Hi! It's me," said Kotick, bobbing in the surf and looking like a little white slug.

"Well! May I be – skinned!" said Sea Vitch, and they all looked at Kotick as you can fancy a club full of drowsy old gentlemen would look at a little boy. Kotick did not care to hear any more about skinning just then; he had seen enough of it; so he called out: "Isn't there any place for seals to go where men don't ever come?"

"Go and find out," said Sea Vitch, shutting his eyes. "Run away. We're busy here."

Kotick made his dolphin-jump in the air and shouted as loud as he could: "Clam-eater! Clam-eater!" He knew that Sea Vitch never caught a fish in his life, but always rooted for clams and seaweeds; though he pretended to be a very terrible person. Naturally the chickies and the gooverooskies and the epatkas, the burgomaster gulls and the kittiwakes and the puffins, who are always looking for a chance to be rude, took up the cry, and – so Limmershin told me – for nearly five minutes you could not have heard a gun fired on Walrus Islet. All the population was yelling and screaming: "Clam-eater! Stareek!" while

叫醒。他们一个个瞪着眼睛朝各个方向看,唯独落下正确的方向。

"嗨!朝我这儿看,"可迪克说。他在漂浮的海浪中晃动着,好像一条白色的小毛虫。

"好吧,把我的皮剥了吧!"海威兹说。海象们都看着可迪克,那是你可以想象得出的场景,就像老绅士俱乐部,一个个昏昏欲睡地看着小男孩。可迪克不想听到任何关于剥皮的字眼,他不想再看见了。于是他喊道:"是不是存在人类没有踏足过,海豹可以去的地方?"

"去找吧。"海威兹说这话的时候闭上了双眼,"离开这儿,我们这里很忙。"

可迪克像海豚一样跳到空中,尽可能大声地喊:"吃蛤蜊的家伙!吃蛤蜊的家伙!"他了解海威兹一生中都没捉到一条鱼,他一直都是吃蛤蜊和海草。虽然他假装出一副非常可怕的样子。当然,那些一直在寻找机会粗鲁一把的北极鸥、三趾鸥和海雀抓住机会一起叫唤开来。利莫辛是这样告诉我的,在差不多五分钟的时间里,你在岛上连枪响的声音都听不到。岛上所有的民众都在大叫:"吃蛤蜊的家伙!

Sea Vitch rolled from side to side grunting and coughing.

"Now will you tell?" said Kotick, all out of breath.

"Go and ask Sea Cow," said Sea Vitch. "If he is living still, he'll be able to tell you."

"How shall I know Sea Cow when I meet him?" said Kotick, sheering off.

"He's the only thing in the sea uglier than Sea Vitch," screamed a burgomaster gull, wheeling under Sea Vitch's nose. "Uglier, and with worse manners! Stareek!"

Kotick swam back to Novastoshnah, leaving the gulls to scream. There he found that no one sympathized with him in his little attempts to discover a quiet place for the seals. They told him that men had always driven the holluschickie – it was part of the day's work - and that if he did not like to see ugly things he should not have gone to the killing-grounds. But none of the other seals had seen the killing, and that made the difference between him and his friends. Besides, Kotick was a white seal.

"What you must do," said old Sea Catch, after he had heard his son's adventures, "is to grow up and be a big

老家伙

斯达瑞克[1]!"这让海威兹咕咕哝哝打着滚儿,嘴里还不断咳嗽着。

"你现在能告诉我了吗?"可迪克要喘不上气了。

"去问海牛吧,"海威兹说,"倘若他没死,他会告诉你的。"

"当我看见他的时候,我怎么知道他是海牛呢?"可迪克边说边转过身子。

"他是海洋中比海威兹还丑的唯一的一个,"海鸥尖叫着说,盘旋在海威兹的鼻子下面,"更加丑,更加无礼!斯达瑞克!"

可迪克游回诺瓦斯托什纳,留下海鸥在那里尖叫。回到了诺瓦斯托什纳,他发现他只是想试着为海豹发掘一个安宁的栖息地,然而没有一个同伴支持他。他们告诉他,人们一直驱赶霍鲁斯奇基,这是日常工作的一部分,若是他不愿意看见这么丑陋的事情,他就不应该跟到屠宰场。可是因为其他的海豹都没有见过杀戮,这使他跟朋友之间有不同的想法。此外,可迪克是一只白色的海豹。

"你必须要做的是,"老海捕手听说他儿子的冒险经历之

seal like your father, and have a nursery on the beach, and then they will leave you alone. In another five years you ought to be able to fight for yourself." Even gentle Matkah, his mother, said: "You will never be able to stop the killing. Go and play in the sea, Kotick." And Kotick went off and danced the Fire-dance with a very heavy little heart.

That autumn he left the beach as soon as he could, and set off alone because of a notion in his bullet-head. He was going to find Sea Cow, if there was such a person in the sea, and he was going to find a quiet island with good firm beaches for seals to live on, where men could not get at them. So he explored and explored by himself from the North to the South Pacific, swimming as much as three hundred miles in a day and a night. He met with more adventures than can be told, and narrowly escaped being caught by the Basking Shark, and the Spotted Shark, and the Hammerhead, and he met all the untrustworthy ruffians that loaf up and down the high seas, and the heavy polite fish, and the scarlet-spotted scallops that are moored in one place for hundreds of years, and grow very proud of it; but he never met Sea Cow, and he never found an island that he could

后，说道，"好好长大，像爸爸一样成为一只大海豹，在海滩上拥有自己的繁衍之地，然后他们就会远离你了。五年之后，你应该能为自己而战了。"即使是温和的玛特卡，他的妈妈也说："你永远不能阻挡杀戮。到海中去玩儿吧，可迪克。"可迪克离开了，跳起了火焰舞，小小的心里却非常沉重。

那年秋天，可迪克尽早离开海滩，独自出发了，就因为他脑袋中那个执着的念头。如果大海中真有这样的动物，他就要找到海牛；他要为海豹找一个安宁的海岛，那里有坚固的海滩，人类无法抓到他们。他就这样独自开启了探险之旅，从北太平洋到南太平洋，每天要游三百英里，他遇到的冒险经历说都说不完。他险些被姥鲨、斑点鲨、双髻鲨抓住。他碰到了海中上下穿梭的不可靠的恶棍，笨重却有礼貌的鱼，在同一个地方停泊了几百年的并引以为傲的、身上有着红色斑点的扇贝。可是他从来没有见过海牛，他也没有发现他理想中的海岛。

If the beach was good and hard, with a [s]lope behind it for seals to play on, there [w]as always the smoke of a whaler on the [h]orizon, boiling down blubber, and [K]otick knew what that meant. Or else he [c]ould see that seals had once visited the [i]sland and been killed off, and Kotick [k]new that where men had come once [t]hey would come again.

He picked up with an old [s]tumpy-tailed albatross, who told him [t]hat Kerguelen Island was the very place [f]or peace and quiet, and when Kotick [w]ent down there he was all but smashed [t]o pieces against some wicked black [c]liffs in a heavy sleet-storm with [l]ightning and thunder. Yet as he pulled [o]ut against the gale he could see that [e]ven there had once been a seal nursery. [A]nd it was so in all the other islands that [h]e visited.

Limmershin gave a long list of them, [f]or he said that Kotick spent five seasons [e]xploring, with a four months' rest each [y]ear at Novastoshnah, where the [h]olluschickie used to make fun of him [a]nd his imaginary islands. He went to the [G]allapagos, a horrid dry place on the [E]quator, where he was nearly baked to [d]eath; he went to the Georgia Islands, the

如果海滩又好又坚固，后面还有让海豹玩耍的斜坡，地平线上就总会出现捕鲸船冒着烟。而可迪克知道这是什么意思。要不然他也得出海豹曾经到访过岛屿，然后被杀死了。可迪克清楚，人们去过的地方，就会再去。

他遇到了一只短尾巴老信天翁，信天翁跟他讲，凯尔盖朗岛是和平宁静的理想之地。当可迪克赶到那里的时候，正赶上一场特大的雷雨，他差点就被险恶的黑色悬崖撞得粉碎。然而，当他在大风中离开的时候，他可以看到即使是这样的地方，也曾是海豹的繁衍之地。他到过的所有其他岛屿都是如此。

利莫辛说出了一个长长的名单。他说，可迪克用了五年的时间去探索，每年在诺瓦斯托什纳休整四个月。霍鲁斯奇基常常嘲笑他和他想象中的岛屿。他到过赤道上可怕的干燥之地，加拉帕戈斯，在那里他几乎要被烤死了。他去了乔治亚岛、奥克尼岛、翡翠岛、小夜莺岛、戈大岛、布

Orkneys, Emerald Island, Little Nightingale Island, Gough's Island, Bouvet's Island, the Crozets, and even to a little speck of an island south of the Cape of Good Hope. But everywhere the People of the Sea told him the same things. Seals had come to those islands once upon a time, but men had killed them all off. Even when he swam thousands of miles out of the Pacific, and got to a place called Cape Corientes (that was when he was coming back from Gough's Island), he found a few hundred mangy seals on a rock, and they told him that men came there too.

That nearly broke his heart, and he headed round the Horn back to his own beaches; and on his way north he hauled out on an island full of green trees, where he found an old, old seal who was dying, and Kotick caught fish for him and told him all his sorrows. "Now," said Kotick, "I am going back to Novastoshnah, and if I am driven to the killing-pens with the holluschickie I shall not care."

The old seal said: "Try once more. I am the last of the Lost Rookery of Masafuera, and in the days when men killed us by the hundred thousand there was a story on the beaches that some day a white seal would come out of the north

韦岛、位于南印度洋的克罗泽特群岛，甚至去了好望角南端一个小不点的岛。可是无论在那里，大海居民都告诉他同样的情况。海豹很久以前就来过这些岛屿，可是人类杀光了他们。即使他从太平洋游了几千英里，到达了一个名叫科伦特斯角的地方（那时他刚从戈夫岛回来），他在岩石上发现了几百只长了疥癣的海豹。他被告知，人类也来过这里了。

这几乎击碎他的心。他从恩角绕过，前往自己的海滩。在向北的归途，他在一个满是绿色树木的岛上看到一只年老的、就要死去的海豹。可迪克给他抓鱼吃，跟他讲述了所有的悲伤。"现在，"可迪克说，"我要返回诺瓦斯托什纳，倘若我与霍鲁斯奇被一同赶去被杀，我也不管了。"

老海豹说："再多试一次。我是灭绝的玛莎夫艾拉族群里最后一只海豹了。在十万只海豹被屠杀的日子里，海滩上有这样的传说，说是终有一日，会出现一只来自北方的白海豹，带领着

nd lead the seal people to a quiet place. am old and I shall never live to see that ay, but others will. Try once more."

And Kotick curled up his mustache (it vas a beauty), and said: "I am the only vhite seal that has ever been born on the eaches, and I am the only seal, black or vhite, who ever thought of looking for ew islands."

That cheered him immensely; and vhen he came back to Novastoshnah that ummer, Matkah, his mother, begged him o marry and settle down, for he was no onger a holluschick, but a full-grown ea-catch, with a curly white mane on his houlders, as heavy, as big, and as fierce s his father. "Give me another season," e said. "Remember, Mother, it is always he seventh wave that goes farthest up he beach."

Curiously enough, there was another eal who thought that she would put off narrying till the next year, and Kotick anced the Fire-dance with her all down ukannon Beach the night before he set ff on his last exploration.

This time he went westward, because e had fallen on the trail of a great shoal f halibut, and he needed at least one undred pounds of fish a day to keep him n good condition. He chased them till he

海豹们寻找到一片安宁的栖息之地。我老了，不会活着见到那一天了，不过其他的海豹会看到。再多试一次。"

可迪克翘起了他的胡须（胡子真美），说道："出生在海滩上的海豹，我是唯一一只白色的，我是唯一的一只，不管黑还是白，唯一想要寻找新岛屿的海豹。"

可迪克因此受到了巨大的鼓舞，当他在那个夏季回到诺瓦斯托什纳的时候，他的妈妈玛特卡恳求他成家并安定下来。他不再是霍鲁斯奇基，他已经成年，肩上长着白色的卷曲鬃毛，身形体重都跟他父亲一样凶猛了。"再让我寻找一个季节吧，"他说，"不要忘了，妈妈，海滩上冲得最远的永远是第七朵浪花。"

奇怪的是，另一只雌海豹正好觉得她应该将婚事推迟到下一年。在可迪克出发进行最后一次探索之前的晚上，他跟这只雌海豹沿着整个鲁坎农跳起了火焰舞。

他这次朝西出发，因为他跟在了一大群比目鱼的后面。每天他至少要食用一百磅的鱼来维持体能充沛。他追着这群比目鱼，直到他累了，然后蜷起身子，

was tired, and then he curled himself up and went to sleep on the hollows of the ground-swell that sets in to Copper Island. He knew the coast perfectly well, so about midnight, when he felt himself gently bumped on a weed bed, he said: "Hm, tide's running strong to-night," and turning over under water opened his eyes slowly and stretched. Then he jumped like a cat, for he saw huge things nosing about in the shoal water and browsing on the heavy fringes of the weeds.

"By the Great Combers of Magellan!" he said, beneath his mustache. "Who in the Deep Sea are these people?"

They were like no walrus, sea-lion, seal, bear, whale, shark, fish, squid, or scallop that Kotick had ever seen before. They were between twenty and thirty feet long, and they had no hind flippers, but a shovel-like tail that looked as if it had been whittled out of wet leather. Their heads were the most foolish-looking things you ever saw, and they balanced on the ends of their tails in deep water when they weren't grazing, bowing solemnly to one another and waving their front flippers as a fat man waves his arm.

"Ahem!" said Kotick. "Good sport, gentlemen?" The big things answered by bowing and waving their flippers like the

在冲往科珀岛的浪涛中睡觉。他非常熟悉那片海岸，因此在午夜时分，他感到自己轻轻地撞上草床时，说道："嗯，今晚的潮汐很猛烈。"然后他在水下翻了个身，慢慢睁开眼睛，舒展了一下筋骨。就像猫似的跳了起来，因为他看到有庞大的东西在浅水区东一下西一下，啃食着海草的边缘。

"以麦哲伦海峡的巨浪起誓！"可迪克嘴巴在胡须下面说，"这些在深海中的族类是谁？"

他们不同于可迪克见过的海象、海狮、海豹、熊、鲸、鲨鱼、鱼类、乌贼，还有扇贝。他们有二三十英尺那么长，又没有后面的鳍肢，不过有铲子状的尾巴，看起来好像湿的皮革削出来的。他们的头是你曾见过的长得最愚蠢的东西。当他们不食草的时候，他们用深水中的尾巴末端保持平衡，彼此郑重地鞠躬，像胖子挥动手臂一样挥动他们的前鳍肢。

"嗯哼！"可迪克说，"捕猎愉快吗，先生？"那些大块头们鞠躬回应，挥动着鳍肢有如青蛙

'rog-Footman. When they began feeding
gain Kotick saw that their upper lip was
plit into two pieces, that they could
witch apart about a foot and bring
ogether again with a whole bushel of
eaweed between the splits. They tucked
he stuff into their mouths and chumped
olemnly.

"Messy style of feeding that," said
Kotick. They bowed again, and Kotick
egan to lose his temper. "Very good," he
aid. "If you do happen to have an extra
oint in your front flipper you needn't
how off so. I see you bow gracefully,
ut I should like to know your names."
he split lips moved and twitched, and
he glassy green eyes stared; but they did
ot speak.

"Well!" said Kotick, "you're the only
eople I've ever met uglier than Sea
Vitch – and with worse manners."

Then he remembered in a flash what
he Burgomaster Gull had screamed to
im when he was a little yearling at
Valrus Islet, and he tumbled backward in
he water, for he knew that he had found
Sea Cow at last.

The sea cows went on schlooping and
grazing, and chumping in the weed, and
Kotick asked them questions in every
anguage that he had picked up in his

男仆。当他们再次开始吃草的时候，可迪克看见他们的上唇裂成了两半，可以瞬间张开一英尺，将整整一蒲式耳的海草放进口中再合上。他们将东西放进嘴里后，郑重其事地嚼起来。

"这样进食太糟糕了。"可迪克说。他们再次鞠躬回应。可迪克开始发怒了。"非常好，"他说，"如果你们恰巧前鳍肢上多长出一节，也无需这样卖弄。你们的鞠躬姿势在我眼里很优雅，不过我想要知道你们叫什么。"那些分裂的嘴唇抽动着，玻璃一般的绿眼睛怔怔地瞪着，不过他们没有说话。

"那好吧！"可迪克说，"你们是唯一的我见过的比海威兹还丑陋的族类，并且更加无礼。"

然后他瞬间想起，他一周岁的时候在海象小岛上北极海鸥尖叫的话语。他在水中来了一个后翻，因为他知道他终于找到了海牛。

海牛们继续慢吞吞地撕扯啃食着海草，可迪克用他在旅途之中掌握的各种语言询问他们——大海民众的语言和人类一样多种

travels; and the Sea People talk nearly as many languages as human beings. But the Sea Cow did not answer, because Sea Cow cannot talk. He has only six bones in his neck where he ought to have seven, and they say under the sea that that prevents him from speaking even to his companions; but, as you know, he has an extra joint in his fore flipper, and by waving it up and down and about he makes what answers to a sort of clumsy telegraphic code.

By daylight Kotick's mane was standing on end and his temper was gone where the dead crabs go. Then the Sea Cow began to travel northward very slowly, stopping to hold absurd bowing councils from time to time, and Kotick followed them, saying to himself: "People who are such idiots as these are would have been killed long ago if they hadn't found out some safe island; and what is good enough for the Sea Cow is good enough for the Sea Catch. All the same, I wish they'd hurry."

It was weary work for Kotick. The herd never went more than forty or fifty miles a day, and stopped to feed at night, and kept close to the shore all the time; while Kotick swam round them, and over them, and under them, but he could not

多样。但是他没有得到海牛的回应，因为海牛不会讲话，他们的脖子上只有六根骨头，但他们原本应该长七根。海底有种说法，这样甚至不能让他们和同伴之间交流。可是正如你所知道的那样，他们的前鳍肢多了一个关节，可以上下挥动，这样就能使他们发出一种类似笨拙的电报代码一样的讯息。

天亮以后，可迪克的鬃毛被气得都竖起来了，他的耐性也去了死蟹才去的地方。海牛开始慢慢地向北行进，不时举行着荒谬的鞠躬集会。可迪克跟在后面，自言自语道："这么白痴的家伙，要是没有安全的岛屿栖身，人们早就将他们杀光了。对海牛而言够理想的地方，对大海捕手一定是够理想的。虽然如此，我仍然盼着他们能快点。"

这样的行进方式让可迪克很厌烦。每天海牛的行程不会超过四十或五十英里，晚上的时间还要停下来进食；他们的路线一直沿着海岸。尽管可迪克围绕着他们，前后左右地游，可他连半

hurry them up one half-mile. As they went farther north they held a bowing council every few hours, and Kotick nearly bit off his mustache with impatience till he saw that they were following up a warm current of water, and then he respected them more.

One night they sank through the shiny water – sank like stones – and, for the first time since he had known them, began to swim quickly. Kotick followed, and the pace astonished him, for he never dreamed that Sea Cow was anything of a swimmer. They headed for a cliff by the shore, a cliff that ran down into deep water, and plunged into a dark hole at the foot of it, twenty fathoms under the sea. It was a long, long swim, and Kotick badly wanted fresh air before he was out of the dark tunnel they led him through.

"My wig!" he said, when he rose, gasping and puffing, into open water at the farther end. "It was a long dive, but it was worth it."

The sea cows had separated, and were browsing lazily along the edges of the finest beaches that Kotick had ever seen. There were long stretches of smooth worn rock running for miles, exactly fitted to make seal nurseries, and there were playgrounds of hard sand, sloping

英里都催促不了他们。海牛们又到北方后，他们的鞠躬集会几个小时就举行一次，可迪克耐性全无几乎咬断了自己的胡子。直到他发觉海牛们是随着一股暖流而行，才平添了对海牛的几分敬意。

一天晚上，海牛们沉入闪亮的水下——像石头一般沉下——自从可迪克认识他们以后，他们第一次这样快速游泳。可迪克紧随其后，他惊讶于海牛的速度，因为他连做梦也不会想到海牛是游泳高手。他们朝着岸边的一处悬崖前进，悬崖深深地扎根海底，他们游进悬崖底部一个黑洞中，黑洞距离海面有二十丈英寸。这一下游了好久好久，在他们带领他游出黑洞之前，可迪克就等不及要呼吸新鲜空气。

"我的脑袋呀！"当他从洞口的另一端游出，钻出宽阔的水面，气喘吁吁时，说道，"这次水潜得够久，但是非常值得。"

海牛们各自分开，懒洋洋地沿着可迪克见过的最上等的海滩边缘漫步。这里有绵延数英里的光溜溜的岩石，非常适合海豹在这里生儿育女；岩石后面有用来嬉笑玩耍的硬沙地，倾斜着深入内陆；这里有供海豹跳舞的浪

inland behind them, and there were rollers for seals to dance in, and long grass to roll in, and sand-dunes to climb up and down, and best of all, Kotick knew by the feel of the water, which never deceives a true Sea Catch, that no men had ever come there.

The first thing he did was to assure himself that the fishing was good, and then he swam along the beaches and counted up the delightful low sandy islands half hidden in the beautiful rolling fog. Away to the northward out to sea ran a line of bars and shoals and rocks that would never let a ship come within six miles of the beach; and between the islands and the mainland was a stretch of deep water that ran up to the perpendicular cliffs, and somewhere below the cliffs was the mouth of the tunnel.

"It's Novastoshnah over again, but ten times better," said Kotick. "Sea Cow must be wiser than I thought. Men can't come down the cliffs, even if there were any men; and the shoals to seaward would knock a ship to splinters. If any place in the sea is safe, this is it."

He began to think of the seal he had left behind him, but though he was in a hurry to go back to Novastoshnah, he

涛，有可以打滚儿的肥美草地，还有可以爬上爬下的山丘。最关键的是，可迪克凭感觉这里的海水得知——这种感觉从不会欺骗一个真正的大海捕手——人类从未到过此地。

他要做的第一件事是亲身验证一下在这里钓鱼是否容易。然后他沿着海滩开始游，统计着美丽的迷雾中有多少个若有若无的宜人的低矮沙岛。在遥远的北方，出了海的位置是一片沙洲、浅滩和礁石，这让船只永远被截在了海滩六英里之外。岛屿和大陆之间是一条延伸到垂直悬崖的深水区，而隧道口就在悬崖下面的某个地方。

"这是诺瓦斯托什纳的翻版，不过比诺瓦斯托什纳还要好十倍，"可迪克说，"海牛肯定比我想得更聪明。就算人类到访这里，他们也不能从峭壁上下来；向海的滩涂会使船只撞碎。倘若有什么地方在大海中是安全的，必定是这里。"

可迪克开始想起他留在身后的海豹，不过虽然他迫切要赶

thoroughly explored the new country, so that he would be able to answer all questions.

Then he dived and made sure of the mouth of the tunnel, and raced through to the southward. No one but a sea cow or a seal would have dreamed of there being such a place, and when he looked back at the cliffs even Kotick could hardly believe that he had been under them.

He was six days going home, though he was not swimming slowly; and when he hauled out just above Sea-Lion's Neck the first person he met was the seal who had been waiting for him, and she saw by the look in his eyes that he had found his island at last.

But the holluschickie and Sea Catch, his father, and all the other seals laughed at him when he told them what he had discovered, and a young seal about his own age said: "This is all very well, Kotick, but you can't come from no one knows where and order us off like this. Remember we've been fighting for our nurseries, and that's a thing you never did. You preferred prowling about in the sea."

The other seals laughed at this, and the young seal began twisting his head from side to side. He had just married that

回诺瓦斯托什纳，他仍要先将新的国度探个究竟，以便他返回后能回答所有的疑虑。

然后他跳入水中，确定好隧道的入口，就向南行进了。除了海牛和一只海豹之外，没有什么动物能梦想着有这样的一处地方。当他回头看悬崖的时候，可迪克自己都不敢相信他从那个底下游进游出。

他回家的路上花了六天的时间，即使他一点都没有放慢速度。当他在海狮颈上方出现时，他遇到的第一个海豹就是在等待他的那只。从他的眼中，她看到他终于找到了理想的岛屿。

可是当可迪克告诉霍鲁斯奇基、他的父亲大海捕手，还有其他所有的海豹他的发现时，却被大家嘲笑了。一只和可迪克年纪相仿的海豹冒出来说："听起来非常好，可迪克，不过你不能从一个谁都不知晓的地方回来就命令我们这样离开。不要忘了，我们一直战斗在繁衍窝的争夺中，你却从未做过这件事。你更喜欢徘徊在大海之中。"

其他海豹也为此而取笑他，年轻的海豹开始左右扭动他的脑袋。他那年刚刚成家，正为此

year, and was making a great fuss about it.

"I've no nursery to fight for," said Kotick. "I want only to show you all a place where you will be safe. What's the use of fighting?"

"Oh, if you're trying to back out, of course I've no more to say," said the young seal, with an ugly chuckle.

"Will you come with me if I win?" said Kotick; and a green light came into his eyes, for he was very angry at having to fight at all.

"Very good," said the young seal, carelessly. "If you win, I'll come."

He had no time to change his mind, for Kotick's head darted out and his teeth sunk in the blubber of the young seal's neck. Then he threw himself back on his haunches and hauled his enemy down the beach, shook him, and knocked him over. Then Kotick roared to the seals: "I've done my best for you these five seasons past. I've found you the island where you'll be safe, but unless your heads are dragged off your silly necks you won't believe. I'm going to teach you now. Look out for yourselves!"

Limmershin told me that never in his life – and Limmershin sees ten thousand big seals fighting every year – never in

殚精竭虑。

"我没有要争斗的繁衍窝,"可迪克说,"我就是想让你们大家知道,有一个地方对你们来说是安全的。打斗的用处是什么?"

"哦,倘若你要后退的话,我自然是不再多言。"年轻的海豹很难听地笑着。

"若是我打败了你,你愿意和我一起去吗?"可迪克说。他的眼里折射出绿光,必须要打斗来解决让他非常恼火。

"非常好,"年轻的海豹漫不经心地说,"倘若你赢了,我就去。"

年轻的海豹连改变主意的时间都没有,因为可迪克的头都射出来了,他的牙齿也咬进了年轻海豹的颈部的脂肪。然后他往后蹲去,将对手拖到海滩上,来回摇晃,再将其撞翻。接着可迪克朝着海豹们吼道:"五个春夏秋冬过去了,我已经为你们竭尽全力。我找到了那个保你们平安的岛屿,可是不将你们的脑袋从愚蠢的脖子上扯下来,你们是不会相信的。我现在就教你们怎么做,小心点儿!"

利莫辛跟我讲,他每年要见

all his little life did he see anything like Kotick's charge into the nurseries. He flung himself at the biggest sea-catch he could find, caught him by the throat, choked him and bumped him and banged him till he grunted for mercy, and then threw him aside and attacked the next. You see, Kotick had never fasted for four months as the big seals did every year, and his deep-sea swimming-trips kept him in perfect condition, and, best of all, he had never fought before. His curly white mane stood up with rage, and his eyes flamed, and his big dog-teeth glistened, and he was splendid to look at.

Old Sea Catch, his father, saw him tearing past, hauling the grizzled old seals about as though they had been halibut, and upsetting the young bachelors in all directions; and Sea Catch gave one roar and shouted: "He may be a fool, but he is the best fighter on the Beaches. Don't tackle your father, my son! He's with you!"

Kotick roared in answer, and old Sea Catch waddled in, his mustache on end, blowing like a locomotive, while Matkah and the seal that was going to marry Kotick cowered down and admired their men-folk. It was a gorgeous fight, for the two fought as long as there was a seal

到上万大海豹打斗，不过在他短短的一辈子，他未曾见过像可迪克冲进繁衍窝那样的阵仗。他扑倒在他能找到的最大海捕手身上，咬住他的喉咙，使他窒息，把他撞到一直到他求饶为止。再把他扔到一边，攻击下一个。你要清楚，可迪克从未像其他大海豹那样每年禁食四个月，他一直在深海中旅行让他保持着最佳状态，而且最关键的是，他之前从未打斗过。他卷起的白色鬃毛也因愤怒竖了起来，眼睛通红，大大的犬牙发出闪亮的光芒，看起来真是棒极了。他拖拽那些老海豹就好像是对付大比目鱼一般，年轻的单身汉们被他打得四处乱窜。

老海捕手，他的父亲，看见他正撕扯过来，便给了一嗓子，喊道："你的父亲可能是个笨蛋，不过他是这海滩上最优秀的武士。不要对你的父亲下手，我的儿子！他是支持你的。"

可迪克大声回应。老海捕手摇摇摆摆地加入了战斗，鬃毛竖起，像火车头一样气喘吁吁。而玛特卡和要嫁给可迪克的雌海豹蜷缩在一边，仰慕着他们的英雄。这场战斗使人愉悦，可迪克父子打到没有一只海豹敢再抬

that dared lift up his head, and then they paraded grandly up and down the beach side by side, bellowing.

At night, just as the Northern Lights were winking and flashing through the fog, Kotick climbed a bare rock and looked down on the scattered nurseries and the torn and bleeding seals. "Now," he said, "I've taught you your lesson."

"My wig!" said old Sea Catch, boosting himself up stiffly, for he was fearfully mauled. "The Killer Whale himself could not have cut them up worse. Son, I'm proud of you, and what's more, I'll come with you to your island – if there is such a place."

"Hear you, fat pigs of the sea! Who comes with me to the Sea Cow's tunnel? Answer, or I shall teach you again," roared Kotick.

There was a murmur like the ripple of the tide all up and down the beaches. "We will come," said thousands of tired voices. "We will follow Kotick, the White Seal."

Then Kotick dropped his head between his shoulders and shut his eyes proudly. He was not a white seal any more, but red from head to tail. All the same he would have scorned to look at or touch one of his wounds.

起头来。接下来他们在海滩上并肩游行，到处吆喝。

夜晚来临的时候，北极光透过迷雾闪烁着，可迪克爬上裸露的岩石，向下俯看零零散散的繁衍窝，还有打斗中受伤流血的海豹们。"现在，"他说，"我已经给了你们教训。"

"我的脑袋！"老海捕手说的时候，僵硬地挺直了身子，因为他也伤得不轻。"即使和虎鲸对抗，也不可能将他们打得更狠。我的儿子，我为你自豪，更重要的是，我会和你去你说的岛屿——倘若这样的地方存在的话。"

"你们听着，大海的肥猪！要跟我一起去海牛的那条隧道都有谁？回答我，要不然我还会教训你们。"可迪克吼道。

海滩上到处充满了如潮水一般的细声碎语。"我们要去，"数千只疲倦的声音说，"我们将跟随可迪克，白色的海豹。"

然后可迪克将脑袋低低地放在肩膀上，自豪地闭上了双眼。他的皮毛不再是白白的，此刻从头到尾都已经是鲜红的。尽管如此，他还是不屑于看看或者碰一下自己的伤口。

A week later he and his army (nearly ten thousand holluschickie and old seals) went away north to the Sea Cow's tunnel, Kotick leading them, and the seals that stayed at Novastoshnah called them idiots. But next spring when they all met off the fishing-banks of the Pacific, Kotick's seals told such tales of the new beaches beyond Sea Cow's tunnel that more and more seals left Novastoshnah.

Of course it was not all done at once, for the seals need a long time to turn things over in their minds, but year by year more seals went away from Novastoshnah, and Lukannon, and the other nurseries, to the quiet, sheltered beaches where Kotick sits all the summer through, getting bigger and fatter and stronger each year, while the holluschickie play round him, in that sea where no man comes.

一周之后，可迪克带领着他的队伍（将近一万只霍鲁斯奇基和老海豹）向北方海牛的隧道游去。选择留在诺瓦斯托什纳的海豹称呼他们为白痴。但是到了下一年的春季，当两伙海豹在太平洋渔岸相遇的时候，可迪克队伍的海豹说了很多海牛隧道以外的新海滩的故事。越来越多的海豹从诺瓦斯托什纳离开了。

这当然不是一次就全部完成的，海豹需要很长的时间在心里不断盘算这件事。不过每年越来越多的海豹从诺瓦斯托什纳、鲁坎农和其他繁衍窝搬离，去安宁、平和的海滩。每年的整个夏季，可迪克都会在那里栖息，他变得越来越大只、越来越肥硕、越来越强壮。而霍鲁斯奇基就围绕在他身边嬉笑玩耍，在那片人类不曾到访的海域。

LUKANNON

鲁坎农

THIS is a sort of very sad seal National Anthem.

这是一首非常忧伤的海豹族歌。

I met my mates in the morning (and oh, but I am old!)

Where roaring on the ledges the summer ground-swell rolled;

I heard them lift the chorus that dropped the breakers' song –

The beaches of Lukannon – two million voices strong!

清晨我遇见了我的同伴（哦，但是我老了），

夏季的涌浪在暗礁上怒吼。

我听到他们在鲁坎农合唱，

掩盖了浪涛喧嚣的两百万个壮音！

The song of pleasant stations beside the salt lagoons,

The song of blowing squadrons that shuffled down the dunes,

The song of midnight dances that churned the sea to flame –

The beaches of Lukannon – before the sealers came!

这歌声中是盐礁湖旁宜人的驻地，

这歌声中是成群结队屏气冲下沙丘，

这歌声中是搅动大海的火焰之舞，

海豹猎人来临之前的鲁坎农海滩！

I met my mates in the morning (I'll never meet them more!);

清晨我遇到了我的同伴（我再也不会遇见他们了），

They came and went in legions that darkened all the shore.

And through the foam-flecked offing as far as voice could reach

We hailed the landing-parties and we sang them up the beach.

The beaches of Lukannon – the winter-wheat so tall –

The dripping, crinkled lichens, and the sea-fog drenching all!

The platforms of our playground, all shining smooth and worn!

The beaches of Lukannon – the home where we were born!

I meet my mates in the morning, a broken, scattered band.

Men shoot us in the water and club us on the land;

Men drive us to the Salt House like silly sheep and tame,

And still we sing Lukannon – before the sealers came.

Wheel down, wheel down to southward; oh, Gooverooska go!

And tell the Deep-Sea Viceroys the story of our woe;

他们来来回回，将整个海岸都淹没了。

只要声音能够到达，我们朝着泡沫飞扬的海面欢呼，

我们向登陆队伍呼喊，在沙滩上有歌声迎接他们。

鲁坎农海滩——冬小麦已经那么高——

皱巴巴的青苔还在滴水，海雾打湿了一切！

供我们玩乐的平台，全部闪亮而光滑！

鲁坎农海滩——那是我们出生的家。

清晨我遇到我的同伴，零零散散一队，

人类在水中将我们射杀，在陆地上将我们敲晕，

人类将我们赶往盐宅，就像对待温顺的绵羊，

可我们仍在歌唱鲁坎农——在海豹猎人来临之前。

掉转朝向，掉转向南；哦，去吧，海豹们，出发！

去告诉深海总督我们遭遇的悲惨，

Ere, empty as the shark's egg the tempest flings ashore,

The beaches of Lukannon shall know their sons no more!

暴风雨猛扫海岸，空如鲨鱼之卵，

鲁坎农海滩将不再识得他们的子孙！

CHAPTER 5   "RIKKI-TIKKI-TAVI"

第五章   "里奇-提奇-塔维"

AT the hole where he went in
Red-Eye called to Wrinkle-Skin.
Hear what little Red-Eye saith:
"Nag, come up and dance with death!"

就在他踏足的洞口，
红眼对皱皮大声叫吼。
听听小红眼的喊声：
"纳格，来，与死神共舞吧！"

Eye to eye and head to head,
(Keep the measure, Nag.)
This shall end when one is dead;
(At thy pleasure, Nag.)
Turn for turn and twist for twist –
(Run and hide thee, Nag.)
Hah! The hooded Death has missed!
(Woe betide thee, Nag!)

眼对眼，头对头，
（掌握好节奏，纳格。）
一方死了，舞蹈才会结束；
（随你的便，纳格。）
它转动你转动，它扭转你扭转——
（快逃，躲起来，纳格。）
哈！戴头巾的死神错过了你！
（灾难正在袭来，纳格！）

THIS is the story of the great war that Rikki-tikki-tavi fought single-handed, through the bath-rooms of the big bungalow in Segowlee cantonment. Darzee, the tailor-bird, helped him, and Chuchundra, the muskrat, who never comes out into the middle of the floor, but always creeps round by the wall, gave him advice; but Rikki-tikki did

这场大战的故事说的是，里奇-提奇-塔维孤身一人在席高利军营营地大平房浴室独自作战的伟大事迹。长尾缝叶莺达西助了他一臂之力。麝鼠楚春德拉一直不到地板中间，总是绕着墙根给他建议。只有里奇-提奇真正大战了一场。

the real fighting.

He was a mongoose, rather like a little cat in his fur and his tail, but quite like a weasel in his head and his habits. His eyes and the end of his restless nose were pink; he could scratch himself anywhere he pleased, with any leg, front or back, that he chose to use; he could fluff up his tail till it looked like a bottle-brush, and his war-cry as he scuttled through the long grass, was: "Rikk-tikk-tikki-tikki-tchk!"

One day, a high summer flood washed him out of the burrow where he lived with his father and mother, and carried him, kicking and clucking, down a roadside ditch. He found a little wisp of grass floating there, and clung to it till he lost his senses. When he revived, he was lying in the hot sun on the middle of a garden path, very draggled indeed, and a small boy was saying: "Here's a dead mongoose. Let's have a funeral."

"No," said his mother; "let's take him in and dry him. Perhaps he isn't really dead."

They took him into the house, and a big man picked him up between his finger and thumb and said he was not dead but half choked; so they wrapped

里奇是一只猫鼬。他的皮毛和尾巴就像一只小猫，可是他的头和习性又很像鼬鼠。他的眼睛和不安分的鼻尖是粉红色的。他能够凭喜好将自己的任意一条腿，前腿或者后腿，挠身上的随便什么地方。他能让自己的尾巴蓬开，直到看起来像个奶瓶刷。他跋涉在高高的草丛中时，他的战斗呐喊是："里克-提克-提奇-提奇-戚克！"

有一天，夏季的一场大洪水将他从与父母共同居住的洞里冲了出来，尽管他一路又踢又叫，还是被洪水带到了路边的沟渠。他发现了一缕草漂浮在水面上，便紧紧地抓住它，直到失去了知觉。当他清醒的时候，正躺在花园小路中间的烈日下，满身泥污。一个小男孩恰巧开口："这只猫鼬死了，咱们给他举行一个葬礼吧。"

"不，"小男孩的妈妈说，"咱们将他弄进屋里，烘干他，他可能不是真的死了。"

他们将他弄进了屋里，一个高个子男人用拇指和食指把里奇拎起来，然后说他只是呛得要断气了，并没有死。所以大家用棉絮包

him in cotton-wool, and warmed him, and he opened his eyes and sneezed.

"Now," said the big man (he was an Englishman who had just moved into the bungalow); "don't frighten him, and we'll see what he'll do."

It is the hardest thing in the world to frighten a mongoose, because he is eaten up from nose to tail with curiosity. The motto of all the mongoose family is, "Run and find out"; and Rikki-tikki was a true mongoose. He looked at the cotton-wool, decided that it was not good to eat, ran all round the table, sat up and put his fur in order, scratched himself, and jumped on the small boy's shoulder.

"Don't be frightened, Teddy," said his father. "That's his way of making friends."

"Ouch! He's tickling under my chin," said Teddy.

Rikki-tikki looked down between the boy's collar and neck, snuffed at his ear, and climbed down to the floor, where he sat rubbing his nose.

"Good gracious," said Teddy's mother, "and that's a wild creature! I suppose he's so tame because we've been kind to him."

裹着他，用温暖的小火烘着他，他睁开了眼睛，打了个喷嚏。

"现在，"高个男人说（他是个英国人，刚刚搬进这幢平房），"不要把他吓着，我们来瞧瞧他要做些什么。"

世界上最难的事就是吓唬住一只猫鼬了，因为他的好奇心从鼻子一直蔓延到尾巴尖。所有的猫鼬家族的座右铭是："跑去看看，弄明白怎么回事。"而里奇-提奇是一只真正的猫鼬。他瞧了瞧棉絮，认准这东西不好吃，就在桌子四周乱跑，最后坐了起来，整理自己的皮毛，挠挠痒，一下子跳到了小男孩的肩膀上。

"不要怕，泰迪，"小男孩的爸爸说，"这是他在和你交朋友。"

"哎哟！我的下巴让他弄得发痒。"泰迪说。

里奇-提奇低头看看男孩的领子和脖子中间，闻了闻他的耳朵，接着爬到了地上，坐在那里揉起自己的鼻子。

"好家伙，"泰迪的妈妈说，"这就是野生动物啊！我想是因为我们善待他，他才这么温顺。"

"All mongooses are like that," said her husband. "If Teddy doesn't pick him up by the tail, or try to put him in a cage, he'll run in and out of the house all day long. Let's give him something to eat."

They gave him a little piece of raw meat. Rikki-tikki liked it immensely, and when it was finished he went out into the veranda and sat in the sunshine and fluffed up his fur to make it dry to the roots. Then he felt better.

"There are more things to find out about in this house," he said to himself, "than all my family could find out in all their lives. I shall certainly stay and find out."

He spent all that day roaming over the house. He nearly drowned himself in the bath-tubs, put his nose into the ink on a writing-table, and burned it on the end of the big man's cigar, for he climbed up in the big man's lap to see how writing was done. At nightfall he ran into Teddy's nursery to watch how kerosene lamps were lighted, and when Teddy went to bed Rikki-tikki climbed up too; but he was a restless companion, because he had to get up and attend to every noise all through the night, and find out what made it.

"所有的猫鼬都是这样的，"她的丈夫说，"如果泰迪不拽他的尾巴，或者把他关在笼子里，他就会整天在屋子里跑来跑去。我们给他些吃的吧。"

里奇从人们的手里得到了一小块生肉，他非常喜欢吃。吃完以后，他就到外面的阳台上，坐在阳光下，让皮毛蓬松起来，好彻底晒干它。这下他觉得他更舒服了。

"在这个房子里，还有更多的事情要弄清楚，"他自言自语道，"比我一家人一生能发现的还多，我一定要留下来并找出答案。"

里奇一整天都在屋子里漫游。他几乎把自己淹没在浴缸里，还把鼻子插进了写字台上的墨水里。鼻子还被高个子男人的雪茄头烫着了，因为他爬到高个子男人的腿上，看人家是怎样写字的。傍晚时分，他跑到泰迪的儿童房，看油灯是如何点燃的。泰迪上床以后，里奇-提奇也跟着爬了上去。可他是个不老实的伙伴，一到晚上，但凡有任何声响，他就会起来查看，找出声音的来源。泰迪的爸爸妈妈睡前最后一件事，就是看看自己的孩子，里奇-提奇此时正清醒地躺在

Teddy's mother and father came in, the last thing, to look at their boy, and Rikki-tikki was awake on the pillow. "I don't like that," said Teddy's mother; "he may bite the child." "He'll do no such thing," said the father. "Teddy's safer with that little beast than if he had a bloodhound to watch him. If a snake came into the nursery now –"

But Teddy's mother wouldn't think of anything so awful.

Early in the morning Rikki-tikki came to early breakfast in the veranda riding on Teddy's shoulder, and they gave him banana and some boiled egg; and he sat on all their laps one after the other, because every well-brought-up mongoose always hopes to be a house-mongoose some day and have rooms to run about in, and Rikki-tikki's mother (she used to live in the General's house at Segowlee) had carefully told Rikki what to do if ever he came across white men.

Then Rikki-tikki went out into the garden to see what was to be seen. It was a large garden, only half cultivated, with bushes as big as summer-houses of Marshal Niel roses, lime and orange trees, clumps of bamboos, and thickets of high grass.

枕头上。"我不喜欢这样，"泰迪的妈妈说，"他可能会咬孩子。""他不会那么做的，"爸爸说，"和这只小野兽在一起，会比一只猎犬跟着泰迪更安全。如果有一条蛇现在进了儿童室……"

不过泰迪的妈妈不会想那么恐怖的事情。

一大清早，里奇-提奇就骑着泰迪的肩膀，走到阳台上吃早餐。他们给了里奇香蕉和一些煮鸡蛋。里奇一个接一个地在每个人的膝盖上都坐了一下，因为每一只教养良好的猫鼬都渴望有一天可能做一只家养的猫鼬，然后在很多房间里到处跑。里奇的母亲（她过去常常住在席高利的将军房）详细地嘱咐过他若是遇到了白人要怎么办。

早餐结束以后，里奇-提奇跑到了花园，去看看有什么东西。这个花园很大，不过只有一半栽种了花草，如凉亭一般大的尼尔元帅玫瑰丛、酸橙和橘子树、竹丛和高深的草丛。里奇-提奇舔了舔嘴唇。"这个狩猎场棒极了。"他说着，

Rikki-tikki licked his lips. "This is a splendid hunting-ground," he said, and his tail grew bottle-brushy at the thought of it, and he scuttled up and down the garden, snuffing here and there till he heard very sorrowful voices in a thorn-bush.

It was Darzee, the tailor-bird, and his wife. They had made a beautiful nest by pulling two big leaves together and stitching them up the edges with fibers, and had filled the hollow with cotton and downy fluff. The nest swayed to and fro, as they sat on the rim and cried.

"What is the matter?" asked Rikki-tikki.

"We are very miserable," said Darzee. "One of our babies fell out of the nest yesterday and Nag ate him."

"Hm!" said Rikki-tikki," that is very sad – but I am a stranger here. Who is Nag?"

Darzee and his wife only cowered down in the nest without answering, for from the thick grass at the foot of the bush there came a low hiss – a horrid cold sound that made Rikki-tikki jump back two clear feet. Then inch by inch out of the grass rose up the head and spread hood of Nag, the big black

这个想法让他蓬开了瓶刷子一样的尾巴。他沿着花园，跳上跳下，到处嗅了嗅，直到荆棘丛中非常悲伤的声音引起了他的注意。

这是长尾缝叶莺达西和他妻子的哭声。他们之前把两片大叶子拉在一起，用纤维将边缘缝上，并用棉花和松软的绒毛将空洞的地方填满，从而制作了一个美丽的巢穴。此时他巢穴来回摇摆着，他们坐在边上哭泣。

"发生了什么事？"里奇问道。

"我们太痛苦了，"达西说，"我们的一个宝宝昨天从窝里掉出来，纳格把他给吃了。"

"嗯！"里奇说，"是很难过，不过我刚来到这里。纳格是谁？"

达西和他的妻子只是蜷缩进巢穴里，没有应答，因为低沉的嘶嘶声从灌木丛根部浓密的草丛中传了出来。这可怕的冰冷的声音使里奇向后跳出了足有两英尺那么远。然后，嘶嘶声一寸一寸地从草地上爬起来，展开了一条黑色大眼镜蛇的兜帽。他从舌头到尾巴，长

cobra, and he was five feet long from tongue to tail. When he had lifted one-third of himself clear of the ground, he stayed balancing to and fro exactly as a dandelion-tuft balances in the wind, and he looked at Rikki-tikki with the wicked snake's eyes that never change their expression, whatever the snake may be thinking of.

"Who is Nag?" he said, "I am Nag. The great god Brahm put his mark upon all our people when the first cobra spread his hood to keep the sun off Brahm as he slept. Look, and be afraid!"

He spread out his hood more than ever, and Rikki-tikki saw the spectacle-mark on the back of it that looks exactly like the eye part of a hook-and-eye fastening. He was afraid for the minute; but it is impossible for a mongoose to stay frightened for any length of time, and though Rikki-tikki had never met a live cobra before, his mother had fed him on dead ones, and he knew that all a grown mongoose's business in life was to fight and eat snakes. Nag knew that too, and at the bottom of his cold heart he was afraid.

"Well," said Rikki-tikki, and his tail began to fluff up again, "marks or no

有五英尺。他将自己身体的三分之一抬离地面,像蒲公英在风中寻找平衡一样,左右摇摆着身体。他用邪恶的双眼望着里奇,不管蛇脑子里怎么想,他的眼神一向如此。

"纳格是谁?"他说,"我是纳格。当第一条眼镜蛇为睡觉的天神布拉姆撑开兜帽挡住太阳的时候,伟大的天神布拉姆就将印记刻在了我们整个族类的身上,看看,吓着了吧!"

他的兜帽比以往任何时候都张得更大,里奇看见了兜帽后面的印记,那印记看起来就像衣服上面风纪扣的扣眼。他害怕了片刻,不过不可能让一只猫鼬害怕更长时间。尽管里奇从未见过活的眼镜蛇,可他妈妈喂过他死的蛇肉。他清楚,所有的成年猫鼬一生就是要与蛇斗争,将其吃掉。纳格也清楚这一点,在他冰冷的心底,他也很害怕。

"好吧,"里奇说着,抖起了尾巴,"不管有没有印记,你吃掉

marks, do you think it is right for you to eat fledglings out of a nest?"

Nag was thinking to himself, and watching the least little movement in the grass behind Rikki-tikki. He knew that mongooses in the garden meant death sooner or later for him and his family; but he wanted to get Rikki-tikki off his guard. So he dropped his head a little, and put it on one side.

"Let us talk," he said. "You eat eggs. Why should not I eat birds?"

"Behind you! Look behind you!" sang Darzee.

Rikki-tikki knew better than to waste time in staring. He jumped up in the air as high as he could go, and just under him whizzed by the head of Nagaina, Nag's wicked wife. She had crept up behind him as he was talking, to make an end of him; and he heard her savage hiss as the stroke missed. He came down almost across her back, and if he had been an old mongoose he would have known that then was the time to break her back with one bite; but he was afraid of the terrible lashing return-stroke of the cobra. He bit, indeed, but did not bite long enough, and he jumped clear of the whisking tail, leaving Nagaina torn and angry.

了巢穴外面的幼鸟，你觉得自己有权这样做吗？"

纳格暗自盘算着，注视着里奇身后的草丛中最细微的动静。他清楚猫鼬出现在花园里，对他和他的家人来说，意味着终有一日会有灭顶之灾，但是他想让里奇放下戒备。于是他稍微低下他的头，歪在一边。

"咱们谈谈吧，"他说，"你吃鸡蛋，我为什么不应该吃鸟呢？"

"在你后面，看看你身后！"达西大叫。

里奇明白最好不要浪费时间对视。他尽可能高地跳到空中。就在此时，他的身下嗖地射出了纳格的恶妻纳格爱娜的脑袋。原来里奇在和纳格说话的时候，她鬼鬼祟祟地爬到了他身后，想趁机了断他。他听到了她因为袭击失手发出的可怕的嘶嘶声。他几乎正落在她的背上。倘若他是一只老猫鼬，他会知道那时候正好咬上它一口，不过他惧怕眼镜蛇的回身一击。他的确咬了她，可是咬的时间短，随后就跳起躲开了摆动的蛇尾，留下被咬伤的纳格爱娜气愤不已。

"Wicked, wicked Darzee!" said Nag, lashing up as high as he could reach toward the nest in the thorn-bush; but Darzee had built it out of reach of snakes, and it only swayed to and fro.

Rikki-tikki felt his eyes growing red and hot (when a mongoose's eyes grow red, he is angry), and he sat back on his tail and hind legs like a little kangaroo, and looked all around him, and chattered with rage. But Nag and Nagaina had disappeared into the grass. When a snake misses its stroke, it never says anything or gives any sign of what it means to do next. Rikki-tikki did not care to follow them, for he did not feel sure that he could manage two snakes at once. So he trotted off to the gravel path near the house, and sat down to think. It was a serious matter for him.

If you read the old books of natural history, you will find they say that when the mongoose fights the snake and happens to get bitten, he runs off and eats some herb that cures him. That is not true. The victory is only a matter of quickness of eye and quickness of foot, – snake's blow against mongoose's jump, – and as no eye can follow the motion of a snake's head when it strikes, that makes things much

"可恶，可恶的达西！"纳格咆哮着，用尽全力向高扫向荆棘丛中的巢穴。可是达西将巢穴建在了蛇能企及的高度之上，所以巢穴只是在来回摇摆着。

里奇-提奇察觉到他的眼睛越来越红，越来越热（猫鼬的眼睛发红表示他很生气），他用尾巴和后腿支撑着坐下，像一只小袋鼠，看着周围，气呼呼地叫着。但是纳格和纳格爱娜已经消失于草丛中。一条蛇失手后，不会讲，也不会发出任何信号说明下一步会怎么做。里奇不愿意跟着他们，因为他不确定他能否同时应对两条蛇。于是他小跑到房子附近的碎石路上，坐下来衡量。这对他来说是件很重大的事情。

如果你阅读过自然历史的古书，你会发现有这样一种说法，当一只猫鼬与蛇搏斗碰巧被咬时，猫鼬会跑掉然后食用一种草药而治愈。那其实是不对的。胜利就取决于哪一方眼疾脚快，是蛇的出击和猫鼬的跳跃的较量；蛇头出击的时候，任何一双眼睛都跟不上他的速度，这使得事情本身比什么神奇的草药都更加精彩。里奇清楚自己太年轻了，他很高兴自己逃过了一

more wonderful than any magic herb. Rikki-tikki knew he was a young mongoose, and it made him all the more pleased to think that he had managed to escape a blow from behind. It gave him confidence in himself, and when Teddy came running down the path, Rikki-tikki was ready to be petted.

But just as Teddy was stooping, something flinched a little in the dust, and a tiny voice said: "Be careful. I am death!" It was Karait, the dusty brown snakeling that lies for choice on the dusty earth; and his bite is as dangerous as the cobra's. But he is so small that nobody thinks of him, and so he does the more harm to people.

Rikki-tikki's eyes grew red again, and he danced up to Karait with the peculiar rocking, swaying motion that he had inherited from his family. It looks very funny, but it is so perfectly balanced a gait that you can fly off from it at any angle you please; and in dealing with snakes this is an advantage. If Rikki-tikki had only known, he was doing a much more dangerous thing than fighting Nag, for Karait is so small, and can turn so quickly, that unless Rikki bit him close

击。这也让他对自己充满了信心，泰迪顺着小路跑向他的时候，里奇已经准备好接受爱抚了。

但是正当泰迪弯腰的时候，有东西在尘土中退缩了一下，一个小小的声音说："当心，我能要你的命！"这是卡莱特，一种浑身灰尘的褐色小蛇，就喜欢在尘土中躺着，被他咬了，就等同于被眼镜蛇咬到那么危险。不过他太小了，人们都不留意他，所以他对人的伤害其实更大。

里奇的眼睛再次变红，他用从家族继承的那套独特的动作，摇摆着，跳舞一样冲向卡莱特。这套动作看起来很搞笑，但是这种步态平衡得很完美，让你任何角度都可以迎战。这在迎战一条蛇的时候，是有利的。里奇如果知道自己正在面对的战斗，比和纳格的战斗要凶险就好了，卡莱特实在是小，转身的速度可能更快。除非是里奇咬住了卡莱特靠近头后方的位置，要不然蛇一转身，里奇的眼睛或者嘴巴就惨了。可是里奇并不晓得这一点。

to the back of the head, he would get the return-stroke in his eye or lip. But Rikki did not know: his eyes were all red, and he rocked back and forth, looking for a good place to hold. Karait struck out. Rikki jumped sideways and tried to run in, but the wicked little dusty gray head lashed within a fraction of his shoulder, and he had to jump over the body, and the head followed his heels close.

Teddy shouted to the house: "Oh, look here! Our mongoose is killing a snake"; and Rikki-tikki heard a scream from Teddy's mother. His father ran out with a stick, but by the time he came up, Karait had lunged out once too far, and Rikki-tikki had sprung, jumped on the snake's back, dropped his head far between his fore legs, bitten as high up the back as he could get hold, and rolled away. That bite paralyzed Karait, and Rikki-tikki was just going to eat him up from the tail, after the custom of his family at dinner, when he remembered that a full meal makes a slow mongoose, and if he wanted all his strength and quickness ready, he must keep himself thin.

He went away for a dust-bath under the castor-oil bushes, while Teddy's

他的眼睛完全红了，他来回晃动，寻找一口咬下的好地方。卡莱特发动进攻了，里奇跳到一旁试图迎战，但那个邪恶的小土灰脑袋几乎就击中了他的肩膀。他只得跳过蛇身，卡莱特的脑袋紧贴着他的脚跟。

泰迪朝着房子喊道："快，看这里！我们的猫鼬正杀一条蛇呢。"里奇随后就听到了来自泰迪妈妈的尖叫声。泰迪的爸爸出来的时候，手里拿着一根棍子，不过等他赶到的时候，卡莱特已经冲出了太远，里奇跳起来，蹦到了蛇背上，并把头深埋在两条前腿之间。尽量往蛇背的高处咬，然后就滚到了一边。这口咬得卡莱特一下子瘫痪了。然后里奇刚想从尾巴开始吃掉卡莱特，就用家族食用正餐的方式，猛地记起，吃得过饱会让猫鼬变得迟缓。如果想要时刻保持能量满满，反应迅速，就一定不能变胖。

他走到蓖麻树丛下，洗起了灰尘浴，泰迪的父亲此时仍在殴打咽

father beat the dead Karait. "What is the use of that?" thought Rikki-tikki. "I have settled it all"; and then Teddy's mother picked him up from the dust and hugged him, crying that he had saved Teddy from death, and Teddy's father said that he was a providence, and Teddy looked on with big scared eyes. Rikki-Tikki was rather amused at all the fuss, which, of course, he did not understand. Teddy's mother might just as well have petted Teddy for playing in the dust. Rikki was thoroughly enjoying himself.

That night at dinner, walking to and fro among the wine-glasses on the table, he could have stuffed himself three times over with nice things; but he remembered Nag and Nagaina, and though it was very pleasant to be patted and petted by Teddy's mother, and to sit on Teddy's shoulder, his eyes would get red from time to time, and he would go off into his long war-cry of "Rikk-tikk-tikki-tikki-tchk!"

Teddy carried him off to bed, and insisted on Rikki-tikki sleeping under his chin. Rikki-tikki was too well bred to bite or scratch, but as soon as Teddy was asleep he went off for his nightly walk round the house, and in the dark

了气的卡莱特。"继续打他的用处何在？"里奇想着，"我已经将他结了。"接下来，泰迪的母亲将里奇从尘土中拎起来抱着，哭着说是他救了泰迪。泰迪的父亲说他是上帝的恩赐，泰迪则惊恐地看着。里奇看着他们如此大惊小怪，也觉得十分有趣，当然了，他是不明白人们为何这样的。里奇想要是泰迪也像他一样在尘土中滚一滚，他的妈妈也会这样爱抚他的。里奇非常享受这一刻。

到了用晚餐的时候，里奇在餐桌的酒杯之间来回走动。他是可以往嘴里塞进三倍的美食的，可是他记起了纳格和纳格爱娜。所以即使泰迪的母亲轻轻地爱抚他，他也可以坐在泰迪的肩膀上，这都让他非常愉悦，他的眼睛仍然会时常变红。然后还会发出长长的迎战呐喊："里克-提克-提奇-提奇-戚克！"

泰迪将里奇抱着一起去睡觉，并且坚持要他在自己下巴底下睡觉。里奇非常有教养，他不咬人也不会将人抓伤，泰迪睡着了，他就会下床绕着屋子夜巡。他在黑暗中碰到了楚春德拉，沿着墙根爬行的

he ran up against Chuchundra, the muskrat, creeping round by the wall. Chuchundra is a broken-hearted little beast. He whimpers and cheeps all the night, trying to make up his mind to run into the middle of the room, but he never gets there.

"Don't kill me," said Chuchundra, almost weeping. "Rikki-tikki, don't kill me."

"Do you think a snake-killer kills muskrats?" said Rikki-tikki scornfully.

"Those who kill snakes get killed by snakes," said Chuchundra, more sorrowfully than ever. "And how am I to be sure that Nag won't mistake me for you some dark night?"

"There's not the least danger," said Rikki-tikki; "but Nag is in the garden, and I know you don't go there."

"My cousin Chua, the rat, told me –" said Chuchundra, and then he stopped.

"Told you what?"

"Hsh! Nag is everywhere, Rikki-tikki. You should have talked to Chua in the garden."

"I didn't – so you must tell me. Quick, Chuchundra, or I'll bite you!"

Chuchundra sat down and cried till the tears rolled off his whiskers. "I am a very poor man," he sobbed. "I never

麝鼠。楚春德拉很心碎，每个夜里都在不停地呜咽，他试图下定决心溜到房子中央，可是他从未到达过那里。

"不要杀我，"楚春德拉几乎都哭了，"里奇，不要杀我！"

"你觉得一个杀蛇者会去杀麝鼠吗？"里奇语气很轻蔑。

"杀蛇的那些家伙会被蛇杀掉，"楚春德拉用比以往更加悲伤的语气说，"我要如何确信纳格不会在某个黑夜当中把我错认成你呢？"

"这种危险性一点儿都不存在，"里奇说，"纳格是在花园的，我知道你是不往那里去的。"

"我的表弟老鼠楚阿跟我说……"楚春拉德话没说完就停下了。

"跟你说了什么？"

"嘘！哪里都能见到纳格。里奇，在花园里，你应该跟楚阿聊一聊的。"

"我没跟他聊。因此你必须告诉我。快点，楚春拉德，要不然我咬你了。"

楚春德拉干脆坐下来哭了，哭

had spirit enough to run out into the middle of the room. Hsh! I mustn't tell you anything. Can't you hear, Rikki-tikki?"

Rikki-tikki listened. The house was as still as still, but he thought he could just catch the faintestscratch-scratchin the world – a noise as faint as that of a wasp walking on a window-pane – the dry scratch of a snake's scales on brickwork.

"That's Nag or Nagaina," he said to himself; "and he is crawling into the bath-room sluice. You're right, Chuchundra; I should have talked to Chua."

He stole off to Teddy's bath-room, but there was nothing there, and then to Teddy's mother's bath-room. At the bottom of the smooth plaster wall there was a brick pulled out to make a sluice for the bath-water, and as Rikki-tikki stole in by the masonry curb where the bath is put, he heard Nag and Nagaina whispering together outside in the moonlight.

"When the house is emptied of people," said Nagaina to her husband, "he will have to go away, and then the garden will be our own again. Go in quietly, and remember that the big man

到泪水都顺着他的胡须滚落。"我真的非常可怜,"他抽泣着,"我从未有足够的勇气跑到房子的中间。嘘!我什么也不能告诉你。你听不到吗,里奇?"

里奇仔细听着。屋子里还是那么安静,不过他认为他捕捉到了世界上最微弱的剐蹭声,就仿佛窗玻璃上有黄蜂在爬行,这声音是蛇鳞在砖头上的刮擦声。

"这是纳格或者纳格爱娜的声音,"他自言自语,"他正往浴室的排水槽爬。你说得没错。我本该跟楚阿聊聊。"

他偷偷溜到泰迪的浴室,但里什么也没有,然后他又跑到了泰迪母亲的浴室。光滑的石膏墙的底部,一块砖被拉出来,用做排放浴池水的槽口。里奇沿着放浴盆的石栏边爬过去,听到外面的月光下纳格和纳格爱娜正一起低声谋划着。

"当房子空无一人的时候,"纳格爱娜对她的丈夫说,"他就不得不走,然后花园再次为我们所有。悄悄地爬进去,记得先把杀掉卡莱特的高个子男人咬死。随后就

who killed Karait is the first one to bite. Then come out and tell me, and we will hunt for Rikki-tikki together."

"But are you sure that there is anything to be gained by killing the people?" said Nag.

"Everything. When there were no people in the bungalow, did we have any mongoose in the garden? So long as the bungalow is empty, we are king and queen of the garden; and remember that as soon as our eggs in the melon-bed hatch (as they may to-morrow), our children will need room and quiet."

"I had not thought of that," said Nag. "I will go, but there is no need that we should hunt for Rikki-tikki afterward. I will kill the big man and his wife, and the child if I can, and come away quietly. Then the bungalow will be empty, and Rikki-tikki will go."

Rikki-tikki tingled all over with rage and hatred at this, and then Nag's head came through the sluice, and his five feet of cold body followed it. Angry as he was, Rikki-tikki was very frightened as he saw the size of the big cobra. Nag coiled himself up, raised his head, and looked into the bath-room in the dark, and Rikki could see his eyes glitter.

出来告诉我,我们再一同去捕获里奇。"

"但是你确定我们杀掉房子里的人有什么好处吗?"纳格说。

"什么都好。房子里无人居住的话,我们还能在花园看见猫鼬吗?一旦房子空了,我们就成了花园的国王和王后了。要记得,我们的蛋在甜瓜圃里孵化出来的话(他们可能明天就孵出来),我们的孩子需要空间,也需要安静的环境。"

"我没想过这个,"纳格说,"我马上就去,不过之后我们不必去猎杀里奇。我要把高个子男人和他的妻子都杀掉,倘若可以,他的孩子我也不会放过,再悄悄地回来。那时候房子就空了,里奇就会离开了。"

听到这些话,里奇全身充满了愤怒和仇恨。纳格的脑袋此时从水槽钻出来了,他那五英尺长的身子也随后露出来。尽管里奇非常气愤,可他看到大眼镜蛇的长躯时,也是相当恐惧的。纳格盘起自己的身子,抬起头,于黑暗之中朝着浴室看,里奇能够看到他的眼睛在闪闪发光。

"Now, if I kill him here, Nagaina will know; and if I fight him on the open floor, the odds are in his favor. What am I to do?" said Rikki-tikki-tavi.

Nag waved to and fro, and then Rikki-tikki heard him drinking from the biggest water-jar that was used to fill the bath. "That is good," said the snake. "Now, when Karait was killed, the big man had a stick. He may have that stick still, but when he comes in to bathe in the morning he will not have a stick. I shall wait here till he comes. Nagaina – do you hear me? – I shall wait here in the cool till daytime."

There was no answer from outside, so Rikki-tikki knew Nagaina had gone away. Nag coiled himself down, coil by coil, round the bulge at the bottom of the water-jar, and Rikki-tikki stayed still as death. After an hour he began to move, muscle by muscle, toward the jar. Nag was asleep, and Rikki-tikki looked at his big back, wondering which would be the best place for a good hold. "If I don't break his back at the first jump," said Rikki, "he can still fight; and if he fights – O Rikki!" He looked at the thickness of the neck below the hood, but that was too much

"此刻,我要是在这儿把他杀死,纳格爱娜一定知道,若是我在开阔的地板上与他对抗,他就会占据上风。我要怎么做呢?"里奇心里嘀咕着。

纳格来回挥舞着,里奇接着听到了他在那个用于填满浴缸的最大的水罐里喝水。"不错,"蛇说,"好了,当卡莱特遇难的时候,高个子男人手里有根棍子。他现在可能还拿着,不过他清早来洗澡的时候,不会带着棍子的。我要在这里等着他来。纳格爱娜,听到我讲话了吗?我就在这阴凉的地方等到天明。"

外面没有回应。这让里奇明白纳格爱娜离开了。在水罐底端鼓起的地方,纳格将自己自上而下,一圈圈盘在上面。里奇好像死了一样,一动不动地守着。过了一个小时,他开始慢慢向水罐方向移动。纳格睡了,里奇望着他宽阔的后背,琢磨着从哪里下口可以一口致命。"倘若我第一跳没有将他的背咬断,"里奇心里嘀咕着,"他就还能抗争。若是他对抗起来……哦,里奇!"他看了看纳格蛇兜帽西面粗厚的脖颈,对他来说那个位置太厚了;要是在尾巴附近咬上一口,只会让纳格疯狂起来。

or him; and a bite near the tail would only make Nag savage.

"It must be the head," he said at last: "the head above the hood; and, when I am once there, I must not let go."

Then he jumped. The head was lying a little clear of the water-jar, under the curve of it; and, as his teeth met, Rikki braced his back against the bulge of the ed earthenware to hold down the head. This gave him just one second's purchase, and he made the most of it. Then he was battered to and fro as a rat is shaken by a dog – to and fro on the floor, up and down, and round in great circles; but his eyes were red, and he held on as the body cart-whipped over the floor, upsetting the tin dipper and the soap-dish and the flesh-brush, and banged against the tin side of the bath. As he held he closed his jaws tighter and tighter, for he made sure he would be banged to death, and, for the honor of his family, he preferred to be found with his teeth locked. He was dizzy, aching, and felt shaken to pieces when something went off like a thunderclap just behind him; a hot wind knocked him senseless and red fire singed his fur. The big man had been wakened by the noise, and had fired both barrels of

"一定要咬他的头，"里奇最后想，"兜帽之上的脑袋，我一旦咬住，决不能松口。"

然后他跳了起来。纳格的脑袋与水罐之间有些空隙，在盘起的蛇身下方。当里奇咬住蛇头以后，将背抵在红色罐子凸起的地方，以便按住蛇头。这让他获得了一秒钟的时间，他将这一秒钟充分利用。接着，他就像一只狗叼住的老鼠那样被来回甩动，上下左右，里奇被纳格一圈一圈地摔打。可是里奇双眼通红，就算蛇身如赶车的鞭子一般抽打着地板，他也紧紧咬住蛇头不松口，纳格打翻了罐勺、肥皂盒和浴刷，哐哐地撞击在浴缸的锡面上。里奇死死地咬着蛇头，下巴收得更紧了。因为他确信自己会被打死了，但是为了家人的荣誉，他宁愿人们发现他的时候，他的牙齿是紧咬着蛇头的。他头晕目眩，全身疼痛，觉得自己要被震裂成碎片了。就在这个时候，他的身后发出了炸雷一样的轰声。他被热浪震晕了，红火烧焦了些他的皮毛。是高个子男人被噪声惊醒了，拿着双管猎枪朝着纳格开了两枪，正好打在他的兜帽后面。

a shot-gun into Nag just behind the hood.

Rikki-tikki held on with his eyes shut, for now he was quite sure he was dead; but the head did not move, and the big man picked him up and said: "It's the mongoose again, Alice; the little chap has saved our lives now." Then Teddy's mother came in with a very white face, and saw what was left of Nag, and Rikki-tikki dragged himself to Teddy's bedroom and spent half the rest of the night shaking himself tenderly to find out whether he really was broken into forty pieces, as he fancied.

When morning came he was very stiff, but well pleased with his doings. "Now I have Nagaina to settle with, and she will be worse than five Nags, and there's no knowing when the eggs she spoke of will hatch. Goodness! I must go and see Darzee," he said.

Without waiting for breakfast, Rikki-tikki ran to the thorn-bush where Darzee was singing a song of triumph at the top of his voice. The news of Nag's death was all over the garden, for the sweeper had thrown the body on the rubbish-heap.

"Oh, you stupid tuft of feathers!"

里奇-提奇紧闭双眼，嘴里紧咬着纳格，因为他相当确定他已经死了，不过蛇头不动了。高个子男人抱起猫鼬，说："这次又是猫鼬，艾丽斯，这个小家伙这次可是救了我们大伙的性命啊。"跟着进来的泰迪母亲脸色惨白，瞅了瞅死去的纳格。里奇十分费力地挪回泰迪的卧室。在余下的夜晚，他一半时间都用来摇晃自己的身体，他想确认他是否被摔裂成四十块，就像他想象的那样。

到了早晨，里奇周身僵硬，不过他很满意自己的所作所为。"我现在还要去对付纳格爱娜，她比五个纳格还要难对付，而且我不清楚她提到的蛇蛋什么时候孵化出来。老天！我必须去瞧瞧达西。"他说。

没有吃早饭，里奇就跑去了荆棘丛。此时达西正声嘶力竭地哼唱着胜利之歌。纳格已死的消息整个花园的生物都已知晓，清洁工将尸体就扔在了垃圾堆上。

"哦，你这个浑身羽毛的蠢家

said Rikki-tikki, angrily. "Is this the time to sing?"

"Nag is dead – is dead – is dead!" sang Darzee. "The valiant Rikki-tikki caught him by the head and held fast. The big man brought the bang-stick and Nag fell in two pieces! He will never eat my babies again."

"All that's true enough; but where's Nagaina?" said Rikki-tikki, looking carefully round him.

"Nagaina came to the bath-room sluice and called for Nag," Darzee went on; "and Nag came out on the end of a stick – the sweeper picked him up on the end of a stick and threw him upon the rubbish-heap. Let us sing about the great, the red-eyed Rikki-tikki!" and Darzee filled his throat and sang.

"If I could get up to your nest, I'd roll all your babies out!" said Rikki-tikki. "You don't know when to do the right thing at the right time. You're safe enough in your nest there, but it's war for me down here. Stop singing a minute, Darzee."

"For the great, the beautiful Rikki-tikki's sake I will stop," said Darzee. "What is it, O Killer of the terrible Nag!"

伙！"里奇说的时候很生气，"这是要唱歌的时候吗？"

"纳格死了，死了，死了！"达西不停地唱着，"是勇敢的里奇将蛇头咬住不松口。高个子男人拿来了棍子砰砰响，纳格被分裂成两截！他再也不能吞下我的宝宝了。"

"你唱的这些全都属实，不过纳格爱娜在哪里？"里奇-提奇说这话的时候，警惕地看着周围。

"纳格爱娜爬到浴室的排水槽里寻纳格了，"达西继续唱着，"纳格被一根棍子挑着拿出来，清洁工用棍子挑着他将他往垃圾堆上一扔。让我们歌颂一下了不起的红眼睛里奇！"达西提高了嗓门唱道。

"如果我能爬进你的巢穴，我会把你的孩子们都弄出去！"里奇说，"你不知道什么时间该做什么事。你在你的巢穴里是安全了，可是我在下面，这对我来说是一场战争。停下，待一分钟，达西。"

"为了了不起的漂亮的里奇，我不唱了，"达西说，"怎么了，杀死纳格的伟大猎手？"

"Where is Nagaina, for the third time?"

"On the rubbish-heap by the stables, mourning for Nag. Great is Rikki-tikki with the white teeth."

"Bother my white teeth! Have you ever heard where she keeps her eggs?"

"In the melon-bed, on the end nearest the wall, where the sun strikes nearly all day. She had them there weeks ago."

"And you never thought it worth while to tell me? The end nearest the wall, you said?"

"Rikki-tikki, you are not going to eat her eggs?"

"Not eat exactly; no. Darzee, if you have a grain of sense you will fly off to the stables and pretend that your wing is broken, and let Nagaina chase you away to this bush? I must get to the melon-bed, and if I went there now she'd see me."

Darzee was a feather-brained little fellow who could never hold more than one idea at a time in his head; and just because he knew that Nagaina's children were born in eggs like his own, he didn't think at first that it was fair to kill them. But his wife was a sensible bird, and she knew that cobra's

"第三次问你，纳格爱娜在哪里？"

"在马厩的垃圾堆上，为纳格哀悼呢。伟大的里奇有着洁白的牙齿。"

"不要讨论我的白牙！你听说她要把蛋放在哪里吗？"

"就在瓜圃当中，离墙最近，整天都可以晒到太阳的地方。几个星期前她就把蛋放在那里了。"

"你从未想过要花点时间告诉我这个吗？你说的是最靠近墙边的那里？"

"里奇，你不是想要把她的蛋吃掉吧？"

"准确地讲，不是吃，达西。倘若你稍微动一动脑子，你就会飞到马厩那里，假装你的翅膀断了，让纳格爱娜追着你来到荆棘丛。我必须去瓜圃那里，可是我要是此刻就去，她就会看见我。"

达西是个毛头小子，脑子里永远装不下一个以上的念头。只是因为他清楚纳格爱娜的孩子就像自己的宝宝，也是卵生，于是他的第一想法就是杀死这些孩子不公平。不过他的妻子很明智，她清楚眼镜蛇蛋就是以后年幼的眼镜蛇。所以她飞出巢穴，留下达西温暖巢窝，

ggs meant young cobras later on; so he flew off from the nest, and left Darzee to keep the babies warm, and continue his song about the death of Nag. Darzee was very like a man in some ways.

She fluttered in front of Nagaina by the rubbish-heap, and cried out, "Oh, my wing is broken! The boy in the house threw a stone at me and broke it." Then she fluttered more desperately than ever.

Nagaina lifted up her head and hissed, "You warned Rikki-tikki when I would have killed him. Indeed and truly, you've chosen a bad place to be lame in." And she moved toward Darzee's wife, slipping along over the dust.

"The boy broke it with a stone!" shrieked Darzee's wife.

"Well! It may be some consolation to you when you're dead to know that I shall settle accounts with the boy. My husband lies on the rubbish-heap this morning, but before night the boy in the house will lie very still. What is the use of running away? I am sure to catch you. Little fool, look at me!"

Darzee's wife knew better than to do that, for a bird who looks at a snake's

继续哼唱着纳格已死。达西在一些方面跟男人有些相似。

她飞向垃圾堆,在纳格爱娜面前边扑腾翅膀边哭喊着:"哦,我的翅膀折断了!屋里的男孩朝我扔石头,将它打断了。"接着她又比之前扑腾得更厉害。

纳格爱娜把脑袋抬起,轻声说:"我原本可以杀了里奇的时候,是你警告了他。的确,你折断翅膀的地方很糟糕。"然后她就顺着达西妻子的方向,一路滑过尘土。

"那个男孩用石头把我的翅膀打断了!"达西的妻子尖叫着。

"好吧!让你在临死之前知道我会去跟那个男孩算账,对你也算有些安慰。我的丈夫今天清晨躺在垃圾堆上,屋子里的男孩用不了晚上,就会安安静静地躺下。逃跑的意义何在?我一定能抓住你。小蠢货,看着我!"

达西的妻子知道不能那么做,若是一只鸟注视一条蛇的眼睛,她

eyes gets so frightened that she cannot move. Darzee's wife fluttered on, piping sorrowfully, and never leaving the ground, and Nagaina quickened her pace.

Rikki-tikki heard them going up the path from the stables, and he raced for the end of the melon-patch near the wall. There, in the warm litter about the melons, very cunningly hidden, he found twenty-five eggs, about the size of a bantam's eggs, but with whitish skin instead of shell.

"I was not a day too soon," he said; for he could see the baby cobras curled up inside the skin, and he knew that the minute they were hatched they could each kill a man or a mongoose. He bit off the tops of the eggs as fast as he could, taking care to crush the young cobras, and turned over the litter from time to time to see whether he had missed any. At last there were only three eggs left, and Rikki-tikki began to chuckle to himself, when he heard Darzee's wife screaming:

"Rikki-tikki, I led Nagaina toward the house, and she has gone into the veranda, and – oh, come quickly – she means killing!"

Rikki-tikki smashed two eggs, and

就会被吓得动弹不了。达西的妻子扑腾着，哀鸣着，一直都在地面上，纳格爱娜加快了速度。

里奇-提奇听到她们顺着小路离开了马厩，他立马跑向墙边的瓜圃。在那里，他找到了被巧妙隐藏在温暖的瓜床中的蛇蛋二十五个，大小就和矮脚鸡的蛋类似，只是只有一层白色膜，没有壳。

"我真是一天也没有早来。"他说。因为他可以看到蜷缩在蛋膜里的小眼镜蛇已经发育好。他很清楚他们一旦被孵化出，每一条都可以杀掉一个人或是一只猫鼬。他竭尽全力咬碎蛇蛋的顶端，谨慎地碾碎眼镜蛇幼崽，而且还要不断翻动褥草看是否留下活口。最后，只有三枚蛇蛋了，里奇提奇开始暗自高兴，这时却听到了达西妻子的尖叫声。

"里奇-提奇，纳格爱娜被我引到了房屋这边，她进了走廊。哦，快点过来，她要杀人！"

里奇砸了两枚蛇蛋，然后叼起

tumbled backward down the melon-bed with the third egg in his mouth, and scuttled to the veranda as hard as he could put foot to the ground. Teddy and his mother and father were there at early breakfast; but Rikki-tikki saw that they were not eating anything. They sat stone-still, and their faces were white. Nagaina was coiled up on the matting by Teddy's chair, within easy striking distance of Teddy's bare leg, and she was swaying to and fro singing a song of triumph.

"Son of the big man that killed Nag," she hissed, "stay still. I am not ready yet. Wait a little. Keep very still, all you three. If you move I strike, and if you do not move I strike. Oh, foolish people, who killed my Nag!"

Teddy's eyes were fixed on his father, and all his father could do was to whisper, "Sit still, Teddy. You mustn't move. Teddy, keep still."

Then Rikki-tikki came up and cried: "Turn round, Nagaina; turn and fight!"

"All in good time," said she, without moving her eyes. "I will settle my account with you presently. Look at your friends, Rikki-tikki. They are still and white; they are afraid. They dare not move, and if you come a step

第三个，向后一滚，翻出了瓜圃。他用上全力飞奔，跑向走廊的方向。泰迪和他的爸爸妈妈在那里用早餐。不过里奇看到他们什么都没吃。他们像石头一样一动不动地定在那里，脸都是惨白的。纳格爱娜盘起蛇身，就在泰迪椅子旁边的地垫上，泰迪光秃秃的小腿儿轻易就能被她咬到。纳格爱娜来回摇摆，唱起了歌。

"杀了纳格的高个子男人的儿子啊，"她嘶声唱着，"不要动。我还没有做好准备。等一下。老实待着，你们三个。一旦你们动了，我就出击了，就算你们不动，我也要出击的。愚蠢的人类，竟然把我的纳格杀了。"

泰迪双眼紧盯着父亲，他父亲只能低声说："安静地坐着，泰迪。你不要动，泰迪，不要动。"

里奇-提奇随后来到了走廊，叫道："转身，纳格爱娜，转过来我们战一场！"

"一切都刚刚好，"她说，却并没有转移视线，"很快我就会和你算账。看看你的这些朋友吧，里奇。他们一动都不敢动，他们脸色苍白，他们吓坏了。他们没有胆量

nearer I strike."

"Look at your eggs," said Rikki-tikki, "in the melon-bed near the wall. Go and look, Nagaina."

The big snake turned half round, and saw the egg on the veranda. "Ah-h! Give it to me," she said.

Rikki-tikki put his paws one on each side of the egg, and his eyes were blood-red. "What price for a snake's egg? For a young cobra? For a young king-cobra? For the last – the very last of the brood? The ants are eating all the others down by the melon-bed."

Nagaina spun clear round, forgetting everything for the sake of the one egg; and Rikki-tikki saw Teddy's father shoot out a big hand, catch Teddy by the shoulder, and drag him across the little table with the tea-cups, safe and out of reach of Nagaina.

"Tricked! Tricked! Tricked! Rikk-tck-tck!" chuckled Rikki-tikki. "The boy is safe, and it was I – I – I that caught Nag by the hood last night in the bath-room." Then he began to jump up and down, all four feet together, his head close to the floor. "He threw me to and fro, but he could not shake me off. He was dead before the big man blew him in two. I did

动一动，要是你再向前一步，我就咬了。"

"看看你的蛋，"里奇说，"就在围墙附近的瓜圃。去那里瞧瞧吧，纳格爱娜。"

大蛇的半个身子转了过来，她看到了走廊上的那枚蛇蛋。"啊！将蛋给我。"她说。

里奇-提奇两只前爪夹着蛋，双眼涨得通红："一枚蛇蛋值什么价？一条眼镜蛇幼崽呢？一条眼镜蛇王幼崽呢？这是最后一枚，整个窝里的最后一枚蛋啊？蚂蚁们正在瓜圃当中吃所有其余的蛋呢。"

纳格爱娜掉转了整个蛇身。因为这最后一枚蛇蛋让她忘记了所有，里奇看到泰迪的父亲快速伸出一只大手，把泰迪的肩膀抓住，将他拽过小茶桌。泰迪安全了，纳格爱娜够不到他了。

"骗你的！骗你的！骗你的！里奇-戚克-戚克，"里奇-提奇咯咯地笑起来，"那个男孩现在安全了，是我——昨天晚上在浴室咬住纳格脖子兜帽的是我。"然后他开始四脚并用上下跳动，脑袋靠着地板，"他来回摇晃着我，就是甩不掉。他在高个子男人把他炸成两截之前就死翘翘了。我杀了他。里奇-提克-戚克-戚克！来呀，纳格爱娜，

it.Rikki-tikki-tck-tck! Come then, Nagaina. Come and fight with me. You shall not be a widow long."

Nagaina saw that she had lost her chance of killing Teddy, and the egg lay between Rikki-tikki's paws. "Give me the egg, Rikki-tikki. Give me the last of my eggs, and I will go away and never come back," she said, lowering her hood.

"Yes, you will go away, and you will never come back; for you will go to the rubbish-heap with Nag. Fight, widow! The big man has gone for his gun! Fight!"

Rikki-tikki was bounding all round Nagaina, keeping just out of reach of her stroke, his little eyes like hot coals. Nagaina gathered herself together, and flung out at him. Rikki-tikki jumped up and backward. Again and again and again she struck, and each time her head came with a whack on the matting of the veranda and she gathered herself together like a watch-spring. Then Rikki-tikki danced in a circle to get behind her, and Nagaina spun round to keep her head to his head, so that the rustle of her tail on the matting sounded like dry leaves blown along by the wind.

来和我干一场。你不会做很久的寡妇的。"

纳格爱娜看到杀掉泰迪的机会被自己错失,蛇蛋还被里奇两只爪子夹着。"给我蛇蛋,里奇。给我最后的蛇蛋,我会离开这里,永远也不回来。"她说着,将兜帽垂下。

"没错,你会离开这里,永远都不再回来。因为你会和纳格一起去垃圾堆。出击吧,寡妇!那个高个子男人已经起身去拿枪了!开战吧!"

里奇-提奇在纳格爱娜周围转着圈跳跃,一直保持着她够不到的距离,里奇-提奇的小眼睛变成热炭一般红。纳格爱娜使出浑身的劲儿,扑向他。里奇-提奇向前跳一下,再向后跳一下。纳格爱娜一次又一次地扑向他,每回她的脑袋都会在走廊的草垫子上重击一下,随后又像手表弹簧一般重振旗鼓。里奇在她的后面转着圈跳舞,纳格爱娜也转着圈想要头对着他的头。结果就是她的蛇尾像狂风扫落叶一样在草垫上沙沙作响。

He had forgotten the egg. It still lay on the veranda, and Nagaina came nearer and nearer to it, till at last, while Rikki-tikki was drawing breath, she caught it in her mouth, turned to the veranda steps, and flew like an arrow down the path, with Rikki-tikki behind her. When the cobra runs for her life, she goes like a whiplash flicked across a horse's neck.

Rikki-tikki knew that he must catch her, or all the trouble would begin again. She headed straight for the long grass by the thorn-bush, and as he was running Rikki-tikki heard Darzee still singing his foolish little song of triumph. But Darzee's wife was wiser. She flew off her nest as Nagaina came along, and flapped her wings about Nagaina's head. If Darzee had helped they might have turned her; but Nagaina only lowered her hood and went on. Still, the instant's delay brought Rikki-tikki up to her, and as she plunged into the rat-hole where she and Nag used to live, his little white teeth were clenched on her tail, and he went down with her – and very few mongooses, however wise and old they may be, care to follow a cobra into its hole. It was dark in the hole; and

里奇-提奇忘记了蛇蛋。它就在走廊上放着,纳格爱娜慢慢靠近,最后,在里奇-提奇喘气的空档,将蛋叼进嘴中。然后立马转向走廊的台阶,像离弦的箭顺着小路飞滑而走,里奇-提奇紧跟其后。纳格爱娜真是在逃命,快得就像马鞭抽打在马脖子上一样。

里奇-提奇明白他必须抓住她,否则一切的祸端会卷土重来。纳格爱娜直奔荆棘丛旁边高深的草丛,里奇-提奇奔跑追赶的时候听见达西还在唱愚蠢的胜利之歌。不过他有个聪明的妻子,纳格爱娜过来的时候,她飞出了巢穴,在纳格爱娜的脑袋上方扑腾着翅膀。若是达西也能帮上点忙,他们或许就能让她转过身来。但是纳格爱娜只是低下她的兜帽,继续飞奔向前。尽管如此,这一瞬间的延迟还是让里奇-提奇追上了她,正当她要钻进她和纳格之前居住的老鼠洞时,里奇-提奇白色的小牙紧咬住了蛇尾。并且随她一起进了洞——很少有猫鼬,不管如何聪明如何老道的猫鼬都不会愿意追眼镜蛇追到洞里。那里面一片漆黑,里奇-提奇无从知道哪会会开阔起来,让纳格爱娜有空间可以转身击打他。他狠

Rikki-tikki never knew when it might open out and give Nagaina room to turn and strike at him. He held on savagely, and struck out his feet to act as brakes on the dark slope of the hot, moist earth.

Then the grass by the mouth of the hole stopped waving, and Darzee said: "It is all over with Rikki-tikki! We must sing his death-song. Valiant Rikki-tikki is dead! For Nagaina will surely kill him underground."

So he sang a very mournful song that he made up all on the spur of the minute, and just as he got to the most touching part the grass quivered again, and Rikki-tikki, covered with dirt, dragged himself out of the hole leg by leg, licking his whiskers. Darzee stopped with a little shout. Rikki-tikki shook some of the dust out of his fur and sneezed. "It is all over," he said. "The widow will never come out again." And the red ants that live between the grass stems heard him, and began to troop down one after another to see if he had spoken the truth.

Rikki-tikki curled himself up in the grass and slept where he was – slept and slept till it was late in the afternoon, for he had done a hard day's

狠地咬着她不松口,猛然停下,伸直了脚刹车一般抵在又黑又热又湿的泥土上。

然后洞口的草停止了晃动,达西说:"里奇-提奇被干掉了!我们必须为他唱死亡之歌了。勇敢的里奇-提奇牺牲了!纳格爱娜在洞中一定会把咬死他的。"

于是他唱着一首非常悲伤的歌,这首歌是他一分钟之内创作出来的。就在他唱到最感人的部分时,草地再次颤动起来。满身污泥的里奇-提奇将自己从洞口中拖了出来,舔起他的髭须。达西停下,小小地惊叫了一声。里奇-提奇把他皮毛上的一些尘土抖了抖,打了个喷嚏。"这回都结束了,"他说,"寡妇蛇永远不会再出来了。"居住在草茎之间的红蚂蚁听到了这些话,开始依次排队前去探究他的话是否属实。

里奇-提奇蜷缩在草地上睡着了,他就这样一直睡,睡到了下午很晚的时候,因为这一天他实在是太辛苦了。

work.

"Now," he said, when he awoke, "I will go back to the house. Tell the Coppersmith, Darzee, and he will tell the garden that Nagaina is dead."

The Coppersmith is a bird who makes a noise exactly like the beating of a little hammer on a copper pot; and the reason he is always making it is because he is the town-crier to every Indian garden, and tells all the news to everybody who cares to listen. As Rikki-tikki went up the path, he heard his "attention" notes like a tiny dinner-gong; and then the steady "Ding-dong-tock! Nag is dead – dong! Nagaina is dead! Ding-dong-tock!" That set all the birds in the garden singing, and the frogs croaking; for Nag and Nagaina used to eat frogs as well as little birds.

When Rikki got to the house, Teddy and Teddy's mother (she looked very white still, for she had been fainting) and Teddy's father came out and almost cried over him; and that night he ate all that was given him till he could eat no more, and went to bed on Teddy's shoulder, where Teddy's mother saw him when she came to look late at night.

"现在，"他醒来后说，"我要回到房子那里了。把消息告诉铜匠，达西，他会告诉整个花园纳格爱娜已死的。"

铜匠是一只鸟，他的声音就像敲在铜锅上的一把小锤子。他之所以一直这样做，是因为他是印度所有花园的消息传递者，他将所有消息传达给想要倾听的人。当里奇-提奇踏上小路的时候，他听到了铜匠小晚餐锣一样的"请注意"，然后稳定持续地喊声"叮——咚——噹克！纳格死了——咚！纳格爱娜死了！叮——咚——噹克！"所有的鸟儿都开始放声歌唱，青蛙也随着呱呱直叫。因为纳格和纳格爱娜过去吃小鸟，也不放过青蛙。

当里奇-提奇走到房子的时候，泰迪和泰迪的妈妈（她因为刚刚晕倒，此时脸色还是很白），还有他的爸爸出门迎接，他们几乎是哭着抱起他。他那晚吃掉了所有给他的东西，直到他再也吃不下。然后就睡在了泰迪的肩膀上，泰迪的妈妈深夜回来看他的时候，他依旧睡在那里。

"He saved our lives and Teddy's life," she said to her husband. "Just think, he saved all our lives."

Rikki-tikki woke up with a jump, for all the mongooses are light sleepers.

"Oh, it's you," said he. "What are you bothering for? All the cobras are dead; and if they weren't, I'm here."

Rikki-tikki had a right to be proud of himself; but he did not grow too proud, and he kept that garden as a mongoose should keep it, with tooth and jump and spring and bite, till never a cobra dared show its head inside the walls.

"他救了我们,也救了泰迪,"她跟她的丈夫说,"你想想,是他救了我们一家子。"

里奇-提奇一下子就醒了,所有的猫鼬睡眠都很浅。

"哦,原来是你们,"他说,"什么事令你们烦恼?没有存活的眼镜蛇了,就算是有,我在这里守护着你们呢。"

里奇-提奇有权自豪,可是他没有太骄傲。他看守着花园,做一个尽职尽责的猫鼬,用牙齿、用弹跳、用咬的方式守卫着一切,直到没有一条眼镜蛇再敢往围墙内探头。

DARZEE'S CHANT

达西唱的颂歌

SUNG IN HONOR OF
RIKKI-TIKKI-TAVI

致敬里奇-提奇-塔维

Singer and tailor am I –
Doubled the joys that I know –
Proud of my lilt through the sky,
Proud of the house that I sew –
Over and under, so weave I my music – so weave
I the house that I sew.

歌手和裁缝都是我，
我能体会双倍的快乐——我
自豪于我的歌声穿过云霄，
我骄傲于亲手缝制的窝房，
我的音乐高低混合，

恰如我缝制我的窝房。

Sing to your fledglings again,
Mother, oh lift up your head!
Evil that plagued us is slain,
Death in the garden lies dead.
Terror that hid in the roses is impotent –
flung on the dung-hill and dead!

再次为你的雏鸟歌唱，
妈妈，哦，抬起你的头！
折磨我们的恶魔已死，
花园里的死神变成躺尸。
隐藏在玫瑰丛中的恐怖已被
灭绝，死后扔在了粪堆之上！

Who hath delivered us, who?
Tell me his nest and his name.
Rikki, the valiant, the true,
Tikki, with eyeballs of flame.
Rik-tikki-tikki, the ivory-fanged, the

谁为我们铲除了威胁，是谁？
告诉我他巢穴在哪儿，姓甚名谁。
是里奇，他英勇又真诚，
是里奇，他双眼冒着火焰，

hunter with eyeballs of flame.

Give him the Thanks of the Birds,
Bowing with tail-feathers spread!
Praise him with nightingale words –
Nay, I will praise him instead.

Hear! I will sing you the praise of the bottle-tailed Rikki, with eyeballs of red!

(Here Rikki-tikki interrupted, and the rest of the song is lost.)

里奇-提奇-提奇，他牙尖嘴利，双眼冒火，是最猛的猎手。

为他献上鸟儿的感激，
张开尾羽，鞠躬致谢！
用夜莺的歌声将他赞颂。
不，还是我来将他赞颂。

听啊！我会为你唱颂歌，瓶刷尾红眼球的里奇！

（里奇在此处打断了达西，剩余的歌也就遗失了。）

CHAPTER 6   TOOMAI OF THE ELEPHANTS

第六章   大象们的图麦

I WILL remember what I was, I am sick of rope and chain –

I will remember my old strength and all my forest affairs.

I will not sell my back to man for a bundle of sugar-cane,

I will go out to my own kind, and the wood-folk in their lairs.

I will go out until the day, until the morning break,

Out to the winds' untainted kiss, the waters' clean caress:

I will forget my ankle-ring and snap my picket-stake.

I will revisit my lost loves, and playmates masterless!

KALA Nag, which means Black Snake, had served the Indian Government in every way that an elephant could serve it for forty-seven years, and as he was fully twenty years old when he was caught, that makes him nearly seventy

我会记得我是什么,我厌烦绳索和链条——

我会记得我曾经的力量和森林里的一切事物。

我不会为了一捆甘蔗出卖我的脊梁;

我会去寻找同族,寻找洞穴中的丛林同伴。

我会出去,直到白天到来,直到黎明破晓,

去感受清风纯洁的亲吻,去感受河水清朗的爱抚;

我会忘记我脚掌上的铁环,会折断将我拴住的木桩。

我会重温我逝去的爱,寻回无主的旧日伙伴!

卡拉·纳格,意思是"黑蛇",他已经用大象能做到的所有方式为印度政府服务四十七年了。他被抓的时候刚满二十岁,如今差不多七十岁了。对一头大象而言,这个年龄已经算老了。他记得在一八四

– a ripe age for an elephant. He remembered pushing, with a big leather pad on his forehead, at a gun stuck in deep mud, and that was before the Afghan war of 1842, and he had not then come to his full strength.

His mother, Radha Pyari, – Radha the darling, – who had been caught in the same drive with Kala Nag, told him, before his little milk tusks had dropped out, that elephants who were afraid always got hurt: and Kala Nag knew that that advice was good, for the first time that he saw a shell burst he backed, screaming, into a stand of piled rifles, and the bayonets pricked him in all his softest places. So, before he was twenty-five, he gave up being afraid, and so he was the best-loved and the best-looked-after elephant in the service of the Government of India. He had carried tents, twelve hundred pounds' weight of tents, on the march in Upper India: he had been hoisted into a ship at the end of a steam-crane and taken for days across the water, and made to carry a mortar on his back in a strange and rocky country very far from India, and had seen the Emperor Theodore lying dead in Magdala, and

二年阿富汗战争之前，他的前额上垫上一块大皮垫，推出一门陷在泥潭里的大炮，那时的他还没有使出全身力气。

他的母亲拉德阿·皮阿丽——亲爱的拉德阿，她和卡拉·纳格在同一次追捕中被抓到。卡拉·纳格的乳牙还没掉之前，他的妈妈拉德阿·皮阿丽跟他讲过，害怕的大象通常会受到伤害。卡拉·纳格明白这个告诫很有意义，因为他第一次看到一个爆炸的炮弹时，他边后退边叫着，踩到了来复枪堆积的台子，刺刀刺伤了他最柔软的地方。因此，在他二十五岁之前，他放下了害怕。他也因此成为最受喜爱和最受关注的服务印度政府的大象。在北印度的行军队伍中，他运送过一千二百磅重的帐篷。他曾被蒸汽起重机吊起到一艘船上，在海上漂泊了很多天，之后在远离印度的一个陌生而多岩石的国家，背送一枚迫击炮。他看到西奥多皇帝死在了马格达拉。然后，他又再次回到蒸汽船上返航。那艘船后来受封阿比西尼亚[1]战争奖章，士兵们是那样说的。十年之后，他曾在一个叫作阿里·慕斯基德的地方，看到有的

---

[1] 现称埃塞俄比亚。

had come back again in the steamer entitled, so the soldiers said, to the Abyssinian war medal. He had seen his fellow-elephants die of cold and epilepsy and starvation and sunstroke up at a place called Ali Musjid, ten years later; and afterward he had been sent down thousands of miles south to haul and pile big baulks of teak in the timber-yards at Moulmein. There he had half killed an insubordinate young elephant who was shirking his fair share of the work.

After that he was taken off timber-hauling, and employed, with a few score other elephants who were trained to the business, in helping to catch wild elephants among the Garo hills. Elephants are very strictly preserved by the Indian Government. There is one whole department which does nothing else but hunt them, and catch them, and break them in, and send them up and down the country as they are needed for work.

Kala Nag stood ten fair feet at the shoulders, and his tusks had been cut off short at five feet, and bound round the ends, to prevent them splitting, with bands of copper; but he could do more with those stumps than any untrained

同伴因寒冷、癫痫、饥饿，或者中暑而死。再后来，他被派往南部数千里之外，在毛尔梅恩的木材场运送、堆放柚木。他在那里差点杀了一头不听话的年轻大象，因为他推卸责任不想干自己分内的活儿。

后来，他被木材场解雇了。他被安排与经过业务培训的其他几十头大象一块，帮助捕捉伽罗山中的野生大象。印度政府严格保护着大象，有一个部门是除了追捕他们以外什么都不干，就是负责抓他们然后训练。当有需要的时候，再把大象派到全国各地。

卡拉·纳格站直的时候，他的肩膀离地面有十英尺那么高。他的象牙在五英尺处被剪了，牙齿尾端用铜环绕上防止裂开。即便如此，卡拉·纳格用残缺的牙桩还是能比未经过训练的有完整牙齿的大

elephant could do with the real sharpened ones.

When, after weeks and weeks of cautious driving of scattered elephants across the hills, the forty or fifty wild monsters were driven into the last stockade, and the big drop-gate, made of tree-trunks lashed together, jarred down behind them, Kala Nag, at the word of command, would go into that flaring, trumpeting pandemonium (generally at night, when the flicker of the torches made it difficult to judge distances), and, picking out the biggest and wildest tusker of the mob, would hammer him and hustle him into quiet while the men on the backs of the other elephants roped and tied the smaller ones.

There was nothing in the way of fighting that Kala Nag, the old wise Black Snake, did not know, for he had stood up more than once in his time to the charge of the wounded tiger, and, curling up his soft trunk to be out of harm's way, had knocked the springing brute sideways in mid-air with a quick sickle-cut of his head, that he had invented all by himself; had knocked him over, and kneeled upon him with his huge knees till the life went out

象做得更多。

经过了几周的谨慎驱赶，零星散落在山中的野生大象，最后有四五十头被赶到最终的围栏当中。围栏闸门是用树干捆在一起制成的，在大象身后被砰地关上。卡拉·纳格在一声令下，进入闪着火光、野象群吼的混乱之地（一般是在晚上，闪烁的火把让大象无法判断距离）。卡拉·纳格会挑出最大的最狂躁的一头野象，狠狠地收拾他一顿，让他老实，骑在其他象背上的人们此时会用绳索捆住小一些的野象。

卡拉·纳格不愧为聪明的老"黑蛇"，他在打斗上精通一切技巧。他曾多次英勇对抗受伤的老虎，他蜷缩着柔软的躯干，以免受到伤害，用快如镰刀砍物的速度挥动着脑袋，在半空中把跳起的老虎侧身撞倒。他自己发明了这一绝招。撞倒老虎以后，他把巨大的膝盖跪跪在他身上，一直压到他断气了为止。老虎被干掉了，只剩下一堆有条纹的毛茸茸的东西堆在地上，等着卡拉·纳格将他拖走。

with a gasp and a howl, and there was only a fluffy striped thing on the ground for Kala Nag to pull by the tail.

"Yes," said Big Toomai, his driver, the son of Black Toomai who had taken him to Abyssinia, and grandson of Toomai of the Elephants who had seen him caught, "there is nothing that the Black Snake fears except me. He has seen three generations of us feed him and groom him, and he will live to see four."

"He is afraid ofmealso," said Little Toomai, standing up to his full height of four feet, with only one rag upon him. He was ten years old, the eldest son of Big Toomai, and, according to custom, he would take his father's place on Kala Nag's neck when he grew up, and would handle the heavy ironankus, the elephant-goad that had been worn smooth by his father, and his grandfather, and his great-grandfather. He knew what he was talking of; for he had been born under Kala Nag's shadow, had played with the end of his trunk before he could walk, had taken him down to water as soon as he could walk, and Kala Nag would no more have dreamed of disobeying his shrill little orders than he would have

"是的，"驱象手大图麦说，大图麦是黑图麦的儿子，黑图麦当年将卡拉·纳格带去阿比西尼亚，他的爷爷"大象们的图麦"是见证他被抓的人，"除了我之外，没有什么能吓到'黑蛇'的。他看到了我们三代人喂养他，训练他，他会活着见到我们第四代人喂养他。"

"他也怕我呀。"小图麦说，站直了身子他已经有四英尺高，只在身上围了一块布。小图麦十岁了，是大图麦的大儿子。而且按照习惯，成年以后，他会接替父亲的职位，骑上卡拉·纳格的脖子，用沉重的铁棍驱赶大象。他父亲、祖父还有曾祖父握过的铁棍如今已经很光滑了。他明白卡拉·纳格的语言，因为他出生在卡拉·纳格的影子之下。学会走路之前，他就抱着卡拉·纳格的鼻子玩耍；学会了走路，他就赶着卡拉·纳格下水。一天，当大图麦将棕色的婴儿放到卡拉·纳格的鼻子下方时，告诉他要尊敬未来的主人。就从那时起，卡拉·纳格从未想过要违背小主人的命令，更没想过要杀他。

dreamed of killing him on that day when Big Toomai carried the little brown baby under Kala Nag's tusks, and told him to salute his master that was to be.

"Yes," said Little Toomai, "he is afraid of me," and he took long strides up to Kala Nag, called him a fat old pig, and made him lift up his feet one after the other.

"Wah!" said Little Toomai, "thou art a big elephant," and he wagged his fluffy head, quoting his father. "The Government may pay for elephants, but they belong to us mahouts. When thou art old, Kala Nag, there will come some rich Rajah, and he will buy thee from the Government, on account of thy size and thy manners, and then thou wilt have nothing to do but to carry gold earrings in thy ears, and a gold howdah on thy back, and a red cloth covered with gold on thy sides, and walk at the head of the processions of the King. Then I shall sit on thy neck, O Kala Nag, with a silverankus, and men will run before us with golden sticks, crying, 'Room for the King's elephant!' That will be good, Kala Nag, but not so good as this hunting in the jungles."

"是的，"小图麦说，"他是怕我。"他大步走向卡拉·纳格，称他为老肥猪，并让他抬起一只又一只脚。

"哇！"小图麦说，"你长得真大，"他摇着蓬松的小脑袋，就像他父亲那样，"政府出钱供大象开销，可是他们属于我们这些看象人。当你年老的时候，卡拉·纳格，会有一些富有的王公出钱给政府买下你，依据你的身量大小，行为举止出价。到那时你的耳朵上带上金耳环，背上金轿，身上再披上一块闪着金光的红布，走在国王的游行队伍前面就行了，其他什么都不用做。卡拉·纳格呀，我就坐在你的脖子上，手上握着银色的驱象棒。人们手持金棍奔跑在我们前方，嘴里喊着'为国王的大象让地方！'那样挺好，卡拉·纳格，可那样没有我们在丛林中狩猎这么好。"

"Umph!" said Big Toomai. "Thou art a boy, and as wild as a buffalo-calf. This running up and down among the hills is not the best Government service. I am getting old, and I do not love wild elephants, Give me brick elephant-lines, one stall to each elephant, and big stumps to tie them to safely, and flat, broad roads to exercise upon, instead of this come-and-go camping. Aha, the Cawnpore barracks were good. There was a bazaar close by, and only three hours' work a day."

Little Toomai remembered the Cawnpore elephant-lines and said nothing. He very much preferred the camp life, and hated those broad, flat roads, with the daily grubbing for grass in the forage-reserve, and the long hours when there was nothing to do except to watch Kala Nag fidgeting in his pickets.

What Little Toomai liked was to scramble up bridle-paths that only an elephant could take; the dip into the valley below; the glimpses of the wild elephants browsing miles away; the rush of the frightened pig and peacock under Kala Nag's feet; the blinding warm rains, when all the hills and valleys smoked; the beautiful misty

"哼！"大图麦说，"你就是个小孩，却狂野得像野牛犊。在山上到处跑可不是最舒服的政府工作。我年纪越来越大，我不喜欢野生大象。给我一座砖砌成的象营，每头大象都分上一间，用大树桩将他们拴住，在平坦宽阔的场地锻炼他们，而不是如今这样到处移动的野营。啊哈，坎普尔军营不赖，那附近有集市，每天只有三个小时的工作。"

小图麦想起了坎普尔象营，没说什么。他特别喜欢生活在野营地，并且对那些广阔而平坦的道路感到厌恶，他不喜欢每天在牧草库中翻草料，他厌烦长时间无所事事，只能眼看着树桩旁边的卡拉·纳格坐立不安。

小图麦喜欢爬上只有一头大象才能通过的道路，喜欢浸入下面的山谷；喜欢看数英里外的野象吃草；喜欢看卡拉·纳格脚下受惊的野猪和孔雀奔跑；喜欢令人炫目的暖雨，所有的丘陵和山谷水烟渺渺；美丽多雾的清晨，无人知晓夜晚的宿营之地；他们小心谨慎地赶着野象，以及前一天夜里驱赶大象

mornings when nobody knew where they would camp that night; the steady, cautious drive of the wild elephants, and the mad rush and blaze and hullabaloo of the last night's drive, when the elephants poured into the stockade like boulders in a landslide, found that they could not get out, and flung themselves at the heavy posts only to be driven back by yells and flaring torches and volleys of blank cartridge.

Even a little boy could be of use there, and Toomai was as useful as three boys. He would get his torch and wave it, and yell with the best. But the really good time came when the driving out began, and the Keddah, that is, the stockade, looked like a picture of the end of the world, and men had to make signs to one another, because they could not hear themselves speak. Then Little Toomai would climb up to the top of one of the quivering stockade-posts, his sun-bleached brown hair flying loose all over his shoulders, and he looking like a goblin in the torch-light; and as soon as there was a lull you could hear his high-pitched yells of encouragement to Kala Nag, above the trumpeting and crashing, and

时的奔跑，火光和喧闹；野象好像山体滑坡时的巨石一样进入围栏，当他们发现自己无法出去，沉重的身体也只能被大声的叫嚷、燃烧的火炬和空空的弹药筒驱赶回去。

即使是个小男孩，这时候也能帮上忙，而且图麦一个就能顶上三个小男孩。他拿着火炬来回挥舞，用最大的嗓门叫嚷着。不过最精彩的时刻，是把野象们赶出围场。科达，也就是印度人诱捕野象的围场，看起来一副世界末日的景象。人们不得不打手势沟通，因为他们连自己的声音都听不到。小图麦这时候会爬上一根颤抖的栅栏柱顶部，他那被太阳晒得褪色的棕色头发散在他的肩上，看起来就像手电筒里的精灵。只要有一瞬间的平息，他就会高声呼喊卡拉·纳格，他的喊声高过大象们的叫唤和碰撞声，绳索断裂声和大象的呻吟声。你会听到他对卡拉·纳格的高亢呐喊："上啊，上啊，卡拉·纳格，出击！当心，当心，出击，出

snapping of ropes, and groans of the tethered elephants. "Maîl, maîl, Kala Nag! Dant do! Somalo! Somalo! Maro! Mar! Mind the post!Arre! Arre! Hai! Yai! Kya-a-ah!" he would shout, and the big fight between Kala Nag and the wild elephant would sway to and fro across the Keddah, and the old elephant-catchers would wipe the sweat out of their eyes, and find time to nod to Little Toomai wriggling with joy on the top of the posts.

He did more than wriggle. One night he slid down from the post and slipped in between the elephants, and threw up the loose end of a rope, which had dropped, to a driver who was trying to get a purchase on the leg of a kicking young calf (calves always give more trouble than full-grown animals). Kala Nag saw him, caught him in his trunk, and handed him up to Big Toomai, who slapped him then and there, and put him back on the post.

Next morning he gave him a scolding, and said: "Are not good brick elephant-lines and a little tent-carrying enough, that thou must needs go elephant-catching on thy own account, little worthless? Now those foolish hunters, whose pay is less than my pay,

击！小心树桩，哎呀！哎呀！哈呀！呀啊！"卡拉·纳格和野象们之间的大战会在科达持续很久；而老驱象手会擦干眼睛上的汗水，找时间向高兴扭动着的小图麦点头示意。

小图麦做的不仅仅是扭动。一天晚上，他滑下柱子，溜到大象之中，并将掉落的绳索松散的一端扔还给一名驱象手，这名驱象手正试图抓住小腿乱蹬的一头小野象（小野象总是比成年野象更棘手）。卡拉·纳格看到了，就用鼻子卷起他，将他交给了大图麦。大图麦随即打了他一巴掌，然后将他放回柱子上。

第二天清早，小图麦受到了大图麦的严厉责备："砖象营里运送小帐篷不好吗？还非得要自己捕象，你这个没用的小家伙。现在那些愚蠢的驱象手，赚的还没我多的伙计已经告诉彼得森·萨比布这件事了。"这吓坏了小图麦。

have spoken to Petersen Sahib of the matter." Little Toomai was frightened. He did not know much of white men, but Petersen Sahib was the greatest white man in the world to him. He was the head of all the Keddah operations – the man who caught all the elephants for the Government of India, and who knew more about the ways of elephants than any living man.

"What – what will happen?" said Little Toomai.

"Happen! The worst that can happen. Petersen Sahib is a madman. Else why should he go hunting these wild devils? He may even require thee to be an elephant-catcher, to sleep anywhere in these fever-filled jungles, and at last to be trampled to death in the Keddah. It is well that this nonsense ends safely. Next week the catching is over, and we of the plains are sent back to our stations. Then we will march on smooth roads, and forget all this hunting. But, son, I am angry that thou shouldst meddle in the business that belongs to these dirty Assamese jungle-folk. Kala Nag will obey none but me, so I must go with him into the Keddah, but he is only a fighting elephant, and he does not help to rope

他不怎么了解白人，不过彼得森·萨比布在他心里是世界上最伟大的白人。所有科达的行动的负责人都是他——他是为印度政府抓住所有大象的人；他比任何人都更了解大象们的习性如何。

"怎么……那会怎么样？"小图麦说。

"会怎么样？可能会发生最糟糕的情况。彼得森·萨比布就是个疯子，否则他为什么要去捕猎这些野怪？他甚至可能要求你成为大象捕手，在这热病横行的丛林中的任何一处睡觉，最后在科达里面被野象践踏而死。好在这些胡言乱语平息了。下个星期这次围捕就结束了，我们这些来自平原的驱象手要被送回车站。然后，我们就可以走在平坦的道路上，忘记所有这些围猎。但是，儿子，我很不高兴，你竟然掺和进肮脏的阿萨姆丛林的事务中。卡拉·纳格只听我的话，所以我不得不跟他一起进入科达，可他只是一头战斗大象，他不会帮忙拴象。所以我安逸地坐着，像一个驱象手的样子——不仅仅是猎夫——是一名驱象手，我的意

them. So I sit at my ease, as befits a mahout, – not a mere hunter, – a mahout, I say, and a man who gets a pension at the end of his service. Is the family of Toomai of the Elephants to be trodden underfoot in the dirt of a Keddah? Bad one! Wicked one! Worthless son! Go and wash Kala Nag and attend to his ears, and see that there are no thorns in his feet; or else Petersen Sahib will surely catch thee and make thee a wild hunter – a follower of elephant's foot-tracks, a jungle-bear. Bah! Shame! Go!"

Little Toomai went off without saying a word, but he told Kala Nag all his grievances while he was examining his feet. "No matter," said Little Toomai, turning up the fringe of Kala Nag's huge right ear. "They have said my name to Petersen Sahib, and perhaps – and perhaps – and perhaps – who knows? Hai! That is a big thorn that I have pulled out!"

The next few days were spent in getting the elephants together, in walking the newly caught wild elephants up and down between a couple of tame ones, to prevent them from giving too much trouble on the downward march to the plains, and in

思是一个在服役期结束后能够获得退休金的人。大象们的图麦家族要在科达的泥土中被野象践踏在脚下吗?坏孩子!不安分的家伙!没用的儿子!去给卡拉·纳格洗一洗,注意下他的耳朵,瞧瞧他脚上是否有刺。否则彼得森·萨比布必定会抓住你,让你成为一名野象捕手,追随着大象的脚步,一只丛林熊。呸!差耻!去吧!"

小图麦走了,一句话都没说,但是在给卡拉·纳格检查脚掌的时候,他说出了心里所有的委屈。"没关系,"小图麦说着的时候,翻过卡拉·纳格巨大的右耳边缘。"他们已经向彼得森·萨比布说了我的名字,或许——或许——或许——谁晓得呢?嗨!我拔出一根好大的刺啊!"

接下来的日子里,大象们被聚集到一起,每对被驯服的大象之间放上一头新捕获的野生象,让他们来回走动,防止他们在向平原下行的过程中有太多麻烦;并清点在森林中被磨损或者丢失的毯子、绳子,以及其他物品。

taking stock of the blankets and ropes and things that had been worn out or lost in the forest.

Petersen Sahib came in on his clever she-elephant Pudmini; he had been paying off other camps among the hills, for the season was coming to an end, and there was a native clerk sitting at a table under a tree, to pay the drivers their wages. As each man was paid he went back to his elephant, and joined the line that stood ready to start. The catchers, and hunters, and beaters, the men of the regular Keddah, who stayed in the jungle year in and year out, sat on the backs of the elephants that belonged to Petersen Sahib's permanent force, or leaned against the trees with their guns across their arms, and made fun of the drivers who were going away, and laughed when the newly caught elephants broke the line and ran about.

Big Toomai went up to the clerk with Little Toomai behind him, and Machua Appa, the head-tracker, said in an undertone to a friend of his, "There goes one piece of good elephant-stuff at least. 'Tis a pity to send that young jungle-cock to moult in the plains."

Now Petersen Sahib had ears all over

彼得森·萨比布骑着他聪明的母象普德米尼走过来，山区中其他营地的人他都已经给了工钱，因为捕象季即将结束了。有个本地的职员坐在树下的一张桌子旁，向驱象手们支付工钱。领到工钱的人一个个回到自己的大象身边，加入到随时准备出发的队伍。捕猎者、猎手和轰赶猎物的人，长期受雇于科达，年复一年地在丛林中待着。他们现在正坐在彼得森·萨比布永久队伍的象背上，或者靠在树上，手里挎着枪，嘲笑着那些正要离开的驱象手们。新捕猎回来的野象从队伍中冲出到处跑的时候，他们大声取笑。

大图麦朝职员走去，小图麦跟在他身后。领头的追踪人马丘阿·阿帕对他的一个朋友低声说道："至少出现了一个捕象的好苗子。丛林小公鸡要被送到平原去换毛，太遗憾了。"

彼得森·萨比布可是全身长

him, as a man must have who listens to the most silent of all living things – the wild elephant. He turned where he was lying all along on Pudmini's back, and said, "What is that? I did not know of a man among the plain-drivers who had wit enough to rope even a dead elephant."

"This is not a man, but a boy. He went into the Keddah at the last drive, and threw Barmao there the rope, when we were trying to get that young calf with the blotch on his shoulder away from his mother."

Machua Appa pointed at Little Toomai, and Petersen Sahib looked, and Little Toomai bowed to the earth.

"He throw a rope? He is smaller than a picket-pin. Little one, what is thy name?" said Petersen Sahib.

Little Toomai was too frightened to speak, but Kala Nag was behind him, and Toomai made a sign with his hand, and the elephant caught him up in his trunk and held him level with Pudmini's forehead, in front of the great Petersen Sahib. Then Little Toomai covered his face with his hands, for he was only a child, and except where elephants were concerned, he was just as bashful as a

满了耳朵,因为一个人若是想听到野象的声音,他就必须能听见最寂静生物的声音。此时他在普德米尼的背上转过身来,说:"什么意思?我不知道那些平原的驱象手们,有谁那么机智,他们甚至都拴不住一头死象啊。"

"不是大人,是个小男孩。他在最后赶象的时候进了科达,向巴尔莫那里扔了一根绳子。我们那时正试图把肩上有斑点的象犊子从他母亲身边拖走。"

马丘阿·阿帕指着小图麦,彼得森·萨比布看了看,小图麦鞠了一躬。

"他扔绳子?他比木桩子都矮。小家伙,叫什么?"彼得森·萨比布说。

小图麦太害怕了,话都不敢说。不过卡拉·纳格就在他身后,小图麦用手示意了一下,大象就卷起他,将他举到普德米尼的前额那么高,就在伟大的彼得森·萨比布的面前。小图麦赶紧用手遮住脸,他毕竟只是个孩子,除了涉及大象的事情,其他时候他和别的小孩一样害羞。

child could be.

"Oho!" said Petersen Sahib, smiling underneath his mustache, "and why didst thou teach thy elephantthattrick? Was it to help thee steal green corn from the roofs of the houses when the ears are put out to dry?"

"Not green corn, Protector of the Poor, – melons," said Little Toomai, and all the men sitting about broke into a roar of laughter. Most of them had taught their elephants that trick when they were boys. Little Toomai was hanging eight feet up in the air, and he wished very much that he were eight feet underground.

"He is Toomai, my son, Sahib," said Big Toomai, scowling. "He is a very bad boy, and he will end in a jail, Sahib."

"Of that I have my doubts," said Petersen Sahib. "A boy who can face a full Keddah at his age does not end in jails. See, little one, here are four annas to spend in sweetmeats because thou hast a little head under that great thatch of hair. In time thou mayest become a hunter too." Big Toomai scowled more than ever. "Remember, though, that Keddahs are not good for children to play in," Petersen Sahib went on.

"哦吼！"彼得森·萨比布说，嘴上满是笑意，"为什么你要教你的大象这样做？是因为可以在晒玉米穗的时候，让他从屋顶帮你偷青玉米吗？"

"不是青玉米，是穷人的保护者，甜瓜。"小图麦说。所有坐着的人都迸发出一阵笑声。这些人当中的大多数都在孩童时代这样教过大象。小图麦被卡拉·纳格举在空中八英尺那么高，他却多么希望自己钻到地下八英尺。

"他是图麦，我的儿子，萨比布，"大图麦说这话的时候，皱着眉头，"这孩子非常坏，最终会进大狱的，萨比布。"

"我对你的话很是怀疑，"彼得森·萨比布说，"在他这个年龄就有胆量面对整个科达的小男孩，他的结局不会是监狱。看，小家伙，给你四个安那，买糖吃吧，因为你浓密的头发下面，长了一颗聪明的脑袋。你最终可能会成为一名猎手。"大图麦的眉头皱得更紧了。

"记得，即便如此，科达也不是小孩子玩耍的好地方。"彼得森·萨比布继续说。

"Must I never go there, Sahib?" asked Little Toomai, with a big gasp.

"Yes." Petersen Sahib smiled again. "When thou hast seen the elephants dance. That is the proper time. Come to me when thou hast seen the elephants dance, and then I will let thee go into all the Keddahs."

There was another roar of laughter, for that is an old joke among elephant-catchers, and it means just never. There are great cleared flat places hidden away in the forests that are called elephants' ball-rooms, but even these are found only by accident, and no man has ever seen the elephants dance. When a driver boasts of his skill and bravery the other drivers say, "And when didst thou see the elephants dance?"

Kala Nag put Little Toomai down, and he bowed to the earth again and went away with his father, and gave the silver four-anna piece to his mother, who was nursing his baby-brother, and they all were put up on Kala Nag's back, and the line of grunting, squealing elephants rolled down the hill-path to the plains. It was a very lively march on account of the new elephants, who gave trouble at every

"我永远都不准去那里了吗，萨比布？"小图麦喘着粗气问。

"没错，"彼得森·萨比布再次笑了起来，"当你看到大象跳舞才是适当的时候。等你看到大象跳舞了，就到我这里来。然后所有的科达我都让你进。"

人们又一阵哈哈大笑，因为这是流传在大象捕手之间的老笑话，它代表着永远不可能。在森林中深藏着很多平坦的地方，那里被称作大象的舞场，不过那些地方即使很偶然才被发现，也没人见过大象跳舞。当一个驱象手向同伴吹嘘自己的技巧和勇气时，他的同伴会说："那什么时候你看到大象跳舞了吗？"

卡拉·纳格放下了小图麦，小图麦再次鞠躬，然后随他的父亲一道离开。他把四安那银币放到了正在喂小弟弟的母亲身上。一家子都坐到了卡拉·纳格的后背，一排排大象咕咕噜噜，尖叫着地顺着山路走向平原。这是一支非常活跃的队伍，因为有新大象在其中。每经过一个浅滩，新大象总要弄出些麻烦，隔一分钟就要哄劝或者鞭打他们。

ford, and who needed coaxing or beating every other minute.

Big Toomai prodded Kala Nag spitefully, for he was very angry, but Little Toomai was too happy to speak. Petersen Sahib had noticed him, and given him money, so he felt as a private soldier would feel if he had been called out of the ranks and praised by his commander-in-chief.

"What did Petersen Sahib mean by the elephant-dance?" he said, at last, softly to his mother.

Big Toomai heard him and grunted. "That thou shouldst never be one of these hill-buffaloes of trackers. That was what he meant. Oh you in front, what is blocking the way?"

An Assamese driver, two or three elephants ahead, turned round angrily, crying: "Bring up Kala Nag, and knock this youngster of mine into good behavior. Why should Petersen Sahib have chosen me to go down with you donkeys of the rice-fields? Lay your beast alongside, Toomai, and let him prod with his tusks. By all the Gods of the Hills, these new elephants are possessed, or else they can smell their companions in the jungle."

Kala Nag hit the new elephant in the

大图麦凶狠地戳了卡拉·纳格一下，因为他非常生气。小图麦却开心得话都说不出来。他受到彼得森·萨比布的关注，并且给了他钱，他觉得自己就像一个被叫出队伍的士兵，受到了总司令的称赞。

"彼得森·萨比布提到大象跳舞是什么意思？"他最后轻声问他的母亲。

大图麦听到他说话，嘟囔道："就是说你永远不能成为捕象的野水牛，这就是他的意思。哦，前面的家伙，什么挡住了道儿？"

一名阿萨姆驱象手，前面隔着两三头大象，愤怒地转过身来，大声说道："将卡拉·纳格领到前头，把我这小象撞一撞，让他老实点儿。彼得森·萨比布为什么选择我和你们这群稻田里的驴子一块儿下山？将你的大象赶过来一起，用他的象牙戳一下。以山上的所有神灵起誓，这些新的野象被什么附体了，或者他们在丛林中闻到了同族的气息。"

卡拉·纳格撞了新象肋骨一

ribs and knocked the wind out of him, as Big Toomai said, "We have swept the hills of wild elephants at the last catch. It is only your carelessness in driving. Must I keep order along the whole line?"

"Hear him!" said the other driver. "We have swept the hills! Ho! ho! You are very wise, you plains-people. Any one but a mud head who never saw the jungle would know that they know that the drives are ended for the season. Therefore all the wild elephants to-night will – but why should I waste wisdom on a river-turtle?"

"What will they do?" Little Toomai called out.

"Ohé, little one. Art thou there? Well, I will tell thee, for thou hast a cool head. They will dance, and it behooves thy father, who has swept all the hills of all the elephants, to double-chain his pickets to-night."

"What talk is this?" said Big Toomai. "For forty years, father and son, we have tended elephants, and we have never heard such moonshine about dances."

"Yes; but a plains-man who lives in a hut knows only the four walls of his hut. Well, leave thy elephants

下，让他收敛了一下风头，大图麦这时说："我们在最后围猎的时候，已经扫荡了有野象的所有山头。就是你赶象的时候太大意，我就不得不维持整个象队的秩序吗？"

"听他都说了什么！"另一个驱象手说，"我们扫荡了所有山头！嗬！嗬！生活在平原的你们够聪明的。除了从未见过丛林的泥巴脑袋，全都清楚这次的围猎季已经结束了。正因如此，所有的野象今天晚上会……不过我为什么要在一只河龟身上浪费我的脑力？"

"野象们会做什么？"小图麦喊道。

"哦，小家伙。你在啊？那么，我就告诉你，因为你头脑清醒。野象们会跳舞，你那扫荡过所有山头的父亲，应该要在木桩上加双层的锁链了。"

"你这话什么意思？"大图麦说，"四十年来，我们一家父子都在照顾大象，可我们却从未听过什么大象跳舞这种瞎话。"

"是啊，平原人住在小屋子里，也就只能知晓屋子的四面墙了。那么，让你的大象今晚都不受

unshackled to-night and see what comes; as for their dancing, I have seen the place where – Bapree-Bap! how many windings has the Dihang River? Here is another ford, and we must swim the calves. Stop still, you behind there."

And in this way, talking and wrangling and splashing through the rivers, they made their first march to a sort of receiving-camp for the new elephants; but they lost their tempers long before they got there.

Then the elephants were chained by their hind legs to their big stumps of pickets, and extra ropes were fitted to the new elephants, and the fodder was piled before them, and the hill-drivers went back to Petersen Sahib through the afternoon light, telling the plains-drivers to be extra careful that night, and laughing when the plains-drivers asked the reason.

Little Toomai attended to Kala Nag's supper, and as evening fell, wandered through the camp, unspeakably happy, in search of a tom-tom. When an Indian child's heart is full, he does not run about and make a noise in an irregular fashion. He sits down to a sort of revel all by himself. And Little Toomai had

束缚，看看会发生什么。至于说跳舞，我看到过那个地方，那里——喔哟——哇！迪航河有多少个拐弯处啊？又一个浅滩，我们必须让小象先游。停下等着，后面的。"

他们就这样一路说着，吵着，在溅起的水花中渡了河。他们路程上的第一个营地是为迎接新大象而设的，可是野象们在距离营地很远的地方就开始变得焦躁。

于是驱象手们把大象后腿用铁链子拴在粗壮的木桩上，并且增加了额外的绳索，把饲料就堆在他们面前。山丘驱象人在下午赶回到彼得森·萨比布那里了，并且嘱咐平原驱象手当晚要格外留意。当被问起原因时，他们只是哈哈大笑。

小图麦照看卡拉·纳格食用了晚餐。夜晚时分，他在象营中散步，内心感到无比快乐，他在寻找一只手鼓。当一个印度的小孩子充满愉悦时，他不会跑来跑去到处叫嚷，他会坐下来自己独自陶醉。彼得森·萨比布可是与小图麦讲过话了！倘若他没有找到想要的定西，

been spoken to by Petersen Sahib! If he had not found what he wanted I believe he would have burst. But the sweatmeat-seller in the camp lent him a little tom-tom – a drum beaten with the flat of the hand – and he sat down, cross-legged, before Kala Nag as the stars began to come out, the tom-tom in his lap, and he thumped and he thumped and he thumped, and the more he thought of the great honor that had been done to him, the more he thumped, all alone among the elephant-fodder. There was no tune and no words, but the thumping made him happy.

The new elephants strained at their ropes, and squealed and trumpeted from time to time, and he could hear his mother in the camp hut putting his small brother to sleep with an old, old song about the great God Shiv, who once told all the animals what they should eat. It is a very soothing lullaby, and the first verse says:

Shiv, who poured the harvest and made the winds to blow,

Sitting at the doorways of a day of long ago,

Gave to each his portion, food and

我相信他会爆发的，不过营地的蜜饯商贩借了一只手鼓给他——一只手掌拍打的鼓。他盘腿坐下，就在卡拉•纳格面前，星星亮起的时候，他敲打着放在膝盖上的手鼓，砰砰砰，砰砰砰，砰砰砰。独自坐在大象饲料当中，他越想自己获得的莫大嘉奖就敲得更加起劲儿。他的拍打没曲调也没唱词，可是却令他很是开心。

新的野象们扭动着绳索，并且时不时地发出尖叫声。小图麦可以听到母亲在营地的小屋里唱一首特别古老的有关湿婆神的歌谣哄弟弟睡觉，歌中的湿婆神曾告诉所有动物他们该吃什么。这是一首非常舒缓的摇篮曲，第一节的歌词是这样的：

湿婆神，你让我们满载而归，顺风顺水，

很久之前的某一天，他就坐在门口，

给每人分上一份食物，一份劳

toil and fate,

From the King upon the guddee to the Beggar at the gate.

All things made he – Shiva the Preserver.

Mahadeo! Mahadeo! he made all, – Thorn for the camel, fodder for the kine,

And mother's heart for sleepy head, O little son of mine!

Little Toomai came in with a joyoustunk-a-tunkat the end of each verse, till he felt sleepy and stretched himself on the fodder at Kala Nag's side.

At last the elephants began to lie down one after another as is their custom, till only Kala Nag at the right of the line was left standing up; and he rocked slowly from side to side, his ears put forward to listen to the night wind as it blew very slowly across the hills. The air was full of all the night noises that, taken together, make one big silence – the click of one bamboo-stem against the other, the rustle of something alive in the undergrowth, the scratch and squawk of a half-waked bird (birds are awake in the night much more often than we

碌和一种命运。

王座上的国王，大门口的乞丐谁都不落。

湿婆守护者，一切由他决定。

马哈德奥！马哈德奥！一切任他创造！

带刺的给骆驼，饲料留给母牛，

妈妈的心里是熟睡的小脑瓜，我的小儿子！

小图麦在母亲每句唱词的末尾都欢快地敲上几下，直到他感到困倦，睡在了卡拉·纳格身旁的饲料堆上。

最后大象们一头一头地躺下了，他们一直是这样。只有卡拉·纳格还站在队列的右边。他慢悠悠地左右摇摆着象身，耳朵向前伸着，听夜风缓缓吹过山丘。各种各样的黑夜之声弥漫在空中，形成了一片巨大的寂静——竹子与竹子的碰撞声，树丛中某种生物的沙沙声，一只半睡半醒的鸟发出的刮擦和粗粝的叫声（鸟儿在夜晚醒来的次数要比我们想象的多得多），还有远处瀑布的落水声。小图麦睡了一段时间，睁开双眼的时候，明亮的月光已洒向大地。卡拉·纳格仍然静静地站在那里，耳朵竖起。

imagine), and the fall of water ever so far away. Little Toomai slept for some time, and when he waked it was brilliant moonlight, and Kala Nag was still standing up with his ears cocked. Little Toomai turned, rustling in the fodder, and watched the curve of his big back against half the stars in heaven, and while he watched he heard, so far away that it sounded no more than a pinhole of noise pricked through the stillness, the "hoot-toot" of a wild elephant.

All the elephants in the lines jumped up as if they had been shot, and their grunts at last waked the sleeping mahouts, and they came out and drove in the picket-pegs with big mallets, and tightened this rope and knotted that till all was quiet. One new elephant had nearly grubbed up his picket, and Big Toomai took off Kala Nag's leg-chain and shackled that elephant fore foot to hind foot, but slipped a loop of grass-string round Kala Nag's leg, and told him to remember that he was tied fast. He knew that he and his father and his grandfather had done the very same thing hundreds of times before. Kala Nag did not answer to the order by gurgling, as he usually did. He stood

小图麦转过身，在沙沙作响的饲料堆上注视着星光照耀下的卡拉·纳格背部的曲线。然而就在他注视卡拉·纳格的时候，他听见了远处传来的小如穿针的声音，那是一头野象发出的"呼嘟"声。

在队列中的大象们都好像被击中了一样，全部跳起来。已经睡着的驱象手们被大象的咕嘟声吵醒，走出帐篷，用大槌又砸了砸拴象的木桩。绳子拧得更紧了一些，又拽了拽绳结，直到一切又安静下来。一头新象几乎要将拴他的木桩拔出来了，大图麦取下卡拉·纳格的腿链，将新象的前后腿连起来绑上。卡拉·纳格的腿上只留下缠的一圈草绳，大图麦叮嘱他记得自己是被牢牢拴着的。他清楚他自己、他父亲还有祖父也曾做过数百次同样的事情。可是卡拉·纳格并未向平时那样咕噜一下回应主人的指令。他静静地站着，微微抬起头，耳朵开得就像大扇子，眼睛透过月光，望向伽罗山的重峦山峰。

still, looking out across the moonlight,his head a little raised and his ears spread like fans, up to the great folds of the Garo hills.

"Tend to him if he grows restless in the night," said Big Toomai to Little Toomai, and he went into the hut and slept. Little Toomai was just going to sleep, too, when he heard the coir string snap with a little "tang," and Kala Nag rolled out of his pickets as slowly and as silently as a cloud rolls out of the mouth of a valley. Little Toomai pattered after him, bare-footed, down the road in the moonlight, calling under his breath, "Kala Nag! Kala Nag! Take me with you, O Kala Nag!" The elephant turned without a sound, took three strides back to the boy in the moonlight, put down his trunk, swung him up to his neck, and almost before Little Toomai had settled his knees, slipped into the forest.

There was one blast of furious trumpeting from the lines, and then the silence shut down on everything, and Kala Nag began to move. Sometimes a tuft of high grass washed along his sides as a wave washes along the sides of a ship, and sometimes a cluster of wild-pepper vines would scrape along

"他若是在夜间不老实的话，看管好他。"大图麦告诉小图麦后，就回到小屋子睡觉了。正在小图麦也要睡觉的时候，他听到了椰壳纤维编制的绳子"嗒"地断了。卡拉·纳格慢慢地从拴他的桩子上挣脱，如同一团云静静地从山谷中滚出。小图麦跟在他身后，赤着脚走在月光下的小路，他压低声音喊："卡拉·纳格！卡拉·纳格！把我带上，哦，卡拉·纳格！"大象默默地转过身，站在月光下向后退了三步，把长鼻子放下来，卷起了小图麦，让他骑在自己的脖子上。小图麦甚至还没有坐稳，卡拉·纳格就进入了森林。

象队中爆发了狂暴的叫嚷，然后又了无声响，卡拉·纳格接着向前走去。有时候身旁会扫过高高的草束，如同行驶的船只被波浪冲刷着。有时候背上会滑过野胡椒藤，或者竹子吱吱地掠过肩膀。不过除此以外，卡拉·纳格前行的时候完全没有发出任何其他的声响。他穿

his back, or a bamboo would creak where his shoulder touched it; but between those times he moved absolutely without any sound, drifting through the thick Garo forest as though it had been smoke. He was going uphill, but though Little Toomai watched the stars in the rifts of the trees, he could not tell in what direction.

Then Kala Nag reached the crest of the ascent and stopped for a minute, and Little Toomai could see the tops of the trees lying all speckled and furry under the moonlight for miles and miles, and the blue-white mist over the river in the hollow. Toomai leaned forward and looked, and he felt that the forest was awake below him – awake and alive and crowded. A big brown fruit-eating bat brushed past his ear; a porcupine's quills rattled in the thicket, and in the darkness between the tree-stems he heard a hog-bear digging hard in the moist warm earth, and snuffing as it digged.

Then the branches closed over his head again, and Kala Nag began to go down into the valley – not quietly this time, but as a runaway gun goes down a steep bank – in one rush. The huge

梭在茂密的伽罗森林里，就像是一缕青烟。他正在朝山上走，尽管小图麦能够在树林的缝隙间看见天上的星星，可是他却不知道往哪个方向走着。

卡拉·纳格到了山顶以后，停留了一小会儿，小图麦能够看见月光下的树尖，连成一片，绵延数英里。蓝白色的雾弥漫在山谷的河上。图麦向前倾身，看了看，他觉得在他身下的森林清醒了，周围挤满各种生灵。一只棕色的食果大蝙蝠擦过他的耳朵，一头豪猪的羽刺在树林间咔咔作响。树干的黑暗之中，他听见了猪熊在湿润温暖的土地上艰难地挖掘着，边挖还边闻。

这时树枝再次在他的头顶合拢，卡拉·纳格开始朝山下的溪谷中走去。他不再像之前那样安静，却像一把不受控的枪，一冲到底。巨大的如同活塞一样的四肢稳稳

limbs moved as steadily as pistons, eight feet to each stride, and the wrinkled skin of the elbow-points rustled. The undergrowth on either side of him ripped with a noise like torn canvas, and the saplings that he heaved away right and left with his shoulders sprang back again, and banged him on the flank, and great trails of creepers, all matted together, hung from his tusks as he threw his head from side to side and plowed out his pathway. Then Little Toomai laid himself down close to the great neck, lest a swinging bough should sweep him to the ground, and he wished that he were back in the lines again.

The grass began to get squashy, and Kala Nag's feet sucked and squelched as he put them down, and the night mist at the bottom of the valley chilled Little Toomai. There was a splash and a trample, and the rush of running water, and Kala Nag strode through the bed of a river, feeling his way at each step. Above the noise of the water, as it swirled round the elephant's legs, Little Toomai could hear more splashing and some trumpeting both up-stream and down – great grunts and angry snortings, and all the mist about him

地移动，一步有八英尺那么远，肘部关节的皮肤也跟着沙沙直响。他两侧的灌木丛被他像撕裂帆布一样拨开，肩上的树苗随着他肩膀的移动向前翘起，然后又反弹回来抽打在他的侧身。一大堆的藤蔓缠在一起，在他左右摇头开辟道路的时候垂在了鼻子上。小图麦紧紧地趴在他的大粗脖子上，免得被摇晃的树枝扫到地上。他多希望自己返回了象群。

草地开始变得湿软，卡拉·纳格的脚踏在上面，陷得咯吱咯吱响。山谷底部的夜雾让小图麦感到寒冷。卡拉·纳格扑通一下踩进去，水花就飞溅起来，流水冲刷着他们，卡拉·纳格走过河床，一步步探路而行。河水围绕着卡拉·纳格的腿打漩，在水漩声之外，小图麦听见了更多的水花飞溅的声音，还有叫唤声从上下游传来——那是其他大象的咕哝声和愤怒的鼻息。似乎在周围的雾气中，充满了波动的阴影。

seemed to be full of rolling wavy shadows.

"Ai!" he said, half aloud, his teeth chattering. "The elephant-folk are out to-night. It is the dance, then."

Kala Nag swashed out of the water, blew his trunk clear, and began another climb; but this time he was not alone, and he had not to make his path. That was made already, six feet wide, in front of him, where the bent jungle-grass was trying to recover itself and stand up. Many elephants must have gone that way only a few minutes before. Little Toomai looked back, and behind him a great wild tusker with his little pig's eyes glowing like hot coals, was just lifting himself out of the misty river. Then the trees closed up again, and they went on and up, with trumpetings and crashings, and the sound of breaking branches on every side of them.

At last Kala Nag stood still between two tree-trunks at the very top of the hill. They were part of a circle of trees that grew round an irregular space of some three or four acres, and in all that space, as Little Toomai could see, the ground had been trampled down as hard as a brick floor. Some trees grew

"啊!"他几乎要喊出来,牙齿都在颤抖,"大象族今晚上都出来了。他们这是要跳舞了。"

卡拉·纳格冲出水面,清理干净鼻子里的水,再一次开始向上攀。不过这次他不再孤单,他也不用自己开路。前面有路了,六英尺宽,被践踏得弯弯的丛林草正在试图恢复原样站起来。肯定有很多大象几分钟之前开辟了这条路。小图麦回头看了一眼,身后有一头巨大的野猪一样的家伙,眼睛就像火红的热炭闪闪发光,从迷雾笼罩的河中上了岸。然后树干再次合拢起来,他们向上走,周围处处是叫嚷声、撞击声和树枝被折断的响声。

最后,卡拉·纳格站在了山顶的两棵树树干之间。这两棵树是周围一圈树的一部分,树群的中间是一片不规则的三四英尺的空地。在这片空地上,正如小图麦看到的一样,地面被踩得像砖地那么硬。长在空地中央的几棵树树皮都被蹭掉了,里面的白色树干在月光下显

in the center of the clearing, but their bark was rubbed away, and the white wood beneath showed all shiny and polished in the patches of moonlight. There were creepers hanging from the upper branches, and the bells of the flowers of the creepers, great waxy white things like convolvuluses, hung down fast asleep; but within the limits of the clearing there was not a single blade of green – nothing but the trampled earth.

The moonlight showed it all iron-gray, except where some elephants stood upon it, and their shadows were inky black. Little Toomai looked, holding his breath, with his eyes starting out of his head, and as he looked, more and more and more elephants swung out into the open from between the tree-trunks. Little Toomai could count only up to ten, and he counted again and again on his fingers till he lost count of the tens, and his head began to swim. Outside the clearing he could hear them crashing in the undergrowth as they worked their way up the hillside; but as soon as they were within the circle of the tree-trunks they moved like ghosts.

There were white-tusked wild males,

得更加光亮。藤蔓从高高的树枝上垂下，倒悬在上面的白色钟形花大得就像牵牛花，闭上了花瓣。只是在这块平地上，除了被践踏的地表，没有一片绿色的叶子。

　　除了大象们站着的地方，月光把空地照成铁灰色，大象们的影子漆黑漆黑。小图麦屏住呼吸注视着，眼睛都要跳出眼眶了。就在他注视的时候，越来越多的大象摇摇晃晃从树干间走出，来到空地。小图麦只能数到十，他用手指一遍一遍地数，直到他想不起来第几个十，他的脑袋都晕了。他能够听见空地之外的大象们从山坡上向下冲时，灌木丛被扰得哗哗直响的声音，可是只要这些大象进入到树干的圈子内，他们就像鬼魂一样移动。

　　这里面有长着白色长牙的野

with fallen leaves and nuts and twigs lying in the wrinkles of their necks and the folds of their ears; fat slow-footed she-elephants, with restless, little pinky-black calves only three or four feet high running under their stomachs; young elephants with their tusks just beginning to show, and very proud of them; lanky, scraggy old-maid elephants, with their hollow anxious faces, and trunks like rough bark; savage old bull-elephants, scarred from shoulder to flank with great weals and cuts of bygone fights, and the caked dirt of their solitary mud-baths dropping from their shoulders; and there was one with a broken tusk and the marks of the full-stroke, the terrible drawing scrape, of a tiger's claws on his side.

They were standing head to head, or walking to and fro across the ground in couples, or rocking and swaying all by themselves – scores and scores of elephants.

Toomai knew that so long as he lay still on Kala Nag's neck nothing would happen to him; for even in the rush and scramble of a Keddah-drive a wild elephant does not reach up with his trunk and drag a man off the neck of a

公象，落叶、坚果和树条夹在他们象脖和耳朵的褶皱处。有身材丰腴、腿脚缓慢的母象，肚子下面还有跑来跑去的三四英尺高的幼年小象。有刚刚开始展示象牙的年轻大象，他们觉得非常骄傲。有长得瘦削的年老的母象，脸上露出焦躁不安的神情，象鼻粗糙得就像树皮。有野蛮的老公象，肩膀到肩胛骨，伤痕累累，都是曾经打斗时留下的痕迹，他们正抖落独自洗泥浆浴时留在身上的泥块。还有一头断了根象牙的大象，身上带着老虎奋力一击时，爪子留下的吓人的抓痕。

他们正头对着头站在一起，或者是一对一对来回走动，或者是几十头大象自行摇摆着。

小图麦清楚，只要他躺在卡拉·纳格的脖子上不动，什么都不会伤害到他。因为就算是在科达围猎时，那么混乱，也没有一头野象伸出鼻子，将一个人从一头驯服的大象脖子上拖下来。并且，这些大

tame elephant; and these elephants were not thinking of men that night. Once they started and put their ears forward when they heard the chinking of a leg-iron in the forest, but it was Pudmini, Petersen Sahib's pet elephant, her chain snapped short off, grunting, snuffling up the hillside. She must have broken her pickets, and come straight from Petersen Sahib's camp; and Little Toomai saw another elephant, one that he did not know, with deep rope-galls on his back and breast. He, too, must have run away from some camp in the hills about.

At last there was no sound of any more elephants moving in the forest, and Kala Nag rolled out from his station between the trees and went into the middle of the crowd, clucking and gurgling, and all the elephants began to talk in their own tongue, and to move about.

Still lying down, Little Toomai looked down upon scores and scores of broad backs, and wagging ears, and tossing trunks, and little rolling eyes. He heard the click of tusks as they crossed other tusks by accident, and the dry rustle of trunks twined together, and the chafing of enormous sides and

象们当晚根本没有留意到人。当他们听到森林里有铁镣叮叮当当的声响时，他们开始将耳朵竖起，不过原来是彼得森·萨比布的宠象，普德米尼来了。断了的铁链子还挂在她的脚脖上，她一路咕哝咕哝，喘着粗气攀上了山顶。她肯定是将拴她的柱子弄断了，直接跑出了彼得森·萨比布的象营。小图麦还看到了一只他不认识的大象，背部和胸部都是绳索勒过的深痕，他也肯定是从山丘的某处象营逃出来的。

最后，没有更多的大象穿梭在树林中，卡拉·纳格站出来，走到象群之中，咯咯地交流起来。全部的大象都开始用他们象族的语言交谈，还边聊边走。

小图麦还趴在象背上，俯视着数十个宽阔的象背，他们摇晃着耳朵，甩着鼻子，滚动着小眼睛。他听到了象牙交错碰撞的咔嗒声，象鼻交缠发出的沙沙声，巨大的肩膀和侧身的相互摩擦声，不断晃动的象尾的拍打声。然后，月亮被一道云彩遮盖，小图麦坐在黑暗之中。

shoulders in the crowd, and the incessant flick andhisshof the great tails. Then a cloud came over the moon, and he sat in black darkness; but the quiet, steady hustling and pushing and gurgling went on just the same. He knew that there were elephants all round Kala Nag, and that there was no chance of backing him out of the assembly; so he set his teeth and shivered. In a Keddah at least there was torch-light and shouting, but here he was all alone in the dark, and once a trunk came up and touched him on the knee.

Then an elephant trumpeted, and they all took it up for five or ten terrible seconds. The dew from the trees above spattered down like rain on the unseen backs, and a dull booming noise began, not very loud at first, and Little Toomai could not tell what it was; but it grew and grew, and Kala Nag lifted up one fore foot and then the other, and brought them down on the ground – one-two, one-two, as steadily as trip-hammers. The elephants were stamping altogether now, and it sounded like a war-drum beaten at the mouth of a cave. The dew fell from the trees till there was no more left to fall,

不过黑暗之中，咕哝声依然安静、平稳而忙碌地继续着。小图麦清楚卡拉·纳格身旁站满了大象，他不可能脱离这场集会。于是他咬紧牙关，全身颤抖。在科达里，起码有火炬和人类的呐喊，可是在这黑暗之中，他却是独自一人。有那么一下子，一根象鼻子举起来碰到了他的膝盖。

然后，一头大象大声地吼叫，其他的大象跟着大叫了五到十秒钟，那声音很恐怖。树上的露水掉落在看不见的象背上，就像下雨一样一阵沉闷的轰鸣声开始了，最初的声音很小，小图麦不知道那是什么声响，可是声响越来越大。卡拉·纳格一只前脚抬起来，另外一只也抬起来，最后两只一起落在地上——一二、一二，规律得如杵锤一般。此时大象全都开始跺脚，听起来就像一只战鼓，放在山洞口击打。树上的露水滴落下来，一滴不剩。轰鸣声持续不断，震得大地跟着摇晃。小图麦为了挡住那声音，把双手放在耳朵上。可是他被巨大

and the booming went on, and the ground rocked and shivered, and Little Toomai put his hands up to his ears to shut out the sound. But it was all one gigantic jar that ran through him – this stamp of hundreds of heavy feet on the raw earth. Once or twice he could feel Kala Nag and all the others surge forward a few strides, and the thumping would change to the crushing sound of juicy green things being bruised, but in a minute or two the boom of feet on hard earth began again. A tree was creaking and groaning somewhere near him. He put out his arm and felt the bark, but Kala Nag moved forward, still tramping, and he could not tell where he was in the clearing. There was no sound from the elephants, except once, when two or three little calves squeaked together. Then he heard a thump and a shuffle, and the booming went on. It must have lasted fully two hours, and Little Toomai ached in every nerve; but he knew by the smell of the night air that the dawn was coming.

The morning broke in one sheet of pale yellow behind the green hills, and the booming stopped with the first ray, as though the light had been an order.

的声响贯穿全身——这是数百只沉重的象足一起跺在空地上。他有一两次感受到了卡拉·纳格和其他的大象们都向前进了几步，重击发出的声响最后演变成了多汁的绿色的东西被压伤的声音。一两分钟过后，坚硬的空地上跺脚的轰鸣声再次响起。一棵树，就在他附近吱吱嘎嘎地响。他伸出手臂去摸树皮，可是卡拉·纳格往前动了动，继续跺着脚。他不知道自己到底是在空地的什么位置。象群里没有发出声音，除了有一次，有两三头幼年象一起吱吱尖叫了两声。然后他听到了一声重击和曳脚而行的声音，轰鸣声又继续开始。象群持续了整整两个钟头，小图麦感到痛苦万分，不过他在夜晚的空气中感知，黎明就要到来。

清晨在青山背后射出淡黄色的光芒。当第一缕光线露出，象群就像收到指令一样，停止了轰鸣。小图麦脑袋的嗡嗡声还没有消除，

Before Little Toomai had got the ringing out of his head, before even he had shifted his position, there was not an elephant in sight except Kala Nag, Pudmini, and the elephant with the rope-galls, and there was neither sign nor rustle nor whisper down the hillsides to show where the others had gone.

Little Toomai stared again and again. The clearing, as he remembered it, had grown in the night. More trees stood in the middle of it, but the undergrowth and the jungle-grass at the sides had been rolled back. Little Toomai stared once more. Now he understood the trampling. The elephants had stamped out more room – had stamped the thick grass and juicy cane to trash, the trash into slivers, the slivers into tiny fibers, and the fibers into hard earth.

"Wah!" said Little Toomai, and his eyes were very heavy. "Kala Nag, my lord, let us keep by Pudmini and go to Peterson Sahib's camp, or I shall drop from thy neck."

The third elephant watched the two go away, snorted, wheeled round, and took his own path. He may have belonged to some little native king's establishment, fifty or sixty or a

就连姿势都没有变，就看不到一头大象了，只有眼前的卡拉·纳格、普德米尼，还有身上带着绳索勒痕的那头大象留在原地。没有留下任何痕迹，也没有沙沙的响声表明那些大象去了哪里。

小图麦一遍又一遍地凝视着，整片空地经过一夜之后，比他记忆中宽阔了许多，空地中间有了更多的树，但是周围的灌木丛和丛林草地向后退出不少。小图麦再次瞪大了双眼，此刻他明白了大象们为何踩脚。大象们是为了踩出更多的空间，他们将厚厚的草丛和多汁的甘蔗踩碎，然后再把碎片踩成薄片，把薄片踩至更小的纤维，最终将纤维变成硬土。

"哇！"小图麦说，他的眼皮快睁不开了，"卡拉·纳格，我的象王，让普德米尼带着我们去彼得森·萨比布的象营吧，不然的话，我就从你的象脖上掉下来了。"

第三头大象看那两头大象走了，哼了一声，转了一圈，自己走了。他可能隶属于某个本地小王，距离这里五六十英里，也或者一百英里之外。

hundred miles away.

Two hours later, as Petersen Sahib was eating early breakfast, his elephants, who had been double-chained that night, began to trumpet, and Pudmini, mired to the shoulders, with Kala Nag, very foot-sore, shambled into the camp.

Little Toomai's face was gray and pinched, and his hair was full of leaves and drenched with dew; but he tried to salute Petersen Sahib, and cried faintly: "The dance – the elephant-dance! I have seen it, and – I die!" As Kala Nag sat down, he slid off his neck in a dead faint.

But, since native children have no nerves worth speaking of, in two hours he was lying very contentedly in Petersen Sahib's hammock with Petersen Sahib's shooting-coat under his head, and a glass of warm milk, a little brandy, with a dash of quinine inside of him, and while the old hairy, scarred hunters of the jungles sat three-deep before him, looking at him as though he were a spirit, he told his tale in short words, as a child will, and wound up with:

"Now, if I lie in one word, send men to see, and they will find that the

两个钟头过后，彼得森·萨比布在吃早餐的时候，晚上被加了双层锁链的那些大象们开始吼叫起来。肩膀之下沾满污泥的普德米尼带着双脚疼痛的卡拉·纳格踏进了营地。

小图麦的脸上灰蒙蒙的，头发上沾满树叶，都被露水打湿了，不过他仍然硬撑着给彼得森·萨比布问安，虚弱地喊道："跳舞，大象跳舞了！我看到了大象跳舞，而且，我不行了。"卡拉·纳格坐下的时候，小图麦昏倒了，滑下了象脖。

不过，由于当地的孩子们是不会神经质的，两个小时以后，小图麦非常满足地躺在彼得森·萨比布的吊床上，头下枕着的是彼得森·萨比布捕猎的外衣，还喝下了一杯温热的牛奶、一小杯白兰地和几滴奎宁。满脸胡须、伤疤累累的丛林老猎手里三层外三层地挤在他面前，看着他，就好像看着一个精灵。小图麦非常简短地用小孩子的话说出看到的情景，最后说：

"好了，倘若我有一句虚言，你们派人去那里瞧瞧。他们会看

elephant-folk have trampled down more room in their dance-room, and they will find ten and ten, and many times ten, tracks leading to that dance-room. They made more room with their feet. I have seen it. Kala Nag took me, and I saw. Also Kala Nag is very leg-weary!"

Little Toomai lay back and slept all through the long afternoon and into the twilight, and while he slept Petersen Sahib and Machua Appa followed the track of the two elephants for fifteen miles across the hills. Petersen Sahib had spent eighteen years in catching elephants, and he had only once before found such a dance-place. Machua Appa had no need to look twice at the clearing to see what had been done there, or to scratch with his toe in the packed, rammed earth.

"The child speaks truth," said he. "All this was done last night, and I have counted seventy tracks crossing the river. See, Sahib, where Pudmini's leg-iron cut the bark of that tree! Yes; she was there too."

They looked at each other, and up and down, and they wondered; for the ways of elephants are beyond the wit of any man, black or white, to fathom.

到，大象们在他们跳舞的地方踩踏出了更多的空间。他们也会看到十条又十条，数十条通向那个舞场的小道。他们用双足踏出了更多的空间，我看到了，是卡拉·纳格把我带去的，我真的见到了。卡拉·纳格累得不行了。"

小图麦又睡了，整个下午都没有醒，一直睡到夜幕降临。彼得森·萨比布和马丘阿·阿帕趁着小图麦睡着的时候，跟着两头大象在山中穿越了十五英里的路。彼得森·萨比布在捕象这行干了十八年了，之前就发现过一次大象跳舞的场地。马丘阿·阿帕不需要再次确认那片空地上发生过什么，也无需在夯实的硬地上抠上一脚。

"那孩子没有撒谎，"他说，"所有这些都是昨晚完成的。我已经查过，有七十条越过河流到达此处的小道。瞧瞧，萨比布，普德米尼脚链在那棵树上划开了一个口子！是的，她也来过那儿。"

他们彼此看着，上下打量，心中充满疑惑。大象的行为方式超出了人类，不管是黑人还是白人的理解范畴。

"Forty years and five," said Machua Appa, "have I followed my lord, the elephant, but never have I heard that any child of man had seen what this child has seen. By all the Gods of the Hills, it is – what can we say?" and he shook his head.

When they got back to camp it was time for the evening meal. Peterson Sahib ate alone in his tent, but he gave orders that the camp should have two sheep and some fowls, as well as a double-ration of flour and rice and salt, for he knew that there would be a feast.

Big Toomai had come up hot-foot from the camp in the plains to search for his son and his elephant, and now that he had found them he looked at them as though he were afraid of them both. And there was a feast by the blazing campfires in front of the lines of picketed elephants, and Little Toomai was the hero of it all; and the big brown elephant-catchers, the trackers and drivers and ropers, and the men who know all the secrets of breaking the wildest elephants, passed him from one to the other, and they marked his forehead with blood from the breast of a newly killed jungle-cock, to show that he was a

"四五十年以来，"马丘阿·阿帕说，"我跟随我的大象王，还没听说过有人类的孩子见过这个孩子所见的东西。以所有的山神起誓，那是——我们能说什么呢？"他摇了摇头。

当他们回到营地，已经到了吃晚饭的时候。彼得森·萨比布在他的营帐内单独用餐，不过他下令宰两头羊，杀几只鸡鸭，以及双倍的面粉、大米和盐，因为他知道会有一场盛宴。

大图麦从平原的营地急匆匆地赶来寻找他的儿子和大象。他找到了，但是就那样看着，好像很害怕他们。在熊熊的营火旁，在拴在木桩上的象队面前，正在举行盛大的宴会，小图麦就是宴会上的英雄。高个子棕皮肤的大象捕手，追象人和赶象人、捆绑大象的伙计，还有掌握秘诀能将最疯狂的大象制服的厉害角色，将小图麦从一个人手中传给另外一个人，并且用新鲜的丛林公鸡的血液点在他的前额，表明他是丛林之民，大家承认他身份，所有的丛林之地都任由他出没。

forester, initiated and free of all the jungles.

And at last, when the flames died down, and the red light of the logs made the elephants look as though they had been dipped in blood too, Machua Appa, the head of all the drivers of all the Keddahs – Machua Appa, Petersen Sahib's other self, who had never seen a made road in forty years: Machua Appa, who was so great that he had no other name than Machua Appa – leaped to his feet, with Little Toomai held high in the air above his head, and shouted: "Listen, my brothers. Listen, too, you my lords in the lines there, for I, Machua Appa, am speaking! This little one shall no more be called Little Toomai, but Toomai of the Elephants, as his great-grandfather was called before him. What never man has seen he has seen through the long night, and the favor of the elephant-folk and of the Gods of the Jungles is with him. He shall become a great tracker; he shall become greater than I, even I, Machua Appa! He shall follow the new trail, and the stale trail, and the mixed trail, with a clear eye! He shall take no harm in the Keddah when he runs under their bellies to rope the wild tuskers; and if

最后，当火焰熄灭，原木上的红光使大象们看起来好像被浸入血中。马丘阿·阿帕，所有科达驱象手的老大，另一个彼得森·萨比布，四十年来从未见过一条人工制造出来的道路；马丘阿·阿帕，如此厉害，除了马丘阿·阿帕，没有过其他的名字一下子跳起。他将小小的图麦举过头顶，高喊道："听着，我的兄弟们，还有队列中我的象王们，因为我，马丘阿·阿帕在讲话！这个小家伙不应该再被称作小图麦，他应该被称作大象们的图麦。他的曾祖父在他之前被这样称呼。从未有人见过的东西，他在长长的夜晚看到了。他获得了象民和丛林之神的青睐。他会成长为伟大的捕象手，比我马丘阿·阿帕更加的强大。他清亮的双眼会追踪新的足迹、旧的足迹和混合的足迹！他在科达里奔跑在大象肚腩下面捆绑象牙的时候，大象们不会伤害他。倘若他在横冲直闯的公象面前摔倒的时候，公象们会认出他，不会踩压他。啊嗨！我的拴着铁链的象王们，"他快速行走在尖木桩上，"看见你们在隐秘的地方跳舞的小家伙就在这儿，他见到了人类从未见识过的景象！将荣耀授予他，

he slips before the feet of the charging bull-elephant that bull-elephant shall know who he is and shall not crush him. Aihai! my lords in the chains," – he whirled up the line of pickets, – "here is the little one that has seen your dances in your hidden places – the sight that never man saw! Give him honor, my lords!Salaam karo, my children. Make your salute to Toomai of the Elephants! Gunga Pershad, ahaa! Hira Guj, Birchi Guj, Kuttar Guj, ahaa! Pudmini, – thou hast seen him at the dance, and thou too, Kala Nag, my pearl among elephants! Ahaa! Together! To Toomai of the Elephants.Barrao!"

And at that last wild yell the whole line flung up their trunks till the tips touched their foreheads, and broke out into the full salute – the crashing trumpet-peal that only the Viceroy of India hears, the Salaamut of the Keddah.

But it was all for the sake of Little Toomai, who had seen what never man had seen before – the dance of the elephants at night and alone in the heart of the Garo hills!

我的象王们！萨拉姆卡罗，我的孩子们！向大象们的图麦敬礼！贡嘎·普夏德，啊啊啊！海亚·古基，伯奇·古基，昆塔·古基，啊啊啊！普德米尼，你在舞会上看见他了，还有你，卡拉·纳格，大象之中的珍珠，啊啊啊！一起向大象们的图麦致敬。来吧！"

在马丘阿·阿帕最后一次狂野的叫喊声中，整个队列的大象们都甩出了长鼻子，直到鼻尖碰到额头，用完整的欢呼表达敬意。这属于科达象营的致敬，只有印度总督才能听到的轰鸣声。

但是这一次是小图麦赢得了这份荣耀，他见到了人类从未见过的盛况——象群在伽罗山中心跳舞，就他一个人。

SHIV AND THE GRASSHOPPER

湿婆和蚱蜢

THE SONG THAT TOOMAI'S
MOTHER SANG TO THE BABY

这首歌是图麦妈妈唱给宝宝的

Shiv, who poured the harvest and made the winds to blow,

Sitting at the doorways of a day of long ago,

Gave to each his portion, food and toil and fate,

From the King upon the guddee to the Beggar at the gate.

All things made he – Shiva the Preserver,

Mahadeo! Mahadeo! he made all, –

Thorn for the camel, fodder for the kine,

And mother's heart for sleepy head, O little son of mine!

Wheat he gave to rich folk, millet to the poor,

Broken scraps for holy men that beg from door to door;

Cattle to the tiger, carrion to the kite,

湿婆神，你让我们满载而归，顺风顺水，

很久之前的某一天，他就坐在门口，

给每人分上一份食物，一份劳碌和一种命运。

王座上的国王，大门口的乞丐谁都不落，

湿婆守护者，一切由他决定！

马哈德奥！马哈德奥！一切任他创造！

带刺的给骆驼，饲料留给母牛，

妈妈的心里是熟睡的小脑瓜，我的小儿子！

他把小麦分给富人，小米送给穷人，

挨家乞讨的只有残羹冷炙，

老虎要去战斗，老鹰却有腐

And rags and bones to wicked wolves without the wall at night.

Naught he found too lofty, none he saw too low –

Parbati beside him watched them come and go;

Thought to cheat her husband, turning Shiv to jest –

Stole the little grasshopper and hid it in her breast.

So she tricked him, Shiva the Preserver.

Mahadeo! Mahadeo! Turn and see.

Tall are the camels, heavy are the kine,

But this was least of little things, O little son of mine!

When the dole was ended, laughingly she said,

"Master, of a million mouths is not one unfed?"

Laughing, Shiv made answer,

"All have had their part,

Even he, the little one, hidden 'neath thy heart."

From her breast she plucked it, Parbati the thief,

Saw the Least of Little Things

破烂和骨头留给到处流浪的恶狼。

他不会觉得谁高尚,也不会觉得谁低贱,

站在旁边的帕尔巴蒂看着他们来来往往,

她想骗一骗她的丈夫,就跟湿婆开了个玩笑,

她偷走了小蚱蜢,把它藏在自己的胸窝里。

她成功地欺骗了他,湿婆神保护者。

马哈德奥!马哈德奥!快转身看看,

高个子的是骆驼,沉重的是母牛,

可他才是最小的家伙,我的小儿子!

当分派结束,她笑着问:

"百万生灵之主啊,有谁可被落下?"

湿婆笑着回应:

"所有生灵都分到了一份,

即使你藏在胸口的小家伙,也没被落下。"

她从胸口掏出了小蚱蜢,帕尔巴蒂偷走的那只,

gnawed a new-grown leaf!

Saw and feared and wondered, making prayer to Shiv,

Who hath surely given meat to all that live.

All things made he – Shiva the Preserver.

Mahadeo! Mahadeo! he made all, –

Thorn for the camel, fodder for the kine,

And mother's heart for sleepy head, O little son of mine!

见到它正在啃食一片新鲜的叶子！

她看着，有些害怕也有些疑惑，赶紧向湿婆神祷告，

他确实将食物分给所有的生灵。

湿婆守护者，一切由他决定！

马哈德奥！马哈德奥！一切任他创造！

带刺的给骆驼，饲料留给母牛，

妈妈的心里是熟睡的小脑瓜，我的小儿子！

CHAPTER 7 SERVANTS OF THE QUEEN

第七章 女王陛下的仆人

YOU can work it out by Fractions or by simple Rule of Three,

But the way of Tweedle-dum is not the way of Tweedle-dee.

You can twist it, you can turn it, you can plait it till you drop

But the way of Pilly-Winky's not the way of Winkie-Pop!

分数或者简单的三规则就可以让你算明白，

不过嘀嘟当与嘀嘟嘀不同。

你可以扭动，可以转，可以编，直到你住手，

只是皮里温科的方法不适用温基帕普。

IT had been raining heavily for one whole month – raining on a camp of thirty thousand men, thousands of camels, elephants, horses, bullocks, and mules, all gathered together at a place called Rawal Pindi, to be reviewed by the Viceroy of India. He was receiving a visit from the Amir of Afghanistan – a wild king of a very wild country; and the Amir had brought with him for a bodyguard eight hundred men and horses who had never seen a camp or a locomotive before in their lives – savage men and savage horses from somewhere at the back of Central Asia.

整整一个月都在下大雨，一个名叫拉瓦尔品第的地方聚集了三万士兵，几千匹骆驼、大象、马、公牛和骡子，一切都在等待印度总督审查。总督正在接待来访的阿富汗埃米尔——这是一个野蛮国家的野蛮国王。埃米尔带了八百人马作为保镖随从，他们从未见过营地或火车头——这群来自中亚后方的野蛮人和野蛮的马匹。每个晚上，这群马匹中一定会有几匹挣脱脚链，在漆黑的夜晚在泥泞的营地上到处践踏。或者就是有骆驼挣脱了绳索，跑来跑去，翻倒在帐篷的绳索上。你能想象得出来，对于那

Every night a mob of these horses would be sure to break their heel-ropes, and stampede up and down the camp through the mud in the dark, or the camels would break loose and run about and fall over the ropes of the tents, and you can imagine how pleasant that was for men trying to go to sleep. My tent lay far away from the camel lines, and I thought it was safe; but one night a man popped his head in and shouted, "Get out, quick! They're coming! My tent's gone!"

I knew who "they" were; so I put on my boots and waterproof and scuttled out into the slush. Little Vixen, my fox-terrier, went out through the other side; and then there was a roaring and a grunting and bubbling, and I saw the tent cave in, as the pole snapped, and begin to dance about like a mad ghost. A camel had blundered into it, and wet and angry as I was, I could not help laughing. Then I ran on, because I did not know how many camels might have got loose, and before long I was out of sight of the camp, plowing my way through the mud.

At last I fell over the tail-end of a gun, and by that knew I was somewhere near the Artillery lines

些试图入睡的人们来说，这是多么的有趣。我的帐篷远离骆驼营地，我觉得这样很安全，但是一天晚上，一个人突然冒出脑袋喊道："快点出去把！他们来啦！我的帐篷都没了！"

我清楚"他们"指谁，于是马上将靴子和防水衣穿上，然后溜进烂泥里。我的猎狐犬小维克森在帐篷的另一端跑出去了。然后就是一阵咆哮声、咕噜声和冒泡声，我看到帐篷因支撑它的杆子断了，随即瘪掉，看起来就像疯鬼一样跳舞。是一匹骆驼进入了我的帐篷。我浑身湿透了，气愤得很，不过还是忍不住大笑起来。然后我继续向前跑，因为我不清楚多少匹骆驼挣脱了绳索，我穿行在泥泞中，很快，营地就不在视线之中了。

最后我在一门大炮的尾部摔倒了，这才让我明白我是在炮兵营地周围，晚上的时候大炮都堆积在

where the cannon were stacked at night. As I did not want to plowter about any more in the drizzle and the dark, I put my waterproof over the muzzle of one gun, and made a sort of wigwam with two or three rammers that I found, and lay along the tail of another gun, wondering where Vixen had got to, and where I might be.

Just as I was getting ready to sleep I heard a jingle of harness and a grunt, and a mule passed me shaking his wet ears. He belonged to a screw-gun battery, for I could hear the rattle of the straps and rings and chains and things on his saddle-pad. The screw-guns are tidy little cannon made in two pieces, that are screwed together when the time comes to use them. They are taken up mountains, anywhere that a mule can find a road, and they are very useful for fighting in rocky country.

Behind the mule there was a camel, with his big soft feet squelching and slipping in the mud, and his neck bobbing to and fro like a strayed hen's. Luckily, I knew enough of beast language – not wild-beast language, but camp-beast language, of course – from the natives to know what he was saying.

这里。因为我不想黑夜中再继续淋着细雨到处跑，所以我把防水衣套在一门大炮的炮口上，并用两三根炮管搭了一个简易的小棚子，顺着另一门大炮的尾端躺下。猜想着维克森往哪跑了，自己又栖身何处。

就在我要睡觉的时候，我听到马具叮叮当当的声音和一声咕噜，原来是一头骡子从我身旁经过，摇晃着他湿漉漉的耳朵。他从属于螺式炮炮兵连，因为我能听到皮带、铁环、铁链等东西在他的鞍垫上发出的响声。螺式炮是由两大件组成的小型炮，使用的时候要把它们拧到一起。螺式炮能被送到高山上骡子能找得到路的任何地方，因此在岩石地区的战斗中，作用很大。

一匹骆驼跟在骡子后面，他软软的大脚吧唧吧唧地踩在泥地上，还不断地打滑，脖子像一只迷路的母鸡一样来回晃动。幸运的是，我跟当地人学会了足够多的兽语——当然不是指野兽的语言，而是在兵营中的兽语，因此我知道他说的是什么内容。

He must have been the one that flopped into my tent, for he called to the mule, "What shall I do? Where shall I go? I have fought with a white thing that waved, and it took a stick and hit me on the neck." (That was my broken tent-pole, and I was very glad to know it.) "Shall we run on?"

"Oh, it was you," said the mule, "you and your friends, that have been disturbing the camp? All right. You'll be beaten for this in the morning; but I may as well give you something on account now."

I heard the harness jingle as the mule backed and caught the camel two kicks in the ribs that rang like a drum. "Another time," he said, "you'll know better than to run through a mule-battery at night, shouting 'Thieves and fire!' Sit down, and keep your silly neck quiet."

The camel doubled up camel-fashion, like a two-foot rule, and sat down whimpering. There was a regular beat of hoofs in the darkness, and a big troop-horse cantered up as steadily as though he were on parade, jumped a gun-tail, and landed close to the mule.

"It's disgraceful," he said, blowing

刚才闯进我帐篷的骆驼肯定就是这一匹,因为他跟骡子叫嚷着:"我要怎么做呢?我要去哪儿呢?我同一个白色的摇晃的东西打斗了一场,然后它用一根棍子打我的脖子(那是我帐篷杆子断了,我很高兴听到他这么说)。我们要接着跑吗?"

"哦,是你干的啊,"骡子说,"是你和你的朋友们搅乱了营地?好吧。你们明天早晨会因此挨揍的。但是我现在可以先赊你一些。"

我听到马具叮当的响声,骡子往后退了几下,踢了骆驼肋骨两脚,就好像在打鼓。"下一次,"他说,"你就会知道不要在夜晚跑进螺式炮兵营,喊着:'有小偷,着火了!'坐下来,让你那愚蠢的脖子不要乱晃。"

骆驼用他的方式把身体弓了起来,如同两只脚的尺子[1],坐在那里呜咽着。黑暗之中一阵规律的马蹄声响起,一匹高高大大的战马像游行一样平稳地跑着。他跳过大炮的尾端,落在骡子的附近。

"好丢脸,"他说着,喷了喷

---

[1] 一种老式尺子,形状类似圆规。

out his nostrils. "Those camels have racketed through our lines again – the third time this week. How's a horse to keep his condition if he isn't allowed to sleep? Who's here?"

"I'm the breech-piece mule of number two gun of the First Screw Battery," said the mule, "and the other's one of your friends. He's waked me up too. Who are you?"

"Number Fifteen, E troop, Ninth Lancers – Dick Cunliffe's horse. Stand over a little, there."

"Oh, beg your pardon," said the mule. "It's too dark to see much. Aren't these camels too sickening for anything? I walked out of my lines to get a little peace and quiet here."

"My lords," said the camel humbly, "we dreamed bad dreams in the night, and we were very much afraid. I am only a baggage-camel of the 39th Native Infantry, and I am not so brave as you are, my lords."

"Then why the pickets didn't you stay and carry baggage for the 39th Native Infantry, instead of running all round the camp?" said the mule.

"They were such very bad dreams," said the camel. "I am sorry. Listen! What is that? Shall we run on again?"

鼻息，"那些骆驼再次搅和了我们的兵营。这周已经是第三回了。倘若晚上不让一匹战马睡觉，怎么让他在白天保持状态？谁在这里？"

"我是第一螺式炮炮兵连第二号炮的炮后端骡子，"骡子说，"而另一个是你的朋友。他也把我弄醒了，你是谁呀？"

"第九骑兵团，E连，十五号，我是迪克·库立夫的战马。往旁边站一点儿，那边儿。"

"哦，真抱歉，"骡子说，"太黑了，没看清楚。这些骆驼是不是讨厌得过分？我走出了营地，想在这里找到一些安宁。"

"我的大人们，"骆驼语气很谦恭，"我们晚上的时候做的噩梦，吓到了我们。我只是负责第三十九本土步兵营运送行李的，我没有你们那样有胆识，我的大人们。"

"那为什么你不待在三十九步兵营，好好地运送行李，而是跑到兵营里乱窜？"骡子说。

"那是非常可怕的梦，"骆驼说，"我真的很抱歉。听啊！那是什么？我们要接着跑吗？"

"Sit down," said the mule, "or you'll snap your long legs between the guns." He cocked one ear and listened. "Bullocks!" he said; "gun-bullocks. On my word, you and your friends have waked the camp very thoroughly. It takes a good deal of prodding to put up a gun-bullock."

I heard a chain dragging along the ground, and a yoke of the great sulky white bullocks that drag the heavy siege-guns when the elephants won't go any nearer to the firing, came shouldering along together; and almost stepping on the chain was another battery-mule, calling wildly for "Billy."

"That's one of our recruits," said the old mule to the troop-horse. "He's calling for me. Here, youngster, stop squealing; the dark never hurt anybody yet."

The gun-bullocks lay down together and began chewing the cud, but the young mule huddled close to Billy.

"Things!" he said; "fearful and horrible things, Billy! They came into our lines while we were asleep. D'you think they'll kill us?"

"I've a very great mind to give you a number one kicking," said Billy. "The idea of a fourteen-hand mule with your

"坐下吧，"骡子说，"要不然你会在大炮中间折断你的几条大长腿的。"他竖起了耳朵，听了听，"是公牛！"他说，"炮兵连的公牛。我说啊，你和你的朋友们已经将兵营彻底吵醒了。没有很大的声响，根本吵不醒公牛的。"

我听到了地上拖动着铁链子，同轭的两头公牛气哄哄地一起走了过来。当大象们不肯接近战场的时候，就是这些公牛拉着沉重的炮弹走上前去。随后另外一头骡子也过来了，他几乎踩在了锁链上，嘴里大喊着："比利。"

"这是我们的新成员，"老骡子告诉战马，"他在喊我。在这里，年轻人，不要再喊了。黑夜不会伤到任何人的。"

那两头炮兵团的公牛一起躺下，咀嚼起反刍的食物。年轻的骡子挤在了比利跟前。

"有东西！"他说，"真吓人，真让人讨厌，比利！趁我们熟睡的时候，他们跑进我们的营地，你认为我们会被他们杀掉吗？"

"我有一个想法特别好，我真想好好地踢你一脚，"比利说，"在这位先生面前，你这头受过训练的

training disgracing the battery before this gentleman!"

"Gently, gently!" said the troop-horse. "Remember they are always like this to begin with. The first time I ever saw a man (it was in Australia when I was a three-year-old) I ran for half a day, and if I'd seen a camel I should have been running still."

Nearly all our horses for the English cavalry are brought to India from Australia, and are broken in by the troopers themselves.

"True enough," said Billy. "Stop shaking, youngster. The first time they put the full harness with all its chains on my back, I stood on my fore legs and kicked every bit of it off. I hadn't learned the real science of kicking then, but the battery said they had never seen anything like it."

"But this wasn't harness or anything that jingled," said the young mule. "You know I don't mind that now, Billy. It was Things like trees, and they fell up and down the lines and bubbled; and my head-rope broke, and I couldn't find my driver, and I couldn't find you, Billy, so I ran off with – with these gentlemen."

有十四只手那么高的骡子，竟然给炮兵连丢脸。"

"温和一些，温和一些，"战马说，"记住，他们起初的时候都这样。我第一次见到一个男人（那是我三岁的时候在澳大利亚），我跑了半天。若是我看到的是骆驼，我应该会一直跑。"

几乎所有派驻印度的英国骑兵的战马都是来自澳大利亚，骑兵们会亲自训练这些战马。

"这确实是真话，"比利说，"不要抖了，小伙子。他们第一次将全部的带链子的马具搁到我背上的时候，我前腿直立着，后腿一抬，蹬掉了所有的马具。我那时候还没有学会什么是真正的踢腿，但是炮兵连的人说他们从未见过我那样的。"

"但是那跟马具，还有叮当响的东西不是一回事儿，"年轻的骡子说，"你明白现在那些已经吓不到我了，比利。他们看起来就像树，在营地里上下起伏，还冒泡呢。我头上的绳索断开了，我找不到骑我的那个人，你也不见了，比利。所以我就跑出来了，跟着这两位先生。"

"Hm!" said Billy. "As soon as I heard the camels were loose I came away on my own account, quietly. When a battery – a screw-gun mule calls gun-bullocks gentlemen, he must be very badly shaken up. Who are you fellows on the ground there?"

The gun-bullocks rolled their cuds, and answered both together: "The seventh yoke of the first gun of the Big Gun Battery. We were asleep when the camels came, but when we were trampled on we got up and walked away. It is better to lie quiet in the mud than to be disturbed on good bedding. We told your friend here that there was nothing to be afraid of, but he knew so much that he thought otherwise. Wah!"

They went on chewing.

"That comes of being afraid," said Billy. "You get laughed at by gun-bullocks. I hope you like it, young 'un."

The young mule's teeth snapped, and I heard him say something about not being afraid of any beefy old bullock in the world; but the bullocks only clicked their horns together and went on chewing.

"Now, don't be angryafteryou've been afraid. That's the worst kind of

"哼！"比利说，"一听到骆驼挣脱了绳索，我就悄悄地跑出来了。一头炮兵连———一头螺式炮兵连的骡子称呼公牛为先生，他一定是吓坏了。你们是谁，坐在地上的那两位？"

炮兵团的两头公牛，卷起反刍的食物，一起回应道："大炮兵团第一号大炮的第七轭。骆驼闯进来的时候，我们睡着了，他们踩到了我们，我们就站起来走开了。安静地在泥地里躺着也好过在舒服的草床上被骚扰。我们告诉过你的朋友，没什么好怕的，可是他知道太多的事了，他还有其他的想法。哇！"

两头公牛接着咀嚼食物。

"那是因为他害怕，"比利说，"你被炮兵连的公牛嘲笑了，我希望你能喜欢这样，年轻的小伙子。"

年轻的骡子咬牙切齿，我似乎听到他说了一些不惧怕世界上任何强壮的老公牛。可是那两头公牛只是互相碰了碰牛角，继续咀嚼着食物。

"好了，吓到之后别再生气，这样最糟糕了，"战马说，"不管是

cowardice," said the troop-horse. "Anybody can be forgiven for being scared in the night,Ithink, if they see things they don't understand. We've broken out of our pickets, again and again, four hundred and fifty of us, just because a new recruit got to telling tales of whip-snakes at home in Australia till we were scared to death of the loose ends of our head-ropes."

"That's all very well in camp," said Billy; "I'm not above stampeding myself, for the fun of the thing, when I haven't been out for a day or two; but what do you do on active service?"

"Oh, that's quite another set of new shoes," said the troop-horse. "Dick Cunliffe's on my back then, and drives his knees into me, and all I have to do is to watch where I am putting my feet, and to keep my hind legs well under me, and be bridle-wise."

"What's bridle-wise?" said the young mule.

"By the Blue Gums of the Back Blocks," snorted the troop-horse, "do you mean to say that you aren't taught to be bridle-wise in your business? How can you do anything, unless you can spin round at once when the rein is pressed on your neck? It means life or

谁，在晚上看见了他不知道的东西被吓到，这是能够被原谅的。我们一次又一次地弄断马桩，四五百匹战马，这是因为一个新来的战马一直在给我们讲述在澳大利亚鞭蛇的故事。我们所有的战马最后都被吓坏了，看到谁的头上有松散的绳子都吓得要死。"

"兵营里什么都不错，"比利说，"要是有两天我没有外出转悠，我也会到处窜窜，就是为了好玩儿。不过你当职的时候，都干些什么事情呢？"

"哦，那是完全不同的样子，"战马说，"迪克·库立夫会在我当职的时候骑在我的后背上，用膝盖夹住我。而我所要做的就是看好落脚的地方，并用后腿支撑好整个身体，机警地留意缰绳的指令。"

"机警地留意缰绳的指令是什么意思？"年轻的骡子说。

"以内部街区的蓝桉起誓，"战马哼了一声，"你是说你没有在当职的时候学着怎么机警地听从缰绳的指令？要不然你怎么做事呢？当脖子上的缰绳勒紧的时候，你就要立刻旋转。这关乎着你背上的人的生死，当然也关系到你的性

death to your man, and of course that's life or death to you. Get round with your hind legs under you the instant you feel the rein on your neck. If you haven't room to swing round, rear up a little and come round on your hind legs. That's being bridle-wise."

"We aren't taught that way," said Billy the mule stiffly. "We're taught to obey the man at our head: step off when he says so, and step in when he says so. I suppose it comes to the same thing. Now, with all this fine fancy business and rearing, which must be very bad for your hocks, what do youdo?"

"That depends," said the troop-horse. "Generally I have to go in among a lot of yelling, hairy men with knives, – long shiny knives, worse than the farrier's knives, – and I have to take care that Dick's boot is just touching the next man's boot without crushing it. I can see Dick's lance to the right of my right eye, and I know I'm safe. I shouldn't care to be the man or horse that stood up to Dick and me when we're in a hurry."

"Don't the knives hurt?" said the young mule.

"Well, I got one cut across the chest

命。当你感觉到脖子上的缰绳动了，你就要马上用后腿支撑身体转个身。倘若当时没有足够的空间，你就要向后仰起身子，然后再靠后腿转身。这就是机警地听从缰绳的指令。"

"我们没有被这样训练过，"骡子比利倔强地说，"我们被教导要遵从前面的人：当他说齐步走的时候，我们就齐步走，他说插队的时候，我们就插队。我想这都是一回事。对了，你这些花样，还要用后腿支撑，肯定有损你的腿关节吧，你都干些什么呀？"

"看是什么情形了，"战马说，"基本上我必须要跑到一群大喊大叫、手里握着刀的多毛的人当中。那群人拿着长长的闪着光的大刀，比兽医的刀更可怕。我也必须小心迪克的靴子要恰好碰上另一个人的靴子，但是又不能挤到它。可以看到迪克的长矛就在我右眼的右侧时，我清楚我是安全的。当迪克与我迅速跑动的时候，我可不想变成站在迪克和我对面的那个人和那匹马。"

"那些大刀不会伤到你吗？"年轻的骡问。

"是的，我的胸部有一次被划

once, but that wasn't Dick's fault –"

"A lot I should have cared whose fault it was, if it hurt!" said the young mule.

"You must," said the troop-horse. "If you don't trust your man, you may as well run away at once. That's what some of our horses do, and I don't blame them. As I was saying, it wasn't Dick's fault. The man was lying on the ground, and I stretched myself not to tread on him, and he slashed up at me. Next time I have to go over a man lying down I shall step on him – hard."

"Hm!" said Billy; "it sounds very foolish. Knives are dirty things at any time. The proper thing to do is to climb up a mountain with a well-balanced saddle, hang on by all four feet and your ears too, and creep and crawl and wriggle along, till you come out hundreds of feet above any one else, on a ledge where there's just room enough for your hoofs. Then you stand still and keep quiet, – never ask a man to hold your head, young 'un, – keep quiet while the guns are being put together, and then you watch the little poppy shells drop down into the tree-tops ever so far below."

"Don't you ever trip?" said the

伤了，不过那次不怪迪克……"

"要是伤到了我，我应该会很关心是谁的过错！"年轻的骡子说。

"你必须要这样，"战马说，"倘若你对骑在背上的人不信任，你还是立刻逃走吧。这就是我们一些战马的做法，我不会怪他们。正如我刚刚说的，那不怪迪克。当时的情况是一个人正在地上躺着，为了不踩到他，我拉伸了一下身子起跳，然而他朝上一捅，我被划伤了。下次，我要是必须越过一个躺着的人，我就踩在他身上，用力地踩。"

"哼！"比利说，"这听起来真蠢。任何时候刀都是脏的。正确的做法是架上平衡很好的鞍座，依靠四条腿还有双耳，沿着坡朝上攀爬，一直到你超越其他人爬上数百英尺高的壁架上，那里的空间只能放下你的蹄子接下来站在那里一动不动，保持安静——一定不让人牵着你的脑袋，年轻的小伙子——不要出声，等大炮组装完成，然后你就看着小罂粟花掉落下面遥远的树尖之中。"

"你没被绊倒过吗？"战马

troop-horse.

"They say that when a mule trips you can split a hen's ear," said Billy. "Now and againper-hapsa badly packed saddle will upset a mule, but it's very seldom. I wish I could show you our business. It's beautiful. Why, it took me three years to find out what the men were driving at. The science of the thing is never to show up against the sky-line, because, if you do, you may get fired at. Remember that, young 'un. Always keep hidden as much as possible, even if you have to go a mile out of your way. I lead the battery when it comes to that sort of climbing."

"Fired at without the chance of running into the people who are firing!" said the troop-horse, thinking hard. "I couldn't stand that. I should want to charge, with Dick."

"Oh no, you wouldn't; you know that as soon as the guns are in positionthey'lldo all the charging. That's scientific and neat; but knives – pah!"

The baggage-camel had been bobbing his head to and fro for some time past, anxious to get a word in edgeways. Then I heard him say, as he cleared his throat, nervously:

说。

"人们都说，要是一只骡子被绊倒了，母鸡的耳朵也能被撕裂，"比利说，"有时候，马鞍没有架好的话，骡子可能会翻到一边，不过很少发生这样的事情。我希望能向你展示一下我们怎么干活的。很不错的。为什么呢？花了三年的时间，我才知道人类什么意思。这事儿里面的诀窍就是千万不要让自己暴露在大众面前。因为若是你暴露了自己，你就可能是攻击的目标。不要忘了这个，年轻的小伙子。要尽可能地永远藏好自己，即使你必须因此多走出一英里。当遇到这样爬山的时候，我就会领导整个炮兵团。"

"还没等到冲进开火的人当中，就被炮轰了！"战马边说，边努力思索，"我无法忍受那样，我应该要冲锋，跟着迪克一起。"

"哦，不，你不用的。你了解的，一旦大炮就绪，他们就要全部被填充。那很讲究，也很整洁。可是刀——噗！"

运送行李的骆驼很长一段时间一直在摆动他的脑袋，他急着想要插上一嘴。接下来我听到他清了清嗓子，紧张地说：

"I – I – I have fought a little, but not in that climbing way or that running way."

"No. Now you mention it," said Billy, "you don't look as though you were made for climbing or running – much. Well, how was it, old Hay-bales?"

"The proper way," said the camel. "We all sat down –"

"Oh, my crupper and breastplate!" said the troop-horse under his breath. "Sat down?"

"We sat down – a hundred of us," the camel went on, "in a big square, and the men piled our packs and saddles outside the square, and they fired over our backs, the men did, on all sides of the square."

"What sort of men? Any men that came along?" said the troop-horse. "They teach us in riding-school to lie down and let our masters fire across us, but Dick Cunliffe is the only man I'd trust to do that. It tickles my girths, and, besides, I can't see with my head on the ground."

"What does it matter who fires across you?" said the camel. "There are plenty of men and plenty of other camels close by, and a great many

"我，我，我也打过几仗，不过不是通过爬山，也不是奔跑。"

"不是，你现在提起这事，"比利说，"你看起来确实不太能爬，也不太能跑。好吧，你怎么做的，老干草包？"

"适合我们的方法，"骆驼说，"我们都坐下来……"

"哦，我的臀部和胸部护甲啊！"战马小声说，"坐下来？"

"我们坐下来——能有一百匹，"骆驼接着说，"就在一个方形的场地坐下，人们将我们的鞍具和背上的行李堆在场地外面，他们就在我们背后向外射击，在场地的各个方向。"

"都是些什么样的人？任何一个走上前来的人？"战马说，"在骑术学校的时候，我们被教导躺下，我们的主人会隔着我们射击，可是迪克·库立夫是唯一能让我信任可以这么做的。那样让我肚皮发痒，而且脑袋躺在地上，我什么都看不见了。"

"谁在你身后射击有什么关系？"骆驼说，"有很多的人和很多的骆驼就在身旁，到处是烟雾。那时我一点都不怕，我就老实地坐

clouds of smoke. I am not frightened then. I sit still and wait."

"And yet," said Billy, "you dream bad dreams and upset the camp at night. Well! well! Before I'd lie down, not to speak of sitting down, and let a man fire across me, my heels and his head would have something to say to each other. Did you ever hear anything so awful as that?"

There was a long silence, and then one of the gun-bullocks lifted up his big head and said, "This is very foolish indeed. There is only one way of fighting."

"Oh, go on," said Billy. "Pleasedon't mind me. I suppose you fellows fight standing on your tails?"

"Only one way," said the two together. (They must have been twins.) "This is that way. To put all twenty yoke of us to the big gun as soon as Two Tails trumpets." ("Two Tails" is camp slang for the elephant.)

"What does Two Tails trumpet for?" said the young mule.

"To show that he is not going any nearer to the smoke on the other side. Two Tails is a great coward. Then we tug the big gun all together – Heya – Hullah! Heeyah! Hullah! We do not

在那里等着。"

"然而，"比利说，"你晚上却做噩梦，将整个营地搅和得不得安宁。好了！好了！我还没躺下，不要说什么坐下来让人越过我射击之类的话，我的脚后跟他的脑袋互相要说些什么呢。你们有没有听过那么可怕的事情吗？"

很长时间的沉默，然后其中一只炮兵连的公牛抬起他的大脑袋，说："这种方式真的非常蠢。打仗只有一种方法。"

"哦，接着说，"比利说，"别管我。我猜想你们会尾巴翘起来打仗？"

"只有一种方法，"两头公牛一起说（他们肯定是双生兄弟），"就是这样子的，在双尾吹喇叭的时候，将我们所有的二十轭公牛全套在大炮上。"（"双尾"是营地中大象的俚语叫法。）

"双尾吹喇叭是干什么？"年轻的骡子说。

"为了表明他不会朝另一边的烟雾再靠近了。双尾明显就是个懦夫。然后我们全部用力拉大炮——嗨呀——呼啊！嘿呀！呼啊！我们不会跟猫一样爬，也不会跟小

climb like cats nor run like calves. We go across the level plain, twenty yoke of us, till we are unyoked again, and we graze while the big guns talk across the plain to some town with mud walls, and pieces of the wall fall out, and the dust goes up as though many cattle were coming home."

"Oh! And you choose that time for grazing do you?" said the young mule.

"That time or any other. Eating is always good. We eat till we are yoked up again and tug the gun back to where Two Tails is waiting for it. Sometimes there are big guns in the city that speak back, and some of us are killed, and then there is all the more grazing for those that are left. This is Fate – nothing but Fate. None the less, Two Tails is a great coward. That is the proper way to fight. We are brothers from Hapur. Our father was a sacred bull of Shiva. We have spoken."

"Well, I've certainly learned something tonight," said the troop-horse. "Do you gentlemen of the screw-gun battery feel inclined to eat when you are being fired at with big guns, and Two Tails is behind you?"

"About as much as we feel inclined to sit down and let men sprawl all over

牛一样跑。我们二十轭的公牛拉着大炮穿越平原，直到我们放下装备。当那些大炮越过平原对着一些有泥土城墙的城镇讲话的时候，我们就吃草。城墙掉下碎片，尘土越来越多，好像很多牛在往家跑。"

"哦，那种时候你们竟然选择吃草？"年轻的骡子说。

"那个时候或者其他什么时候，吃东西总是很好的。一直吃到再次将轭套在我们的身上，我们拉着大炮返回双尾等待的地点。一些时候，会有城里的大炮回击我们，我们当中有些牛就是这样被杀的，然后剩下的牛就可以吃更多的草。这是命运，无论如何，双尾明显就是懦夫。这是打仗最适合的方法。我们兄弟来自哈普尔，我们的父亲被献给了湿神婆，这一点我们讲过了。"

"好吧，我今晚确实学到一些什么，"战马说，"当有大炮才朝你们射击，后方还有双尾的时候，两位先生还惦记着吃东西吗？"

"那和我们愿意坐下来让人们趴在我们身上展开手脚，或者拿

us, or run into people with knives. I never heard such stuff. A mountain ledge, a well-balanced load, a driver you can trust to let you pick your own way, and I'm your mule; but the other things – no!" said Billy, with a stamp of his foot.

"Of course," said the troop-horse, "every one is not made in the same way, and I can quite see that your family, on your father's side, would fail to understand a great many things."

"Never you mind my family on my father's side," said Billy angrily; for every mule hates to be reminded that his father was a donkey. "My father was a Southern gentleman, and he could pull down and bite and kick into rags every horse he came across. Remember that, you big brown Brumby!"

Brumby means wild horse without any breeding. Imagine the feelings of Ormonde if a 'bus-horse called him a cocktail, and you can imagine how the Australian horse felt. I saw the white of his eye glitter in the dark.

"See here, you son of an imported Málaga jackass," he said between his teeth, "I'd have you know that I'm related on my mother's side to Carbine,

着大刀冲进人群差不多。我可没听过这种事。山峰的边缘，平衡的鞍座，一个让人信任的骑手，允许自己挑选线路，我就是你的骡子。但是其他的事情，不行！"比利跺了跺脚，说。

"当然啊，"战马说，"每个动物天生都不一样。我非常明白你的家人，从你父亲那边来说的话，是没法儿懂得很多事情的。"

"不要扯上我家族的父系，"比利很生气，因为每头骡子都不喜欢被别人提醒他的父亲是一头驴，"我的父亲是南方的一位绅士，他可以摞倒每一匹他遇到的马，将他们撕咬成碎片。不要忘记这个，你这匹高个子棕色的布朗比！"

布朗比的意思是没有教养的野马。想象一下，要是一匹拉车的马称呼奥曼德为"没用的老东西"，他的感受会怎么样，你就能体会澳大利亚马的心情了。我看到了他的眼睛在黑暗之中闪闪发光。

"往这儿看，进口的马拉加公驴的儿子，"他咬着牙说，"我想让你清楚，我母系这边儿与卡尔宾是亲戚，她可是墨尔本杯冠军得主。

winner of the Melbourne Cup, and where I come from we aren't accustomed to being ridden over roughshod by any parrot-mouthed, pig-headed mule in a pop-gun peashooter battery. Are you ready?"

"On your hind legs!" squealed Billy. They both reared up facing each other, and I was expecting a furious fight, when a gurgly, rumbly voice called out of the darkness to the right – "Children, what are you fighting about there? Be quiet."

Both beasts dropped down with a snort of disgust, for neither horse nor mule can bear to listen to an elephant's voice.

"It's Two Tails!" said the troop-horse. "I can't stand him. A tail at each end isn't fair!"

"My feelings exactly," said Billy, crowding into the troop-horse for company. "We're very alike in some things."

"I suppose we've inherited them from our mothers," said the troop-horse. "It's not worth quarreling about. Hi! Two Tails, are you tied up?"

"Yes," said Two Tails, with a laugh all up his trunk. "I'm picketed for the night. I've heard what you fellows have

在我们老家，我们可看不惯那些鹦鹉嘴、猪脑袋、摆弄着蹩脚的玩具枪的炮兵连的骡子在我们面前横行霸道。你们准备好了吗？"

"抬起你的前腿！"比利尖叫着。他们后脚直立，头对着头，我期待着一场大战的到来。这时候，一个低沉的咕噜咕噜的声音从左边传出："孩子们，你们为什么在那边打斗？安静。"

两头畜生都厌恶地哼了一声，把蹄子落下。因为不管是马或者是骡子，都忍不了大象的声音。

"那是双尾！"战马说，"我无法忍受。他两端都有尾巴，多不公平！"

"我也这么觉得，"比利边说，边挤到战马的边上做伴，"我们在某些事情上非常相似。"

"我想我们是从母亲那里继承下来的，"战马说，"一点都不值得争执。嗨！双尾，你被绑着吗？"

"是的，"双尾抬起长鼻子笑道，"晚上我被拴在木桩上。我听到了你们刚刚说的话。不过不要害

been saying. But don't be afraid. I'm not coming over."

The bullocks and the camel said, half aloud: "Afraid of Two Tails – what nonsense!" And the bullocks went on: "We are sorry that you heard, but it is true. Two Tails, why are you afraid of the guns when they fire?"

"Well," said Two Tails, rubbing one hind leg against the other, exactly like a little boy saying a piece, "I don't quite know whether you'd understand."

"We don't, but we have to pull the guns," said the bullocks.

"I know it, and I know you are a good deal braver than you think you are. But it's different with me. My battery captain called me a Pachydermatous Anachronism the other day."

"That's another way of fighting, I suppose?" said Billy, who was recovering his spirits.

"You don't know what that means, of course, but I do. It means betwixt and between, and that is just where I am. I can see inside my head what will happen when a shell bursts; and you bullocks can't."

"I can," said the troop-horse. "At least a little bit. I try not to think about

怕，我不会过来的。"

两头公牛和骆驼压低声音说："惧怕双尾——真是荒唐！"公牛们继续说："我们很抱歉这样讲，可是这都是事实。双尾，为什么大炮开火的时候，你那么害怕？"

"好吧，"双尾说这话的时候，一条后腿蹭了蹭另外一条后腿，就像一个小男孩在读诗一样，"我不知道你们是否能够理解。"

"我们不能理解，不过我们不得不拉那些大炮。"公牛们说。

"我知道这个，我知道你们比自己认为的更要英勇，可我不同。有一天，我们炮兵团的上尉称呼我们是跟不上时代的厚脸皮。"

"我想这是打仗的另一种方式？"正恢复精神的比利说。

"你当然不知道这是什么意思，但是我知道。这就是说我们介于两者之间，不是马也不是骡子。这就是我所处的位置。我脑袋里明白炮弹爆炸有什么结果，你们公牛不知道。"

"我可以，"战马说，"至少一点点，我尽量不去想它。"

it."

"I can see more than you, and Idothink about it. I know there's a great deal of me to take care of, and I know that nobody knows how to cure me when I'm sick. All they can do is to stop my driver's pay till I get well, and I can't trust my driver."

"Ah!" said the troop-horse. "That explains it. I can trust Dick."

"You could put a whole regiment of Dicks on my back without making me feel any better. I know just enough to be uncomfortable, and not enough to go on in spite of it."

"We do not understand," said the bullocks.

"I know you don't. I'm not talking to you. You don't know what blood is."

"We do," said the bullocks. "It is red stuff that soaks into the ground and smells."

The troop-horse gave a kick and a bound and a snort.

"Don't talk of it," he said. "I can smell it now, just thinking of it. It makes me want to run – when I haven't Dick on my back."

"But it is not here," said the camel and the bullocks. "Why are you so stupid?"

"我看到的比你更多，并且我会思量这个结果。我清楚我要照顾好自己，因为我明白要是我病了，谁也不知道如何治疗。他们所能做的就是把我的骑手的薪水停掉，直到我康复，并且我的骑手不能信赖。"

"啊!"战马说，"这就是原因了。我能够信任迪克。"

"即使你能在我背上放一个团队的迪克，我也不会感觉舒服一些。我尝尽了太多的不舒服，可是也没足够到让我无所谓地继续生活。"

"我们不理解。"两头公牛说。

"我清楚你们不懂，我不是在和你们讲，你们连血是什么都不知道。"

"我们知道，"公牛说，"血是红色的，能浸到地下，闻起来还有味道。"

战马踢了一脚，跳了一下，鼻子一哼。

"不要说这个，"他说，"只是想想，我现在就能闻到血腥味儿。当迪克没有在我后背上的时候，这味道让我想逃跑。"

"可是这地方没有血，"骆驼和两头公牛说，"你为什么这么

"It's vile stuff," said Billy. "I don't want to run, but I don't want to talk about it."

"There you are!" said Two Tails, waving his tail to explain.

"Surely. Yes, we have been here all night," said the bullocks.

Two Tails stamped his foot till the iron ring on it jingled. "Oh, I'm not talking toyou. You can't see inside your heads."

"No. We see out of our four eyes," said the bullocks. "We see straight in front of us."

"If I could do that and nothing else you wouldn't be needed to pull the big guns at all. If I was like my captain – he can see things inside his head before the firing begins, and he shakes all over, but he knows too much to run away – if I was like him I could pull the guns. But if I were as wise as all that I should never be here. I should be a king in the forest, as I used to be, sleeping half the day and bathing when I liked. I haven't had a good bath for a month."

"That's all very fine," said Billy; "but giving a thing a long name doesn't make it any better."

"Hsh!" said the troop-horse. "I think

蠢？"

"血是可恶的，"比利说，"我不想跑，但是我也不想谈论它。"

"你们在那边啊！"双尾说，摇起尾巴解释。

"当然，是的，我们整晚上都在这里啊。"两头公牛说。

双尾跺着脚，直到拴在脚上的铁环叮当作响，"哦，我没有跟你们讲话，脑子里的东西你们看不到。"

"是啊，我们的四只眼睛能看到，"公牛说，"我们笔直地看着前方。"

"倘若我能做到这一点，除此之外什么都看不到，就无需你们拉大炮了。倘若我能像我的上尉一样——射击之前他可以看见脑袋里的东西，全身都在颤抖，可他知道太多，逃不掉——倘若我能像他一样，我就能拉大炮。可是我若有他们那么聪明，我就肯定不待在这里了。我会像过去一样成为森林里的国王，睡半天觉，什么时候想洗澡就去洗。我一个月没有好好洗个澡了。"

"都非常不错，"比利说，"可是说再多好听的也改善不了什么。"

"嘘！"战马说，"我觉得我知

I understand what Two Tails means."

"You'll understand better in a minute," said Two Tails angrily. "Now, just you explain to me why you don't like this!"

He began trumpeting furiously at the top of his trumpet.

"Stop that!" said Billy and the troop-horse together, and I could hear them stamp and shiver. An elephant's trumpeting is always nasty, especially on a dark night.

"I shan't stop," said Two Tails. "Won't you explain that, please? Hhrrmþh! Rrrt! Rrrmph! Rrrhha!" Then he stopped suddenly, and I heard a little whimper in the dark, and knew that Vixen had found me at last. She knew as well as I did that if there is one thing in the world the elephant is more afraid of than another it is a little barking dog; so she stopped to bully Two Tails in his pickets, and yapped round his big feet. Two Tails shuffled and squeaked. "Go away, little dog!" he said. "Don't snuff at my ankles, or I'll kick at you. Good little dog – nice little doggie, then! Go home, you yelping little beast! Oh, why doesn't some one take her away? She'll bite me in a minute."

道双尾意味着什么了。"

"你会在一分钟以后理解得更透彻，"双尾生气地说，"现在，跟我解释一下，为什么你们不喜欢这样！"

他开始用最大的音量喊。

"停下来吧！"比利和战马一起说。我可以听到他们跺起脚，在打战。大象的叫声总是令人讨厌，特别是在黑暗的夜晚。

"我不停下，"双尾说，"请你们解释一下，好吗？嗯呃！噗！啊呃！啊呜！啊哈！"然后他突然停了下来，我在黑暗中听到一丝呜咽声，我知道是维克森终于发现我了。她和我一样清楚要是世界上有一种东西是大象最害怕的，那就是一直狂叫的小狗。于是她停下来，欺负起拴在木桩上的双尾，围绕着他的大脚大声叫嚷。双尾拖着脚尖叫道，"走开！小狗！"他说，"不要在我的脚踝这儿嗅，要不然我会踢你。好小狗，友善的小狗，没完了？！回家去，你这个乱叫的小畜生！哦，为什么没有人带走她？一分钟不到，她就咬我了。"

"Seems to me," said Billy to the troop-horse, "that our friend Two Tails is afraid of most things. Now, if I had a full meal for every dog I've kicked across the parade-ground, I should be as fat as Two Tails nearly."

I whistled, and Vixen ran up to me, muddy all over, and licked my nose, and told me a long tale about hunting for me all through the camp. I never let her know that I understood beast talk, or she would have taken all sorts of liberties. So I buttoned her into the breast of my overcoat, and Two Tails shuffled and stamped and growled to himself.

"Extraordinary! Most extraordinary!" he said. "It runs in our family. Now, where has that nasty little beast gone to?"

I heard him feeling about with his trunk.

"We all seem to be affected in various ways," he went on, blowing his nose. "Now, you gentlemen were alarmed, I believe, when I trumpeted."

"Not alarmed, exactly," said the troop-horse, "but it made me feel as though I had hornets where my saddle ought to be. Don't begin again."

"I'm frightened of a little dog, and

"依我看,"比利对战马说,"大多数的东西都能吓到我们的双尾朋友。如果我能踢一条穿越阅兵场的狗就饱餐一顿,现在我应该胖得就像双尾那样了。"

我吹了一声口哨,维克森跑到了我的身边。她满身是泥,舔了舔我鼻子,并且告诉我在整个兵营里寻找我的漫长过程。我永远不会让她知晓我能听懂动物们的话,要不然她会为所欲为的。于是我将她放在我胸部位置,再系上大衣的扣子。双尾拖着脚,跺着地,自顾自地咆哮起来。

"不寻常!太不寻常!"他说,"我们家族总碰上不寻常的事。现在,那个讨厌的小畜生跑去哪里了?"

我听到他伸着长鼻子到处摸索着。

"我们似乎都会受到方方面面的影响,"他继续说着,鼻子里吹着气,"好吧,我相信刚才我的大声吼叫惊扰到各位了。"

"准确地讲,不是惊扰,"战马说,"但是那使我认为,原本放马鞍的位置变成了黄蜂,不要再叫了。"

"一只小狗能够吓到我,这里

the camel here is frightened by bad dreams in the night."

"It is very lucky for us that we haven't all got to fight in the same way," said the troop-horse.

"What I want to know," said the young mule, who had been quiet for a long time – "whatIwant to know is, why we have to fight at all."

"Because we are told to," said the troop-horse, with a snort of contempt.

"Orders," said Billy the mule; and his teeth snapped.

"Hukm hai!", said the camel with a gurgle; and Two Tails and the bullocks repeated, "Hukm hai!"

"Yes, but who gives the orders?" said the recruit-mule.

"The man who walks at your head – Or sits on your back – Or holds the nose-rope – Or twists your tail," said Billy and the troop-horse and the camel and the bullocks one after the other.

"But who gives them the orders?"

"Now you want to know too much, young un," said Billy, "and that is one way of getting kicked. All you have to do is to obey the man at your head and ask no questions."

"He's quite right," said Two Tails. "I

的骆驼会在晚上被噩梦吓醒。"

"对我们来说幸运的是,我们作战的方式都不相同。"战马说。

"我想要知道,"沉寂了很长时间的年轻骡子说,"我想知道为什么我们必须作战。"

"因为我们收到这样的指令。"战马轻蔑地说。

"那是命令。"骡子比利咬着牙说。

"呼咳嗨![1]",骆驼咕噜着说,双尾和公牛重复着,"呼咳嗨!"

"是的,可是谁下达了命令?"新招来的骡子说。

"在你前面行走的人——或者是骑在你背上的人——或者是手握缰绳的人——或者是拧你尾巴的人。"比利、战马、骆驼还有公牛们一个个说着。

"可是,又是谁命令他们的?"

"现在你想知道的太多了,年轻的小伙子,"比利说,"这是要挨踢。你所要做的就是听从你前面的那个人,不要有任何疑问。"

"他的话非常对,"双尾说,

---

[1] 那是命令!

can't always obey, because I'm betwixt and between; but Billy's right. Obey the man next to you who gives the order, or you'll stop all the battery, besides getting a thrashing."

The gun-bullocks got up to go. "Morning is coming," they said. "We will go back to our lines. It is true that we see only out of our eyes, and we are not very clever; but still, we are the only people to-night who have not been afraid. Good night, you brave people."

Nobody answered, and the troop-horse said, to change the conversation, "Where's that little dog? A dog means a man somewhere near."

"Here I am," yapped Vixen, "under the gun-tail with my man. You big, blundering beast of a camel you, you upset our tent. My man's very angry."

"Phew!" said the bullocks. "He must be white?"

"Of course he is," said Vixen. "Do you suppose I'm looked after by a black bullock-driver?"

"Huah! Ouach! Ugh!" said the bullocks. "Let us get away quickly."

They plunged forward in the mud, and managed somehow to run their yoke on the pole of an ammunition-wagon, where it jammed.

"我不能总是听从，我在两者之间，不是骡子也不是马，但比利的话是对的。听从在你身边人的指令，要不然你就拖停整个队伍，并且被痛打一顿。"

两头炮兵营的公牛起身走了。"就要到早上了，"他们说，"我们要返回队列中。确实，我们只能通过眼睛看事情，并且我们脑子不太灵活，可我们仍然是今晚唯一从未惧怕过什么的。晚安，勇敢的动物们。"

谁都没有回应。战马开口转移了话题："那只小狗在哪里？有小狗就说明有人在跟前。"

"我在这里，"维克森叫道，"和我们主人在大炮尾端。你这个大块头畜生，浮躁的骆驼，我们的帐篷被你掀翻了，我的主人非常恼火。"

"哟！"两头公牛说，"他肯定是个白人吧？"

"他当然是白人，"维克森说，"你认为我会被一个黑人公牛骑手照看吗？"

"呼啊！哦呜啊！呜！"两头公牛说，"我们快点离开吧。"

他们一头扎进泥地，设法抽出他们牛轭，牛轭卡在了弹药车的杆子上了。

"Now youhavedone it," said Billy calmly. "Don't struggle. You're hung up till daylight. What on earth's the matter?"

The bullocks went off into the long hissing snorts that Indian cattle give, and pushed and crowded and slued and stamped and slipped and nearly fell down in the mud, grunting savagely.

"You'll break your necks in a minute," said the troop-horse. "What's the matter with white men? I live with 'em."

"They – eat – us! Pull!" said the near bullock: the yoke snapped with a twang, and they lumbered off together.

I never knew before what made Indian cattle so afraid of Englishmen. We eat beef – a thing that no cattle-driver touches – and of course the cattle do not like it.

"May I be flogged with my own pad-chains! Who'd have thought of two big lumps like those losing their heads?" said Billy.

"Never mind. I'm going to look at this man. Most of the white men, I know, have things in their pockets," said the troop-horse.

"I'll leave you, then. I can't say I'm overfond of 'em myself. Besides, white

"现在你们卡住了吧？"比利冷静地说，"不要挣扎，你们要挂到天亮了。究竟是怎么了？"

两头公牛喷出了只有印度牛才会的嘶嘶声，持续了好久。他们使劲儿往前挤，冲到一起，向下踩，还滑了一脚，几乎摔倒在泥地上。

"一分钟不到你们就得扯断脖子，"战马说，"白人有什么问题？我和他们住在一块儿。"

"他们——吃——我们！拉啊！"近边儿的公牛说。咔嚓一声牛轭断了，他们两个一起挣脱了。

我之前从来不知道是什么让印度牛如此害怕英国人。就是因为我们吃牛肉——牛的骑手不会碰这东西——当然牛不会喜欢被吃掉。

"我自己脚上的铁链打我吧！谁会想到像他们一样的两个大家伙有可能脑袋不保？"比利说。

"不用担心。我要去瞧瞧那个人。就我所知，大多数白人在他们的口袋里都揣东西。"战马说。

"那我就不和你一块了，我不能说自己多喜欢他们。而且，睡觉

men who haven't a place to sleep in are more than likely to be thieves, and I've a good deal of Government property on my back. Come along, young 'un, and we'll go back to our lines. Good-night, Australia! See you on parade to-morrow, I suppose. Good-night, old Hay-bale! – try to control your feelings, won't you? Good-night, Two Tails! If you pass us on the ground to-morrow, don't trumpet. It spoils our formation."

Billy the mule stumped off with the swaggering limp of an old campaigner, as the troop-horse's head came nuzzling into my breast, and I gave him biscuits; while Vixen, who is a most conceited little dog, told him fibs about the scores of horses that she and I kept.

"I'm coming to the parade to-morrow in my dog-cart," she said. "Where will you be?"

"On the left hand of the second squadron. I set the time for all my troop, little lady," he said politely. "Now I must go back to Dick. My tail's all muddy, and he'll have two hours' hard work dressing me for the parade."

The big parade of all the thirty thousand men was held that afternoon, and Vixen and I had a good place close

的地方也没有人，白人很可能是小偷，而我背上还有很多政府的财物。来吧，年轻的小伙子，我们返回到自己的队伍。晚安，澳大利亚战马！我猜，我们明天会在阅兵场上见。晚安，老干草包！试着控制你的情绪，可以吗？晚安，双尾！假如你明天经过我们身旁，不要吹喇叭，那会把我们的队形弄乱。"

骡子比利像个老战士一样，大摇大摆、蹒跚地走了。战马这时候将头蹭到我的胸前。我拿了几块饼干给他。而最自负的小狗维克森跟他吹嘘，她和我喂养了几十匹马。

"我明天会坐狗车参加游行，"她说，"你会在哪里？"

"我会在第二中队的左侧。我掌控着所有战马队伍的行军时间，小女士，"他礼貌地说，"现在我必须得返回到迪克身边。我的尾巴沾满了泥，为了阅兵仪式，他要花上整整两个小时辛苦地打点我的行头。"

那天下午举行了三万人的大阅兵。维克森和我在靠近阿富汗总

to the Viceroy and the Amir of Afghanistan, with his high big black hat of astrakhan wool and the great diamond star in the center. The first part of the review was all sunshine, and the regiments went by in wave upon wave of legs all moving together, and guns all in a line, till our eyes grew dizzy. Then the cavalry came up, to the beautiful cavalry canter of "Bonnie Dundee," and Vixen cocked her ear where she sat on the dog-cart. The second squadron of the lancers shot by, and there was the troop-horse, with his tail like spun silk, his head pulled into his breast, one ear forward and one back, setting the time for all his squadron, his legs going as smoothly as waltz-music. Then the big guns came by, and I saw Two Tails and two other elephants harnessed in line to a forty-pounder siege-gun while twenty yoke of oxen walked behind. The seventh pair had a new yoke, and they looked rather stiff and tired. Last came the screw-guns, and Billy the mule carried himself as though he commanded all the troops, and his harness was oiled and polished till it winked. I gave a cheer all by myself for Billy the mule, but he never looked

督和埃米尔的地方有一个很好的位置。埃米尔头戴一顶高大的阿斯特拉罕羊毛的黑色帽子，一颗显眼的钻石之星镶嵌在中间。阅兵仪式的第一部分阳光明媚，一个方队走过，士兵们的腿整整齐齐地如波浪一般，手中的枪成一条直线，我们看得都晕了。接着是骑兵队伍，他们随着音乐《邦妮·杜迪》，缓慢而有节奏地跑着。维克森翘起她的耳朵，坐在狗车上。第二队骑兵队的中队走过，其中就有那匹战马。他的尾巴如绢丝一般，脑袋向下垂到胸前，一个耳朵向前，一个耳朵往后，控制着整个队列的行进速度，他的双腿就像华尔兹音乐一般顺畅。然后过来的是大炮方队，我看到双尾和其他两头大象排成一行，身上架着四十磅重的攻城炮。二十对同轭的黄牛走在他们的后面，第七对的轭是新的，他们看起来相当僵硬和疲惫。队伍的最后是螺式炮，骡子比利的架势就好像是他在指挥整个部队，他的挽具上过油了，被擦得闪闪亮亮。我独自一人为骡子比利欢呼，可是他从不向右或者向左看。

right or left.

The rain began to fall again, and for a while it was too misty to see what the troops were doing. They had made a big half-circle across the plain, and were spreading out into a line. That line grew and grew and grew till it was three-quarters of a mile long from wing to wing – one solid wall of men, horses, and guns. Then it came on straight toward the Viceroy and the Amir, and as it got nearer the ground began to shake, like the deck of a steamer when the engines are going fast.

Unless you have been there you cannot imagine what a frightening effect this steady come-down of troops has on the spectators, even when they know it is only a review. I looked at the Amir. Up till then he had not shown the shadow of a sign of astonishment or anything else; but now his eyes began to get bigger and bigger, and he picked up the reins on his horse's neck and looked behind him. For a minute it seemed as though he were going to draw his sword and slash his way out through the English men and women in the carriages at the back. Then the advance stopped dead, the ground

雨又开始下了，有好一段时间，根本看不清薄雾中的部队在做什么。他们在平原上绕成了一个很大的半圆，然后展开成一条直线。这条线不断壮大成长，直到两翼绵延出四分之三英里长，一个由人、马和大炮构成的坚实城墙形成了。然后，它朝着总督和埃米尔的正前方推进，并且随着距离越来越短，地面都开始抖动，仿佛发动机快速行驶的时候汽船上的甲板。

除非你去过那里，要不然你不能想象，整个部队稳稳地走过来，会让在场的观众感到何等的震惊，就算大家都清楚这是在阅兵。我看着埃米尔。他之前丝毫没有惊讶，也看不出有任何的其他神情。可是此时他的眼睛瞪得越来越大，他拿起马脖子上的缰绳，看着身后。有那么一会儿，他似乎要抽出他的剑，从后面车厢中英国的男人和女人中间冲出来，随即前进的部队停止了脚步，地面静止不动。整个队列开始敬礼。有三十支乐队一起演奏。阅兵典礼结束，所有的团队在雨中返回自己的营地，一支步兵乐队开始演奏下面的曲目：

stood still, the whole line saluted, and thirty bands began to play all together. That was the end of the review, and the regiments went off to their camps in the rain; and an infantry band struck up with:

The animals went in two by two,
Hurrah!
The animals went in two by two,
The elephant and the battery mul',
and they all got into the Ark,
For to get out of the rain!

Then I heard an old, grizzled, long-haired Central Asian chief, who had come down with the Amir, asking questions of a native officer.

"Now," said he, "in what manner was this wonderful thing done?"

And the officer answered, "There was an order, and they obeyed."

"But are the beasts as wise as the men?" said the chief.

"They obey, as the men do. Mule, horse, elephant, or bullock, he obeys his driver, and the driver his sergeant, and the sergeant his lieutenant, and the lieutenant his captain, and the captain his major, and the major his colonel, and the colonel his brigadier

动物们成双结对地进去了，
欢呼！
动物们成双结对地进去了，
大象还有炮兵营的骡子，
他们全都进入了方舟，
就为了不淋到雨！

然后，我听到一位随同埃米尔一块过来的、留着长长的花白头发的中亚老酋长询问一个本地官员。

"那么，"他说，"是通过怎么的方式实现了这么美妙的事情？"

那个官员回答说："发一项指令，他们就照做了。"

"可是，那些畜生聪明得就像人类？"酋长说。

"他们服从命令，就像人类一样，骡子、马、大象或者公牛，他们听从骑手的指令。骑手们听从中士，中士听从中尉，中尉听从上尉，上尉听从少校，少校听从上校，上校听从三个团的旅长，旅长听从将军，将军听从总督，总督是女王的

commanding three regiments, and the brigadier his general, who obeys the Viceroy, who is the servant of the Empress. Thus it is done."

"Would it were so in Afghanistan!" said the chief; "for there we obey only our own wills."

"And for that reason," said the native officer, twirling his mustache, "your Amir whom you do not obey must come here and take orders from our Viceroy."

奴仆，就是这么实现的。"

"真希望阿富汗也是这样！"酋长说，"因为我们只依从自己的意愿行事。"

"就是由于这一点，"这位本地官员捻起胡须说，"因为你们都不听从埃米尔，他才来到这里，听从我们总督的指令。"

PARADE-SONG OF THE CAMP-ANIMALS

兵营动物的阅兵歌

ELEPHANTS OF THE GUN-TEAM

We lent to Alexander the strength of Hercules,

The wisdom of our foreheads, the cunning of our knees;

We bowed our necks to service; they ne'er were loosed again, – Make way there, way for the ten-foot teams

Of the Forty-Pounder train!

GUN-BULLOCKS

Those heroes in their harnesses avoid a cannon-ball,

And what they know of powder upsets them one and all;

Thenwecome into action and tug the guns again, –

Make way there, way for the twenty yoke

Of the Forty-Pounder train!

大炮队伍的大象

我们将力量借给亚历山大海格力斯，

我们聪慧的头脑，灵巧的膝盖；

我们鞠躬受役，脖颈不再放松。

我们就此开路——为了十只脚的辎重队，

他们拉的是四十磅重的大炮！

拉炮的公牛

马具下的那些英雄躲开了炮弹，

他们知晓炸药的威力，烦恼不已；

就由我们负责接力，拉着大炮继续前行。

我们就此开路——为了二十对同轭的公牛，

我们背负四十磅重的大炮！

CAVALRY HORSES

By the brand on my withers, the finest of tunes

Is played by the Lancers, Hussars, and Dragoons,

And it's sweeter than "Stables" or "Water" to me,

The Cavalry Canter of "Bonnie Dundee"!

Then feed us and break us and handle and groom,

And give us good riders and plenty of room,

And launch us in column of squadrons and see

The way of the war-horse to "Bonnie Dundee"!

SCREW-GUN MULES

As me and my companions were scrambling up a hill,

The path was lost in rolling stones, but we went forward still;

For we can wriggle and climb, my lads, and turn up everywhere,

And it's our delight on a mountain height, with a leg or two to spare!

Good luck to every sergeant, then,

骑士的战马

以我肩上的印痕发誓,

是枪骑手、轻骑手和龙骑手演奏了最美妙的音乐;

对我来说,他甜过马厩或者水,

那就是轻骑兵缓慢的《邦妮·杜迪》!

喂养着我们,训练着我们,打理着我们,培养着我们,

提供我们不错的骑手,还有足够的空间,

让我们加入到骑兵中队的队伍瞧一瞧,

战马是如何随着《邦妮·杜迪》行走!

螺式炮骡子

我和同伴们正在攀爬山峰的小路,

小路被滚石埋没,可我们仍然继续前行;

我们可以扭着身子向上爬,各个方向,都有我们小伙子的身影,

这是我们在高山上的乐趣,只能允许一两条腿落足。

祝福各位中士都有好运气,让

that lets us pick our road;

Bad luck to all the driver-men that cannot pack a load:

For we can wriggle and climb, my lads, and turn up everywhere,

And it's our delight on a mountain height with a leg or two to spare!

COMMISSARIAT CAMELS

We haven't a camelty tune of our own

To help us trollop along,

But every neck is a hairy trombone

(Rtt-ta-ta-ta!is a hairy trombone!)

And this is our marching song:

Can't! Don't! Shan't! Won't!

Pass it along the line!

Somebody's pack has slid from his back,

Wish it were only mine!

Somebody's load has tipped off in the road –

Cheer for a halt and a row!

Urrr! Yarrh! Grr! Arrah!

Somebody's catching it now!

ALL THE BEASTS TOGETHER

Children of the Camp are we,

Serving each in his degree;

我们自己挑选上山的路，

希望所有不能驮运货物的骑手都没好运气；

我们可以扭着身子向上爬，各个方向，都有我们小伙子的身影，

这是我们在高山上的乐趣，只能允许一两条腿落足。

军粮部门的骆驼

我们没有自己的调子，

在路途中鼓舞士气，

可是每个脖子都是长毛的长号。

（啼–嗒–嗒–嗒！我们有长毛的长号！）

这是我们的行军曲调：

不能！别！不该！不要！

将这曲调沿着队列传下去！

有个家伙的背包从后背滑落，

希望是我的就好了！

有个家伙驮的东西倾覆到地上——

停顿一下欢呼起来！

呃！呀！嘎！啊！

有个家伙挨批了！

全部的牲口大合唱

营地的孩子说的就是我们，

Children of the yoke and goad,

Pack and harness, pad and load.

See our line across the plain,

Like a heel-rope bent again.

Reaching, writhing, rolling far,

Sweeping all away to war!

While the men that walk beside,

Dusty, silent, heavy-eyed,

Cannot tell why we or they

March and suffer day by day.

Children of the Camp are we,

Serving each in his degree;

Children of the yoke and goad,

   Pack and harness, pad and load.

我们在各自的位置尽职尽责；

我们是车轭和鞭子、包裹和挽具的孩子。

瞧，我们的队列穿越平原，

就像脚上的铁索又被折弯，

伸展开，扭动着，翻滚着，

横扫整个战场！

走在身旁的人们，

满身灰尘，默默无语，眼皮沉重，

无法说清为什么我们还有他们，忍受日复一日行军的苦难。

营地的孩子说的就是我们，

我们在各自的位置尽职尽责；

我们是车轭和鞭子、包裹和挽具的孩子。

（完）

中英对照全译本系列书目表

英国文学卷

《简爱》

《傲慢与偏见》

《理智与情感》

《爱玛》

《金银岛》

《呼啸山庄》

《双城记》

《雾都孤儿》

《鲁滨逊漂流记》

《一九八四 动物庄园》

《福尔摩斯经典探案集 血字的
　研究 四签名》

《福尔摩斯经典探案集 巴斯克
　维尔的猎犬 恐怖谷》

《福尔摩斯经典探案集 福尔摩
　斯历险记》

《福尔摩斯经典探案集 福尔摩
　斯回忆录》

《福尔摩斯经典探案集 福尔摩
　斯归来记》

《福尔摩斯经典探案集 最后的
　致意》

《福尔摩斯经典探案集 福尔摩
　斯新探案集》

《培根散文集》

《美丽新世界》

《德伯家的苔丝》

《格列佛游记》

《道林·格雷的画像》

《消失的地平线》

《艰难时世》

《弗兰肯斯坦》

《失落的世界》

《月亮和六便士》

《刀锋》

《面纱》

《远大前程》

《丛林之书》

美国文学卷

《红字》

《小妇人》

《伟大的盖茨比》

《瓦尔登湖》

《房龙地理》

《纯真年代》

《秘密花园》

《嘉莉妹妹》

《人类的故事》

《老人与海》

《太阳照常升起》

《乞力马扎罗的雪 海明威短篇
　小说选》

《汤姆·索亚历险记》

《欧·亨利短篇小说选集》

《本杰明·富兰克林自传》

《马克·吐温短篇小说选集》

《爱伦·坡短篇小说选》

《杰克·伦敦小说选 野性的呼唤 海狼》

《小公主》

《永别了，武器》

《丧钟为谁而鸣》

《海明威作品选》

《返老还童 菲茨杰拉德短篇小说选》

《菊与刀》

《睡谷传说 英伦见闻录》

《人猿泰山》

欧洲文学卷

《茶花女》

《高老头》

《欧也妮·葛朗台》

《羊脂球 莫泊桑短篇小说选》

《包法利夫人》

《海底两万里》

《木偶奇遇记》

《爱的教育》

《地心游记》

《八十天环游地球》

《少年维特之烦恼》

《名人传》

《变色龙 契诃夫短篇小说选》

《青鸟 蜜蜂的生活》

《哈克贝利·费恩历险记》

《尼尔斯骑鹅旅行记》

《尼尔斯骑鹅旅行记：续集》

《玩偶之家》

《都柏林人》

《钢铁是怎样炼成的》

《牛虻》

《昆虫记》

《海蒂》

严复译文卷

《国富论（上）》

《国富论（下）》

《天演论》

《论自由》

《社会学研究》

朱生豪译文卷

《罗密欧与朱丽叶》

《威尼斯商人》

《仲夏夜之梦》

《第十二夜》

《皆大欢喜》

《无事生非》

《哈姆莱特》

《李尔王》

《麦克白》

《奥赛罗》

纳尼亚传奇

《纳尼亚传奇1 魔法师的外甥》

《纳尼亚传奇2 狮子、女巫和魔衣橱》

《纳尼亚传奇3 能言马与男孩》

《纳尼亚传奇4 凯斯宾王子》

《纳尼亚传奇5 黎明踏浪号》

《纳尼亚传奇6 银椅》

《纳尼亚传奇7 最后一战》

其他文学卷

《绿山墙的安妮》

《泰戈尔诗歌集 新月集&飞鸟集》